Marx's construction
of social theory

J.M. Barbalet

Marx's construction
of social theory

Routledge & Kegan Paul
London, Boston, Melbourne and Henley

First published in 1983
by Routledge & Kegan Paul plc
39 Store Street, London WC1E 7DD,
9 Park Street, Boston, Mass. 02108, USA,
296 Beaconsfield Parade, Middle Park,
Melbourne, 3206, Australia, and
Broadway House, Newtown Road,
Henley-on-Thames, Oxon RG9 1EN

Set in Press Roman
and printed in Great Britain by
T.J. Press Ltd, Padstow, Cornwall

Library of Congress Cataloging in Publication Data

Barbalet, J.M., 1946-

Marx's construction of social theory.
Bibliography: p.
Includes index.
1. Marx, Karl, 1818-1883 – Sociology. 2. Communism
and social sciences. 3. Communism and society.
4. Marxian school of sociology. I. Title.
HX39.5.B2863 1983   335.4'01   83-4582

ISBN 0-7100-9540-6

Contents

Acknowledgments

I am indebted to friends and colleagues — too many to be enumerated — who contributed to the writing of this book. Any shortcomings which remain in it are entirely the result of my own efforts. Professor Graeme Duncan, of the University of East Anglia, introduced me to Marxist theory, and Mr Paul Nursey-Bray, of Adelaide University, supervised the thesis on which this book is based. I am grateful to them both. Professor Ralph Miliband, of Brandeis University, and Dr Michael Evans, of Manchester University, offered many helpful suggestions in their capacity as examiners. Professor Frank Jones, of the Australian National University, kindly made facilities available for some of the rewriting. Jacki Gray and Vivienne Read are to be thanked for typing the manuscript. The continuous and enduring support and encouragement so essential for thinking and writing came in abundance from my family. My wife Margaret and son Tom especially are thanked for their 'invisible' but indispensable contribution to this book.

Introduction

In this book is presented an argument about Marx's construction of social theory. The building metaphor has a certain appropriateness in the present context, for it highlights three major areas of interest which are developed in the chapters which follow. First, we are concerned with Marx's search for a sound epistemology or foundation on which to build a social theory. Second, there is a concern with the way in which Marx continually modifies the concepts — theoretical building blocks or bricks — he uses in putting up the structure, and the different functions they are given in holding it together. Finally, we examine the manner in which construction entails that at various times the theoretical structure itself is in different ways dismantled, reorganised and in which some material is replaced with other theoretical fabric.

Recent scholarly interest in Marx has focused on two general problems, first the theoretical content of his early thought and second, its intellectual background, in particular its relation to the Hegelian tradition. A number of positions have been taken in the critical literature, but two alternatives immediately present themselves as influential. One argues that Marx's early thought, drawn from an Hegelian background, constitutes the theoretical foundation upon which his later thought is developed. The other maintains that Marx's early thought, drawn from an Hegelian background, does not constitute the theoretical foundation upon which his later thought is developed. These may be characterised as the 'continuity' thesis and the 'discontinuity' thesis. The argument to be presented here takes issue with both of these interpretations of Marx's development.

The common assumption, that Marx's theory bears some relation to Hegel's, while in a sense uncontestable, is quite misleading. Not only does the emphasis on the Hegelian background of Marx's thought present an inadequate picture in itself, it also leads to the neglect of other intellectual influences on Marx which were in many ways more important. It will be demonstrated that in his early writings, where Hegel's influence is almost uniformly considered to be at its strongest, Marx's social and political theory is heavily coloured by English political economy, liberal social thought and the political doctrines of a revolutionary democratic tradition. Any influence of Hegel on Marx was through the prism of a milieu dominated by Feuerbach. The significance of Feuerbach for Marx's theoretical formation and development is considered in detail below.

On the question of Marx's development, it will be suggested that there is a continuity in Marx's thought. Many of his early concerns were not abandoned, but formed the first exploratory attempts to grapple with a set of problems with which Marx continued to deal and of which he continued to achieve a deeper grasp. It will also be argued, however, that alongside this continuity of interests in Marx there is a significant theoretical discontinuity. Marx's explanation of the democratic state, for instance, of alienation and class, to name but some of the concepts Marx continued to use in his writings, are understood through different theoretical frameworks at different stages of his development.

In his early critique of Hegel Marx outlined the idea that the development of the political state must be conceived in terms of human history. It is the elaboration of this idea which leads Marx to formulate a number of theoretical accounts of history and society, and on which he attempted to found a theory of revolution and human emancipation. Up to 1845 Marx seemed to be dissatisfied with the results of his research, for he abandoned several different theories almost as soon as they had been formulated. Marx does find his intellectual feet, however, with *The German Ideology* and thereafter continues to build upon the social and political theory first outlined in that work. This thumbnail sketch of Marx's development, which is argued in detail below, recognises a unity of purpose in Marx's thought while at the same time it suggests that he was more interested in attempting to develop an adequate account of social reality than he was in remaining consistent with a position stated early on.

It is possible to follow a single idea or cluster of ideas through Marx's work and observe the manner in which they are developed and are refined in his long-term treatment of them. Several chapters below do this for many concepts in Marx. There is an obvious continuity of thought when Marx can be observed to use the same concepts through a number of works, modifying them, extending or contracting their application, certainly, but nevertheless continually employing them as part of his intellectual equipment. A large and sophisticated literature, predominantly concerned with the concept of alienation, has demonstrated this type of linear continuity of concepts in Marx. It confirms a unity of thought in Marx which would be foolish to deny. But a unity of this sort can coexist with a theoretical development in which there are many points of new departure.

The concept of alienation is most suitable in demonstrating that despite the various refinements and developments it undergoes in Marx's thought it can be found in his writings from the *Critique of Hegel's Philosophy of Right* through to *Capital*. The development of concepts, however, entails much more than mere changes in their content. The fact that a concept is refined or changed in any way indicates an alteration in the system of thought in which it resides. For concepts derive their meaning from the theory of which they are a part. Outside of a theoretical context which relates concept to concept, provides them with meaning, ascribes them a significance and places them in a hierarchy of logical and explanatory order, concepts can exist only as vacuous categories. Conceptual development, then, entails modifications in the position and function of the concept within the theory in which it is used. Conceptual change *pari passu* amounts to a change in theory, to theoretical change.

This is not to say that such theoretical change will necessarily be of a fundamental nature. Clearly, a conceptual refinement may change a theory by making it internally consistent where it had been inconsistent prior to the modification of a concept or group of concepts. But the important point is that tracing the evolution of a particular concept through the course of Marx's intellectual development, demonstrating that he always had a place for it, without reference to the wider theoretical context, cannot itself confirm a theoretical consistency in Marx's thought. As concepts are dependent on theories for their meaning, the continuity of isolated concepts proves little in itself. The argument in this book, that the theoretical content of Marx's thought is different at various stages of his writing, is maintained by keeping the question of theory as opposed to that of concept at the forefront of discussion.

The theme that is developed here, that there are theoretical dissimilarities between Marx's writings at different stages of his development, is not based on an argument that Marx entertains merely different theories at different times. Marx's theory of surplus value, for instance, was developed in the late 1850s. It might be argued on this basis that Marx's writings prior to the draft *Grundrisse der Kritik der Politischen Oekonomie*, in which the theory was first elaborated, are 'discontinuous' with his writings after the *Grundrisse*. But such an argument, which ignored the fact that the theory of surplus value was constructed through an application of the historical methodology first outlined in *The German Ideology*, would run the risk of triviality. For while *The German Ideology* does not contain Marx's mature theory of exploitation the latter could be developed only on the foundation of the former. Any argument of discontinuity on the basis of an absence of the theory of surplus value in *The German Ideology* would demonstrate little of significance, even though the point itself may be of interest. The absence of an explicit statement of the implications and applications of a theory clearly cannot be regarded as evidence for a claim that a theoretical framework employed at one time is different to that employed at another.

It is probably fair to say that all interpretations of Marx's thought generally accept a descriptive differentiation between a 'young Marx' and a 'mature Marx'. In his writings up to say 1846, Marx employed an expository style which is clearly quite different from the style of his writings after that time. It is also apparent that in the former period words such as 'alienation' frequently appear but are relatively scarce thereafter. A primary concern in Marx with philosophical issues is largely confined to his early writing, while economic analysis occupied his attention in the writings of the later period. Upon these differences of style, language and intellectual focus are based the short-hand terms referring to Marx's 'early' and 'mature' writings. This dichotomous periodisation recommends itself in being both simple and uncontroversial. In itself it implies nothing about the theoretical content of Marx's work. Arguments relating to this question have to be defended on other grounds.

To say that Marx's early works, written before *The German Ideology*, constitute an *ensemble* of thought which does not occupy the same methodological, epistemological and substantive theoretical space as his writings after *The German Ideology*, is not necessarily to deny that Marx's thought underwent significant theoretical development before and also after 1845. Neither does it deny that the early writings provide the latter with a chronological and an intellectual foundation. For in dealing with particular problems which arose in the early writings the later works are furnished with a number of issues requiring resolution. The problem of the relation between the state and civil society, for instance, discussed in detail in the 1843 *Critique*, is dealt with by Marx in one form or another throughout his work. Up to 1845 a range of possibilities are explored, and after 1845 a number of treatments are elaborated. But the theoretical forms of these different endeavours, which focus on what is essentially a common problem, are based in the early writings on fundamentally different methodological, episte-mological and theoretical foundations than those employed in the mature works.

It is important to remember, though, that while Marx's theory of the state as alienated social power remains unchanged from the 1843 *Critique* to *The German Ideology*, three quite different theories of alienation are sequentially presented by Marx during this same period. The theory of social class in Marx is also substantially revised during this time. It must be said, then, that not only was Marx's theoretical development not simply continuous and linear, but that the notion of a clear 'epistemological break' also fails to capture the nature of signifi-cant turning points in Marx's intellectual biography. Crucial aspects of the development of Marx's social and political thought, which are inadequately explored in familiar arguments relating to the 'young' and the 'mature' Marx, are taken up below in a general presentation of Marx's intellectual development as one of disjointed incrementalism.

While Marx's 'mature' writings are not neglected in discussion below, our closest attention is directed to the works of the 'early' period. Marx's commentary on Hegel's *Philosophy of Right*, Sections 257-313, commonly known as the *Critique of Hegel's Philosophy of Right*, is undoubtedly the first significant work of this period.[1] The *Critique* was written between March and August 1843, after Marx had lost his position as editor on the *Rheinische Zeitung*. This, among other journals, had carried articles by him since 1842. In the work Marx criticises both Hegel's treatment of constitutional monarchy and his philosophical formalism. Regarding the first of these Marx argues that there is no unity of the universal and the particular in the political state, as Hegel maintains. Marx holds instead that there is a cleavage between civil society, dominated by individual interest, and the political state, an alienated universality. In his criticisms of Hegel's philosophy Marx applies the ideas of Ludwig Feuerbach to show that there is in Hegel a speculative inversion of historical processes in so far as Hegel treats human institutions, such as the state, as mere predicates of the abstract Idea. This mystifies human history, Marx contends, which is understood by him as the development of mankind itself through the evolution of man's essential rationality.

Two works which immediately follow the *Critique*, the essays *On the Jewish Question* and *A Contribution to the Critique of Hegel's Philosophy of Right: Introduction*, restate some ideas of the preceding manuscript, but also introduce some entirely new ideas. The notion of a fundamental split between civil society and the state outlined in the *Critique* is further elaborated in *On the Jewish Question*. But Marx now argues that political emancipation cannot lead to human emancipation. Commerce and money are located as the source of man's alienation and the basis of civil society. In the *Introduction* Marx goes on to identify the proletariat as the social agency of full human emancipation. In actualising philosophy the proletariat is the universal class which transcends both the atomism of civil society and the abstract universality of the state; the class which is the complete loss of humanity is the instrument of human freedom. *On the Jewish Question* and the *Introduction* were written between the end of 1843 and the beginning of 1844 and published together in the Parisian *Deutsch-Französische Jahrbücher* in 1844.

Marx's best-known work of the early period is a manuscript series, of which three survive, called variously the *Paris Manuscripts*, the *Economic and Philosophic Manuscripts*, and simply the *EPM*. These notebooks, which were written between April and August 1844, constitute Marx's first systematic discussion of political economy, and therefore represent a shift of focus away from the criticism of politics found in the previous works. Following English political economy Marx argues that labour is the source of all wealth, but goes on to elaborate for the first time the proposition that as the product of labour is alienated by the capitalist, private property and the labour which produces it reduce the worker to an estranged being. Human emancipation is identified with communism as the abolition of private property. The final manuscript provides a discussion of Hegel's *Phenomenology*. In this Hegel is criticised for conceiving alienation abstractly, in thought only, and Marx here explores some ramifications of the conception of alienated labour discussed in the earlier manuscripts.

Marx's first joint work with Frederick Engels, *The Holy Family*, employs and develops key ideas set out in the *Economic and Philosophic Manuscripts*. In elaborating a critique of Bruno Bauer and the Berlin Young Hegelians, and incidentally defending Feuerbach's humanist materialism, there is a discussion of the contradiction between the proletariat and wealth and an advocation of proletarian action for human emancipation and communism. There is also a discussion of philosophical materialism and the view is expressed that materialism logically leads to communism. The work, which is largely Marx's, was written in the autumn of 1844 in Paris and published in Frankfurt am Main in February 1845.

After leaving Paris under strained circumstances Marx settled briefly in Brussels, where in the spring of 1845 he wrote the eleven aphoristic *Theses on Feuerbach*. These are no more than short statements jotted for future elaboration, but in their brevity they contain a wealth of insight on Feuerbachian materialism. The *Theses* basically outline an internal critique of Feuerbach's philosophy as it relates to the question of the practical aspect of human activity and the social nature of man's species-being. The final of the *Theses*, summarising the implications of the others and providing a credo for them all, proclaims that 'The philosophers have only interpreted the world in various ways; the point, however, is to change it.'

Many of the questions raised in the *Theses* and cognate works of the period are dealt with in *The German Ideology*, written jointly with Engels in Brussels between November 1845 and October 1846. *The German Ideology* differs from earlier works in so far as it sets out for the first time, and in some detail, the principle tenets of historical materialism. In doing so it implicitly contradicts much of Marx's earlier theorising. In the work is an account of the movement of history in terms of economic development and a critique of the essentialist conception of human nature employed by Feuerbach and critically accepted by Marx up to this time. Although submitted for publication *The German Ideology* remained unfinished and forgotten by its authors. In initiating a significantly new development in Marx's thought *The German Ideology* is often regarded as the final work of his early period.

Chapter One

Epistemology

This first chapter deals with the epistemological foundations of Marx's thought. Beginning with Marx's first important early writing, the *Critique of Hegel's Philosophy of Right*, it is argued that the chronological foundation of Marx's work does not provide the final intellectual foundation of his later thought.

A close examination of the theory of knowledge of the *Critique* reveals that while Marx develops a forceful critique of Hegel's epistemology, he elaborates an alternative to it which nevertheless does not escape the general confines of idealism. The essentialist epistemology of the *Critique* employs a model of reality which is non-empirical and formalist. This contrasts sharply with the epistemology of *Capital*, for instance, which is at once empirical without being empiricist. In *Capital* a notion of essence is developed which avoids conceptualising the phenomenal form of social relations and makes accessible the inner relations of empirical social forces which give rise to their phenomenal form.

It will be shown below, then, that Marx's mature epistemology does not draw on his early thought, but contrasts sharply with it. The chapter begins by elucidating the idealist essentialism of Marx's early epistemology, and progresses to a discussion of the naturalist or scientific nature of his mature epistemology.

A crucial characteristic, which distinguishes Marx's science, is its critical dimension. In his scientific analysis of capitalism Marx both criticises capitalism intellectually and furnishes a revolutionary political movement with cognitive elements necessary for an insurrectionary strategy against capitalism. Marx's early idealist epistemology, too, is of a critical nature. But as it is in substance so it is in this regard quite dissimilar to the mature epistemology. These differences between the essentialism of the *Critique* on the one hand, and *Capital* on the other, are touched upon in the present chapter.

It will be attempted below to demonstrate over all that the epistemology of the *Critique* does not and could not furnish Marx's mature thought with an epistemological foundation, and that the epistemology employed in his later writings is not to be found in the *Critique*.

I

It is through Marx's notion of 'true democracy' and its attendant concepts that the *Critique's* epistemology can be most readily discerned, for it is in this notion that his assumptions concerning the intellectual conditions of knowledge most clearly operate.

While Marx accepted, with Hegel, that the state is a rational organism, he differs with Hegel on the question of the state's democratic element:[1]

> The direct participation of all individuals in deliberating and deciding on political matters of general concern is, according to Hegel, 'tantamount to a proposal to put the democratic element without any rational form into the organism of the state, although it is only in virtue of the possession of such a form that the state is an organism at all'. That is to say that where the state organism is purely formal, the democratic element can enter into it only as a formal element. However, *the democratic element should rather be the real element which confers a rational form on the organism of the state as a whole*. If on the other hand it enters the organism or formalism of the state as a 'particular' element, its 'rational form' will be nothing more than an emasculation, an accommodation, *denying its own particular nature*, i.e. it will function purely as a *formal* principle.

For Marx, but not for Hegel, the democratic element is the element of 'reality' in the state, without which the state denies its own nature, denies its rational form.

Implicit in Marx's claim that the reality of the rational state is its democratic element is the further claim that undemocratic states, while not devoid of empirical existence, are nevertheless 'unreal' in so far as they lack a democratic element, for such states lack also a rational form. It is precisely in terms of their incompleteness in this regard, in their absence of democracy, that Marx describes the state when it takes the monarchic or the republican form.[2] Indeed, it is on this basis that Marx contrasts 'the political state' with 'the real state', the former being deficient of the rational form which is manifest in the latter.[3] As an existing state may be less than 'real', so may existing democracy be less than 'true'. The political state, as it is understood in Marx's terminology, is able to attain no more than a 'formal democracy', as opposed to 'real democracy'. Formal democracy is characterised by the fact that under its regime man leads a merely legal rather than a fully human existence.[4] The condition for existence of the 'real state', on the other hand, is 'true democracy', in which 'the constitution [is] founded on its true ground: real human beings and the real people; not merely implicitly and in essence, but in existence and in reality'.[5] The principle defect of the modern age, according to Marx, and this point summarises and unifies his comments on the state and democracy, is the separation of man from his objective essence.[6] This condition of estrangement is sanctioned, according to Marx, in Hegel's refusal to acknowledge that the reality of the state as the rational organism is in its true democracy.

The full force of Marx's account of the state of true democracy relies upon a distinction between man's condition of alienated legal existence and the associated 'existing' structure of the state on the one hand, and the 'reality' of man's human existence in the rational state on the other. For Marx assumes that what exists, or appears to exist, may be neither real nor true. Marx also assumes, and this is crucial to his argument, that 'reality' is immanent in 'existence', that existing conditions — undemocratic and without rationality though they may be — nevertheless contain unrealised 'reality'. For Marx argues that while the objective essence of man is denied its full expression when the state takes a purely political form, it nevertheless abides in man as a dormant or unrealised determinant.[7] The potential for reality, therefore, is in existence itself. Marx says, for instance, that the contradiction between civil society and the state which is manifest in the merely partial participation in the state 'symbolise[s] the *demand* that this contradiction be *resolved*.'[8]

The transformation of existence into reality, according to these tenets, is the result of a progressive unfolding of the essence inherent in man and inherent in the state as constituted by the people in true democracy. In differentiating existence and reality Marx is not postulating, therefore, an ideal reality of a normative nature which is independent of empirical existence and which functions as an external principle of moral criticism. 'Existence' and 'reality' are for Marx but distinct phases in the state's development as the rational organism. In the state's phase of pre-historical existence, in its political form, the universality proper to it is absent. At this stage man's essence is suppressed in legal or political existence. In the real state, on the other hand, man's essence is realised with true democracy; the state then is a truly universal and rational organism.

The concept 'true democracy' serves at least three purposes in the *Critique*. Firstly, in demonstrating that the political state is not the real state 'true democracy' acts as a critical measure which is held against Hegel's idea of the state. While Hegel attempts to prove that the constitutional monarchy, the political state, represents the fulfilment of the ideal of the rational state, Marx shows the exact opposite. That which Hegel applauds Marx proclaims illusory; the idealist vision is not yet realised. This raises the second purpose of the concept. By showing that the real state is one of true democracy Marx constructs the theoretical base from which he is able to engage the Prussian state in a revolutionary polemic. It is in the letters published in the *Deutsch-Französische Jahrbücher*, written during and just after the drafting of the *Critique*, rather than in the *Critique* itself, that this polemic is conducted. But its theoretical basis is in the *Critique*, and as Marx (sometimes unfairly) regards Hegel's ideal as thoroughly Prussian, his *Critique* of Hegel's *Philosophy of Right* serves as an implicit critique of the Prussian state. Marx does not criticise the existing (Prussian) state for moral default and he does not appeal to such principles as equality and justice. Rather, he argues that the state is inevitably doomed which censors, promulgates tendentious laws and in other ways restricts the full participation of the people in its affairs. In the progressive unfolding of man's inherent essence the Prussian state, therefore, will be democratised out of existence into reality. Finally, the concept 'true democracy' signifies an epistemological position. As 'reality' is not the same as 'existence', but merely immanent in it, knowledge of reality, of what is true, cannot be acquired from experience. This is because one can experience only what exists. Experience cannot give rise to knowledge of the real state, for 'in the modern world the idea of the state can appear only in the abstraction of the "merely political state".'[9] In order to claim knowledge of the real state, in order to know what is true and therefore what is not true about existence, Marx requires the concept 'true democracy'. Marx's commitment to democracy in the *Critique* is as much an epistemological stance as a revolutionary political one.

The political functions and epistemological content of 'true democracy' are interrelated and it is therefore difficult, in particular, to separate the epistemological from the other aspects of the notion.

Even more than his polemic against the Prussian state Marx's epistemology is implicit rather than clearly stated in the *Critique*. Its strands have to be extracted from the text and reconstructed *ab extra*.

To recapitulate briefly: Marx argues that the truth of the state's reality cannot be known from experience of the existing state, for the idea of the real state cannot be obtained from the abstraction of the political state. Marx also maintains that reality is immanent in existence. It is from this latter point that Marx is able to surmount the difficulties presented by the former. The empirical reality of man's essence, although denied its full expression in the political state, provides Marx with evidence of the full nature of reality.

The involvement of individuals in offices of the political state, says Marx, indicates an essential quality in the incumbent. He goes on to criticise Hegel for contending that such offices have only an external and contingent link with the particular individuals engaged in state activity. Hegel forgets, continues Marx,[10]

> that particular individuality is a human function and that the activities and agencies of the state are likewise human functions; he forgets that the essence of the 'particular person' is not his beard and blood and abstract *Physis*, but his *social quality*, and that the affairs of state are nothing but the modes of action and existence of the social qualities of men.

It is in this sense that the 'political state is the *mirror of truth* which reflects the disparate moments of the concrete state.'[11] Instead of abstracting from the political state Marx develops his idea of the real state by projecting from man's essence. Rather than starting with the political state to arrive at a conception of the real state Marx claims the empirical reality of man's essential sociality, from which the faculties of state derive.

But in proving his conception of the real state Marx is no more prepared to abstract from the empirical reality of man's essence than he is prepared to abstract from the political state in which man's essence is evident. While Marx finds evidence for the truth of the real state in man's sociality — it is the mirror of truth when expressed in offices of state — the proof of man's sociality is in democracy, and democracy is the form of the real state. Any apparent confusion in all of this results from the interdependence of true democracy, the real state and man's essential sociality, any one of which must be understood in terms of the other two. What is clear, however, and what must resolve any confusion, is the epistemological primacy of the concept 'true democracy' over the concepts 'real state' and 'man's essence'. Democracy is Marx's guarantee of truth, including the truth of man's essence; it is also, therefore, the foundation of his knowledge of the state and man. He says, for instance, that 'all forms of the state . . . are untrue to the extent that they are not democracy.'[12] And when discussing the real state, in which 'the people is itself the universal concern', Marx is 'thus concerned with a will which can achieve its *true existence* as species-will only in the self-conscious will of the people.'[13] Marx's position, then, can be summarised thus: It is the self-conscious will of the people which is denied in the political state, as the full participation of the people is there prevented. The universality of the real state is constituted in the people's self-conscious will, the true existence of which is found only in the real state, and the truth of its existence can be known only in democracy. Marx's commitment to democracy is therefore a commitment to epistemological guarantees.

Marx's commitment to democracy as a guarantee of truth is not unique to the *Critique*. The same principle is found in his article 'On a Proposed Divorce Law', published in the *Rheinische Zeitung* of December 1842, where it is claimed that 'The guarantee . . . [that law express] reliable knowledge and universal insight . . . will be present only when law is the conscious expression of the will of the people, created with and through it.'[14] Here, as in the *Critique*, the assumption which informs Marx's assertion is that given the opportunity of full participation in the state the people consciously express a will which is rational.[15] It can be confirmed that this is also Marx's position in the *Critique* by recalling that when quoting from that work above we saw Marx hold that the condition or state of true democracy, in which popular will is consciously expressed, 'confers a rational form on the organism of the state as a whole'. This is the final card in Marx's epistemological pack. The truth of democracy and the rationality of the state are connected through the essential sociality of man when fully expressed in self-conscious popular will. In summary: Democracy guarantees true knowledge of man and the state because man's essential sociality ensures a self-conscious popular will, expressed and proved in democracy, which is rational. The rationality of popular will, in turn, ensures the reality of the state as a rational organism. This reality of rationality in democracy, for Marx, is the final stage in the development or evolution of the state organism.

This final point returns the discussion to Marx's agreement with Hegel that the state is the rational organism and, implicitly, to Marx's contention that the contemporary separation of man from his objective essence is sanctioned in Hegel's failure to acknowledge that the reality of the state as the rational organism is in true democracy. Before going on to a fuller discussion of the idealist epistemology of the *Critique* it is necessary to say something further on the nature of Marx's criticisms of Hegel.

While the dialectic of historical development in the *Critique* shares the essential rationality of Hegel's dialectic, Marx is critical of Hegel for constructing a rationality of logical, not human, development. Marx argues that for Hegel the generative force of rational development lies outside man and that man's institutions are merely produced by and subject to the logical development of Absolute Spirit, of the Idea.[16] Marx goes on to argue, following Feuerbach, that this basic flaw in Hegel's account results from his treating man as a predicate of universal determination rather than as its subject.[17] The Feuerbachian critique of Hegel allows Marx to propose a Feuerbachian alternative to him:[18]

> Hegel proceeds from the state and conceives of man as the subjectivised state; democracy proceeds from man and conceives of the state as objectified man.

Rational universality — which finds its expression in the true state — is created not in the 'determinations of the Idea', according to Marx, but through the self-determination of 'man's *real* universality', which is essentially inherent in man and has a pre-historical form in existing institutions in so far as they are '*modes* of man's social existence'.[19] Marx shares with Hegel a conception of the state's universality and its determination in the development of the rational. But whereas Hegel sees man as predicated through this development, that is subject to it externally, Marx sees this rationality as the subject of man's self-development, as the progressive unfolding of man's objective essence. It will be clear that Marx arrives at his own position in the *Critique* through an internal critique of Hegel.[20] Louis Dupre, for instance, is therefore correct to point out that while the dialectic in both Marx and Hegel are essentially rational they are also essentially different; Marx's is the dialectic of man as an empirical flesh and blood being, whereas in Hegel the dialectical development is of the Idea.[21] But it would be misleading if we assumed on this basis that Marx's internal critique of Hegel had led him out of the mire of idealism.

It is true that ontologically, on the level of what there is, Marx's discussion seems to imply a rejection of idealism, a rejection of the view that ultimate and determining reality is the reality of ideas. Indeed, Marx is strongly critical of the fact that in Hegel's formulation:[22]

Reality is not deemed to be itself but another reality instead. The ordinary empirical world is not governed by its own minds but by a mind alien to it; by contrast the existence corresponding to the real Idea is not a reality generated out of itself, but is just the ordinary empirical world.

Marx's complaint here is that Hegel denies that reality is generated in the empirical world through the realisation of man's essence, an essence which in its empirical existence in political institutions demonstrates man's potential to attain rational universality. For, Marx says, Hegel argues that the 'reality' of 'existence' derives from the Idea which is alien to the ordinary empirical world, and thus Hegel conceptualises 'reality' as an epiphenomenon of what Marx regards as being the basis of reality.

Marx therefore criticises Hegel's idealism in so far as it derives reality from the Idea, from a source other than empirical existence. But we should not assume from this that Marx wishes to identify extant existence with 'reality' as universal rationality. On the contrary, Marx's wider point is that man's sociality in its rational form exists empirically only in the final phase of man's development in the state of true democracy, and that this rationality is not expressed in the institutions of the political state, even though man's sociality is evident in them. In the political state, Marx argues, man's sociality is not rational, as it is in the real state. So that while man − as a being of sociality − may exist empirically in both the political state and the state of true democracy, his empirical existence has the status of 'reality' only in the latter.[23] There is no suggestion in this statement of Marx's existence-reality dualism that he accepts an idealist ontology. There is no necessary succour for idealism in Marx's argument that man's sociality exists empirically but not in a rational form at a stage of development prior to its rational existence in the real state of true democracy. There is an idealism, though, in Marx's epistemology.

We say that the *Critique*'s epistemology is idealist because Marx's knowledge of man's rationality in the real state and his knowledge of its absence in the political state derives from the concept 'true democracy', a concept which has no empirical reference and which acquires its meaning from a conception of the real state which, it will be suggested, presents itself as an idea only. According to Marx man's essentially social existence is not equivalent to man's reality in the state of rational universality, and knowledge of man's rationality cannot be acquired by abstracting from man's condition in the political state, for rationality is absent from the political state. The political state can provide evidence of man's sociality in so far as political institutions are modes of man's social existence, but the rational content of sociality is evident only in the state of true democracy, in the real state. Marx, quite correctly, dismisses the possibility of obtaining a conception of the real state through an abstraction of the existing political state. There is no purpose, then, in looking for an empirical reference to Marx's knowledge of man's rationality and the real state.

What Marx has rejected on the ontological level he accepts on the epistemological. Epistemologically, at least, Marx retains the idea of the state as an ideal conception, for knowledge of the real state is devoid of existing empirical referents. The determination of Marx's knowledge of reality is the concept of true democracy. Unlike Hegel's idea of the real state Marx's is a fully democratic state, Marx has democratised the idea of the state. However, the underpinnings of the *Critique*'s idealist epistemology seem not to be Hegelian, for textual formulations suggest that Marx goes beyond Hegel back to Plato's doctrine of ideas.

II

Certain passages in the *Critique* suggest that Marx's model of true democracy bears some relation to the historical example of classical Greek antiquity.[24] While this reference in Marx's conception of the real state to a Greek past has been noted in the literature, the Platonic complexion of the idea of democracy used by Marx, which is central to his epistemology, has gone unnoticed. Yet what could be more Platonic than Marx's claim that:[25]

> it goes without saying that all forms of the state have democracy
> for their truth and that they are untrue to the extent that they are
> not democracy.

In his doctrine of ideas Plato distinguishes between the 'Form' or essential nature of a thing on the one hand, and particular instances of that thing on the other. Only the Form or Idea is real; its particular manifestation or existence imperfectly represents reality and is, to that extent, unreal.[26] Knowledge of a thing is sound only so long as it refers to its Form. Marx's concept of true democracy bears a strong resemblance, therefore, to a Platonic Form. But it is in his qualification of its Platonism that Marx most clearly suggests a conscious debt to Plato. Marx says that:[27]

democracy is the essence of all political constitutions . . . it is related to other forms of constitution as a genus to its various species, *only here* the genus itself comes into existence and hence manifests itself as a particular species in relation to other species whose existence does not correspond to the generic essence.

The insertion of the words 'only here' after describing democracy as the essence of all political constitutions which is related to particular constitutions as a general form to its particular manifestations, indicates that this formulation differs from what might otherwise be understood by the formulation as it is usually presented. The qualification 'only here' is taken to indicate that not all that is ordinarily entailed in a stated position here applies. The need to say 'only here' is the need to differentiate between two versions of a position and the phrase itself implies the author's debt to the usually understood version, from which he departs. Whereas in Plato's doctrine of ideas reality as the Form cannot attain a particular existence, Marx contends that under certain specified conditions, namely when rationality is the expression of man's species-will, true democracy as reality 'comes into existence'. By specifying the peculiar attribute of true democracy in this way Marx, in effect, acknowledges a debt to Platonic epistemology in which knowledge of reality and particular existence derives from the Form of a thing.[28]

It is the Platonic background of the *Critique*'s epistemology which gives sense to Marx's critical comments on Hegel's concept formation.

When he [Hegel] deals with the idea which is to acquire reality in the sovereign, he does not have in mind *the real idea of the executive*, the executive *conceived as an idea*; he thinks instead of the subject of the absolute idea which exists bodily in the sovereign

and, Marx says a little further on, Hegel's speculative mystery results from:[29]

the fact that a concept (existence, etc.) is viewed abstractly, that it is not *treated as something autonomous* but as an abstraction from something else . . . [Hegel's confusion could have been avoided] partly with *autonomous abstractions* (of course not abstractions from something else, but ultimately, *self-abstractions*).

Here we have in Marx a notion of the real idea which does not result from an abstraction of existence but from autonomous or self-abstraction. Marx's epistemology shares with Plato's doctrine of ideas the proposition that an intelligible reality may be without references to empirical existence and that it takes the form of the idea.

This underpinning epistemology of the *Critique* is implicit in other, related writings and is a contributing element in the general theoretical stance which Marx developed in this early period. It has been shown that while Marx's epistemology is idealist his dialectic of development insists that reality is implicit in existence. And, as we have seen, this is where he departs from both Hegel and Plato. Marx's knowledge of man and the state is based on the 'real' idea of the state of true democracy, but the reality which he knows through this idea is immanent in existence. Marx differs from Hegel in so far as he does not regard all existence as real or rational and differs from Plato in so far as he maintains that under certain conditions reality may be manifest in a particular empirical existence.[30] Marx's combination of these views allows him to proclaim that the praxis of criticism apprehends the truth of autonomous, self-abstracted concepts and is instrumental in the realisation of this truth in existence as rational reality.

These views incorporating an idealist epistemology were diffused through Marx's thought from the late 1830s to at least 1843. In his notebooks on Epicurean philosophy begun in 1839, which were preparatory to his doctoral thesis (submitted in 1841), Marx wrote that it 'is criticism which measures individual existence against essence, particular actuality against the Idea.'[31] In his letter to Ruge of September 1843, in which he declared the programme of 'the reform of consciousness', Marx says that:[32]

> Reason has always existed, but not always in a rational form. Hence the critic can take his cue from every existing form of theoretical and practical consciousness and from this ideal and final goal implicit in the actual forms of existing reality he can deduce a true reality.

We can see from this that the epistemology of the *Critique* is not a new departure in Marx's thought, but rather the culmination of an earlier development. Marx came to abandon the epistemology of the *Critique* in his later construction of a wholly different epistemology.

It is not possible here to retrace the steps in Marx's thought which took him from the theory of knowledge implicit in the *Critique* to the epistemology employed in the later writings. We will be able to do no more than briefly indicate that Marx's mature epistemology amounts to a rejection of the early idealist epistemology. It contradicts the *Critique*'s epistemology by denying the conflation of concepts and reality and by recognising that concepts are consequences of existing conditions and not autonomous self-abstractions. The difference between the *Critique*'s epistemology and the epistemology of the writings after *The German Ideology*, where Marx first developed the rudiments of his materialism and its epistemology, is particularly sharp when their similarities are considered. There is in all of Marx's reflections on the foundations of knowledge a continuing rejection of the vulgar empiricist account of knowledge, which claims that sense-experience and perception is a sufficient ground for knowledge, and also a continuing critique of Hegel's view that one can conceptualise reality in abstracting from existence. However, the content of the apparently continuing themes in the mature writings is contrary to the version outlined in the *Critique*.

III

In his unpublished *Introduction*[33] Marx criticises a procedure of concept formation which points to those aspects of Hegel's conceptualisation criticised in 1843: in abstracting from 'The real and concrete elements' Hegel 'attenuates meaningful images to abstract definitions.'[34] But Marx's alternative to Hegel is not now the one he proposed in the *Critique*. He specifically denies the possibility of self-abstracting concepts, concepts which are 'a product of the idea which evolves spontaneously and those thinking proceeds outside and above perception and imagination'.[35] Whereas in the *Critique* knowledge of reality is conceived to derive from such self-abstracting concepts, in the *Introduction* Marx maintains the contrary. Taking exchange-value as an example when discussing how 'thinking assimilates the concrete and reproduces it as a concrete mental category',[36] Marx shows that the conditions of existence of a concept could not be more different from the conditions of existence of the things to which a concept refers. In doing this he demonstrates the fallacy of conflating reality and concepts of reality.

In the *Introduction* Marx rejects the positivist-empiricist account of knowledge, as he did in the *Critique*. 'The concrete concept is concrete because it is a synthesis of many definitions ... [it] leads from abstract definitions *by way of reasoning* to the reproduction of the concrete situation ... as a concrete mental category.'[37] Knowledge of reality, according to Marx, is attained by reason rather than by the mere reception of sense-data. But the reasoning referred to here is not the reasoning employed in the *Critique*, which deduces a real essence in existence which mere abstraction from existing conditions would be blind to. Neither is it the reason of rationalism for which reflective reason is the foundation of certainty in knowledge. Marx's position is that the concepts which provide a knowledge of reality cannot be attained through the passive reception of sensation because not all that constitutes reality can be appreciated through direct sensation, for the sensuous world is 'the product of industry and of the state of society . . . it is an historical product'.[38] The historical dimension of reality is the dimension of man's practical activity in which he relates to others under existing and given conditions. Knowledge of these elements of reality is only possible, therefore, when the 'conceptual entity . . . is a *product* of the *thinking* intellect'.[39] Reason is necessary in Marx's mature epistemology to apprehend in thought the empirical conditions of the sensuous world which are not directly evident in sensation.

Reason plays a part in Marx's account of the attainment of knowledge because reality is here not a static phenomenon to be passively received through sensations but an historical movement of active beings which can be known only by actively constructing a conception of reality. In his mature epistemology Marx argues that knowledge of reality is produced, with the instruments of reason, by the knower. This contrasts with the account in the *Critique* where knowledge is available to the knower through his being privy to self-abstracting concepts. Reality itself is of an essentially historical nature in Marx's mature thought so that it cannot be 'fixed' by concepts such as 'true democracy', for concepts of reality, and therefore knowledge of reality, are ultimately the products of existing empirical conditions.[40] Marx's mature epistemology is in this sense fully materialist in so far as it maintains both that reality is located in material existence and that knowledge of reality is a product of material existence.

IV

Central to Marx's language of analysis in both his early and mature thought is the distinction he draws between a thing's appearance and its essence. This verbal continuity cuts across the epistemological discontinuity discussed above, but in no way diminishes its veracity. The significance and meaning of the appearance/essence distinction in the *Critique* is entirely different from that of the mature writings.

An elaboration of this difference will further confirm the theoretical discontinuity between Marx's early and mature thought in this respect. After indicating above that Marx's mature epistemology amounts to a rejection of the early epistemology, an account of the appearance/ essence distinction will fill out the wider theoretical context of the early and mature epistemologies and detail the specific differences between them.

To point to the essential is to indicate the determinate aspect of reality, to isolate what ultimately defines a thing and distinguishes it from others. In specifying an essence one has already distinguished between the peculiar characteristic quality and the incidental, peripheral and more variable aspects of a thing which, while important in determining its particular appearance or manifestation, are less crucial to its course of development and its relations with others. Given this general statement there are at least two senses in which the concept of essence can be conceived. One regards essence as a reality which truly exists, as a level of reality lying behind the reality of phenomenal form, behind the manifestation of appearance. In this sense essence is thus perceived as a level of real existence lying behind visible appearances, as a mode of being superior to the being of appearance. This idealist or metaphysical conception of essence, while primarily ontological, generally entails a self-conscious critical dimension, for it relates to the facts of appearance by positing an alternative reality which reveals what it holds to be the deficiencies of an existence which is imperfect when measured against the essential reality. The form of this critical aspect of essence serves to emphasise its idealism. Its classic statement is Platonic, discussed above in relation to Marx's conception of 'true democracy'. The other manner of conceiving essence is naturalist and scientific. Here essence is discerned through an analysis of reality which reveals the true nature of appearance. It relates to the facts by bringing out their hidden internal logic, by specifying the nature of existence. It does not posit two realms of reality but conceptualises what exists in a way intended to bring out the truth of reality, to reveal in reality what is not apparent to direct experience and superficial reflection. In this sense essence is conceived epistemologically rather than ontologically, as a knowledge of reality as opposed to a being of reality.

In the *Critique* Marx shares with idealism the characteristic of conceiving essences in predominantly ontological terms. He refers to man's 'objective essence', which is said to be isolated in the modern age, and also to the essence of all constitutions as democracy. He talks of 'essence and true realisation' in the same breath, implying that essence is a particular state of being which constitutes a fully realised reality as opposed to an 'existing' reality and he distinguishes between 'existing reality' and 'true reality'.[41] Marx has been shown to assert that the state and democracy can exist under conditions of being which are respectively not real or true. But it has been argued that while Marx develops an existence-reality dualism he avoids a thoroughly idealist ontology which maintains that there are two distinct levels of reality. He does this by arguing, in effect, for an evolutionary ontology which proposes that reality develops out of existence, that essence is immanent, but unrealised, in existence. It can be seen, though, that while the process is evolutionary it is not open ended; there is a clear teleological component in Marx's position.

In contradistinction to an idealist ontology, then, Marx argues in the *Critique* that man's essence as sociality, for instance, exists empirically but not in a rational form at a stage of development prior to its rational existence in the real state of true democracy. This means that for Marx, in the *Critique*, the essence which is ultimately real already exists prior to its full realisation; indeed, the form of existence is itself a consequence of the unrealised form of man's essence. Marx's conception of essence here, therefore, is in some ways similar to the conception of essence in both idealism and naturalism. In common with idealism Marx holds the view that a thing's essence is the condition of its being. But unlike the idealist conception and in common with the naturalist conception of essence Marx assumes that the essence of a thing — in an alienated form — is included in its appearance. But this is so only in so far as it is implicit in 'non-real' or 'pre-real' existence, and it therefore remains at least a quasi-ontological rather than a thorough epistemological claim in the *Critique*. In naturalism, on the other hand, essence is included in appearance in the sense that the concept of appearance as experience of reality is incorporated in the concept of essence as knowledge of reality. Marx's conception of an ontological essence is relevant to his epistemology only in the sense that intellectual apprehension of the objective essence constitutes knowledge of reality. It has already been shown that this bears no relation to his mature epistemology. This, then, is the content of Marx's conception of essence in the *Critique*.

The appearance/essence distinction is also an important part of the language of *Capital*, but the concept of essence is given a markedly different meaning in that work than Marx gave it in the *Critique*. In *Capital* 'essence' refers to a knowledge of reality rather than to a level of reality; and not just to knowledge but to scientific knowledge, a knowledge which is not directly sensual although fully empirical.[42] In his mature thought the concept of essence is fundamental to Marx's materialist epistemology and to his model of science; it refers to a particular conceptualisation of reality.

The notion of essence developed in *Capital* is most obvious when it is deployed against the conception of reality in so-called 'vulgar economy', which Marx alleges lacks an understanding of essences in this sense. In a note which explicitly makes this point Marx draws the distinction between 'that economy which . . . has investigated the real relations of production in bourgeois society, . . . [and] vulgar economy, which deals with appearances only.'[43]

The defining characteristic of vulgar economy, therefore, is in its concept formation, in its notion of economic knowledge, in its propensity to conceptualise appearances rather than essential or real relations. There are numerous citations available to substantiate that this is Marx's primary criterion for identifying vulgar economy. He says, for instance, that vulgar economy 'sticks to appearances in opposition to the law which regulates and explains them' and that it operates from the 'everyday conceptions of the actual agents of production, and . . . arranges them in a certain rational order'.[44]

Marx's critique of vulgar economy, therefore, implies that the distinction between a thing's appearance and its essence, as it is drawn in *Capital*, refers to two distinct forms of knowledge, to two different general conceptions of reality. The distinction, then, must be conceived as epistemological and not ontological. In what follows the precise meaning of Marx's mature essentialism will be outlined, and the content of 'essence', as it is conceived in *Capital*, will be clarified. A central issue raised by Marx's mature conception of essence, which will also be discussed below, is the seeming paradox of an epistemology which both rejects concepts formed in the direct experience of reality and claims to be materialist.

It has been shown that Marx's persisting criticism of what he calls 'vulgar economy' is that it conceptualises the external phenomena of economic life, and in systematising and interpreting these builds a particular model of reality which is incomplete or otherwise defective in terms of his essentialist canons. Marx's own procedure begins with the premise that the scientific enterprise is possible only when the surface phenomena have been penetrated or bypassed, for 'in their appearance things often represent themselves in inverted form' and an 'exact analysis of the process [es of reality], therefore, demands that we should, for a time, disregard all phenomena that hide the play of its inner mechanism.'[45] This is not a claim on Marx's part that appearance is necessarily false, but merely an assertion that the basis of a full understanding of social reality cannot be attained through an apprehension of its directly perceivable manifestations. Marx does not doubt the reality of appearance, but argues that knowledge of reality cannot rely upon categories of appearance, upon 'phenomenal categories'.[46]

By 'phenomenal categories' Marx means the particular conceptions of the world which appear in the direct experience of reality; that is, categories which are generated in practical activity and employed in the everyday behaviour and thought of the practitioners themselves. Marx's point that phenomenal categories are inadequate to understand reality and, under certain conditions, present a false conception of reality, can perhaps best be made clear by referring to his discussion of commodity fetishism. Marx argues that to the direct producers of commodities 'the relations connecting the labour of one individual with that of the rest *appear*, not as direct social relations between individuals at work, but *as what they really are*, material relations between persons and social relations between things.'[47] Marx does not deny that the commodity appears as it really is, for in the social act of exchange the product of labour acquires a characteristic which makes it commensurate with others as an article of trade. However, this conception of the commodity, formed in the direct experience of commodity production, is both enigmatic and woefully misleading, according to Marx.

To form a conception of commodities on the basis of their appearance, Marx argues, would be to give credence to the false view that the particular properties of commodities derive from their being as physical objects. Indeed, the conception of commodities as objects which 'appear as independent beings endowed with life and entering into relation both with one another and the human race'[48] is not only in itself fantastic, he continues, but denies the fact that the conditions under which commodities *qua* commodities exist is 'the peculiar social character of the labour that produces them'.[49] The social character of the labour expended in commodity production is not apparent to the labourers themselves because of the very nature of commodity production, under which social contact between producers is visible to them only in the act of exchanging their products. For in production for exchange, that is, in commodity production, the labour of society is mediated through the market so that the relations connecting the individual labourers do not become a part of their direct experience. Marx's argument, therefore, is that it is in the nature of commodity production to give rise to phenomenal categories which misrepresent reality; that under capitalist relations of production the categories which arise in practical activity will not reveal the reality of which phenomena are a part. This is a comment about the episte- mological consequences of capitalist social relations,[50] and not a comment on the reality or otherwise of appearance.

Given the unreliability of phenomenal categories for providing a conception of reality Marx begins to construct conceptions of its internal logic or relations which are not apparent to the senses, the knowledge of which he regards as an adequate and correct knowledge of reality, by differentiating between what a commodity, for instance, 'appears, at first sight . . . [and what] analysis shows that it is, in reality'.[51] Marx conceives the essence of reality by 'analysing' and 'criticising' phenomenal categories − to use the words that he repeatedly employs when describing his essentialist procedure. While Marx's knowledge of capitalism's essential nature is the consequence of his applying critical reason to categories of appearance it is not a deductive business of drawing conclusions from pre-given premises or *a priori* axioms, nor is it a nomenological exercise of understanding the world by establishing the meaning of terms. Marx's analysis and critique of categories of appearance is, rather, the result of his ascertaining what is the case in the empirical sense, with regard to entities and the rela- tions between them, as opposed to what merely appears to be the case. A discussion of Marx's critique of the categories 'wages' or 'value and price of labour' as 'categories for the phenomenal forms of essential relations'[52] will establish what he means by 'essence', how he arrives at a conception of essence, and its function within his intellectual pro- gramme.

After opening with the remark that:[53]

On the surface of bourgeois society the wage of the labourer *appears* as the price of labour, a certain quantity of money that is paid for a certain quantity of labour,

and noting that this appearance gives rise to the conception of wages as the value and price of labour as a commodity, Marx immediately makes the simple points of reason that such a conception is tauto- logical, absurd and inconsistent with received theory. Tautological because as the value of a commodity, in this case labour, is deter- mined by the quantity of social labour expended in its production, the value of a day's labour would be equivalent to the quantity of the day's labour it contained, a proposition as meaningless as it is circular. Absurd because for labour to be sold on the market as a commodity it must have an objective existence independent of the labourer, which is ridiculous. And contradictory because the classical labour theory of value holds both that equivalents exchange and that capital is a residue of objectified labour retained by the purchaser of labour after production. If the labourer receives the full value of his labour — as he must if his wages are the value of his labour — then the basis of capitalist production described by classical political economy vanishes, for there is nothing left to transform into capital. If, on the other hand, the labourer receives less than the value of his labour, then equivalents do not exchange and the labour theory of value is thereby faulted.[54] Each of these points are acknowledged by Marx in footnotes to be known to classical economy, but because the latter 'borrowed from everyday life the category "price of labour" without further criticism' it was led into 'inextricable confusion and contradiction'.[55]

Marx's criticism of the concept of 'price of labour' begins with a reassessment of the situation described by the phenomenal category, which leads him then to conceptualise it differently. 'That which comes directly face to face with the possessor of money on the market', says Marx, 'is in fact not labour, but the labourer. What the latter sells is his labour-power.'[56] This is a subtle but highly significant point. Marx says that classical political economy came close to this formulation as a result of its own analysis without being conscious of it because it stuck to the category 'value of labour' for wages. It realised, says Marx, that as with other commodities the value of the commodity sold by the labourer to the capitalist is determined by its cost of production. The issue for classical political economy then became 'what is the cost of production — of the labourer, i.e., the cost of producing or reproducing the labourer himself?'[57] In an earlier chapter of *Capital* Marx had already argued that the means of subsistence necessary for the maintenance of the labourer is that required to ensure his capacity for labour, his labour-power.[58] It is the value of labour-power which is paid to the labourer by the capitalist in the form of wages and it is labour-power which is offered by the labourer for sale as a commodity. 'What economists therefore call value of labour, is in fact the value of labour-power, as it exists in the personality of the labourer, which is as different from its function, labour, as a machine is from the work it performs.'[59] Although Marx's dispute with political economy on this matter is conceptual he has not left the realm of fact, his interest is in providing categories adequate to take full cognisance of the facts.

Turning now to the question of how his reformulation of wages as the value of labour-power affects wider considerations Marx reasons, through an arithmetic example, that the labourer can produce the value of his own labour-power in a time less than the full working-day. As the labourer expends labour-power purchased by the capitalist for the entire working-day, the value it produces is greater than its own value, for 'the value it produces depends, not on its own value, but on the length of time it is in action.'[60] Marx makes the further point that whilst the value of labour-power paid to the worker as his daily wage is produced in a portion only of the working-day, it appears as the value or price of labour for the entire working-day, a working-day which, therefore, includes a portion of unpaid labour. 'The wage-form thus extinguishes every trace of the division of the working-day into necessary labour and surplus-labour, into paid and unpaid labour. All labour appears as paid labour.'[61] Marx's argument, then, is that the money relation of wage-labour conceals the unrequited labour, and that the concept of wages as the value of labour obscures the real relation between the wage-labourer and the purchaser of his labour-power. Thus he is able to form a conception of essential or real relations which, he says, are 'beyond the cognisance of the ordinary mind',[62] by criticising and analysing categories of phenomenal forms.

Marx arrives at his conception of essential relations by considering the logical flaws in phenomenal categories, by reassessing the factual situation of which they attempt to take account, by conceptualising that situation with more adequate categories and by generally attempting to discover what is the case as opposed to what merely appears or seems to be the case. In doing this he argues that the phenomenal category, 'value of labour', for instance, is false in so far as it 'makes the actual relation [of wage-labour] invisible, and, indeed, shows the direct opposite of that relation'.[63] Marx, therefore, rejects sensualist epistemologies which employ phenomenal categories, categories of the directly perceivable manifestation of phenomena, on the grounds that they do not provide the basis for an accurate knowledge of social reality. His own epistemology entails that an adequate knowledge of reality is attained by reason rather than mere sense-experience. Whilst his method of apprehending reality both rejects empiricist sensualism and retains reasoning normally associated with rationalism, Marx's mature epistemology must still be regarded as fully empirical in that his criticism and analysis of phenomenal categories never departs from the realm of fact and attempts to grasp the factual relations necessary for the understanding of social reality.

The essence which Marx discovers, knowledge of which is not available to those who take appearance at face value, is the set of relations crucial to the workings of the social system under consideration and which determine its primary characteristics. Conception of these relations, therefore, provides knowledge of social reality. It is these essential or real relations which are held to be responsible for the content of direct experience of reality as it appears in phenomenal form and also those categories of phenomenal forms which 'appear directly and spontaneously as current modes of thought'.[64] Marx's essentialist analysis therefore specifies the material conditions necessary for the experience described by phenomenal categories themselves.

On his own account Marx is in a position to argue that his analysis of the 'true relation of things' — which, as they are relations not discoverable by experience must, he says, 'be discovered by science'[65] — reveals not only real relations but also the ideological function of phenomenal categories, categories which form 'the basis of all the juridical notions of both labourer and capitalist, of all the mystifications of the capitalist mode of production, of all its illusions as to liberty, of all the apologetic shifts of the vulger economists'.[66] Marx's purpose in establishing knowledge of essential relations is not only to discover the real situation and conceptualise it adequately, which is the classical task of science, but, as the obscuration in phenomenal categories is a normal consequence of the direct experience of capitalist production, his purpose is also to provide the basis of a critique of the social system which masks the reality of its own operation.

V

Quite unlike the role ascribed to criticism in the *Critique* and its cognate writings, the critical dimension of Marx's mature epistemology has a largely intellectual and not an immediately practical importance. Marx has no illusions in *Capital* regarding the ability of a knowledge of capitalist relations of commodity production to undo commodity fetishism and the wage-form. Indeed, he observes with an irony appropriate in dispelling such an unlikely prospect that:[67]

> The recent scientific discovery, that the products of labour, so far as they are values, are but material expressions of the human labour spent in their production, marks, indeed, an epoch in the history of the development of the human race, but, by no means, dissipates the

mist through which the social character of labour appears to us as
an objective character of the products themselves . . . just as . . .
after the discovery by science of the component gases of air, the
atmosphere itself remained unaltered.

The abolition of social forms requires social and political action, not
scientific inquiry. Where a scientific conception of essence does have a
practical relevance, though, is in defining the relations which are the
necessary conditions of the social system and, therefore, those relations
upon which action has the consequence of significantly changing
society. It is in this sense that the critical potential of Marx's mature
essentialism has political consequences.

Marx's materialist conception of history can be understood — as
he understood it — as a set of propositions at the core of which is
the thesis that the essential feature of a social system is the manner
of production which it manifests. The difference between societies,
according to this thesis, is to be located essentially in the specific
manner of production found in and employed by different societies.[68]

This position provides Marx with the basis of a critique of a view
common to political economy and non-revolutionary programmes of
social reform and re-construction. Marx derides 'the banality of those
economists who proclaim production as an eternal truth, and confine
history to the domain of distribution'.[69] For, while he concurs that all
societies must produce in order to live, Marx maintains that the manner
or mode of production is specific to each social system and that it is
this fundamentally historical nature of production which marks the
difference between different historical societies.[70]

As he regards production relations as the essential relations of
economic life Marx also argues that it is erroneous to conceive distribution as an independent variable; distribution has to be seen, rather,
as dependent upon production: 'Any distribution whatever of the
means of consumption is only a consequence of the distribution of
the conditions of production themselves. The latter distribution, however, is a feature of the mode of production itself.'[71] The significance
of these comments concerning the historical nature of production and
the evaluation of distribution as a variable dependent upon production
are not confined to economic considerations alone, as they have a programmatic corollary of political importance. Herein lies the critical
dimension of Marx's epistemological essentialism in *Capital*.

Marx's essentialist conception of capitalism as an historical mode of
production leads him to argue that it is only through the overthrow of

capitalist production that the relations between the class of capital and the class of wage-labour can be abrogated and that nothing short of the overthrow of capitalism itself could lead to the emancipation of labour, could lead to socialism. This conclusion ultimately derives from Marx's epistemological essentialism.

It is the essentialism of Marx's mature thought that is responsible for the unique character of his science. This latter can be summarised by two factors. The first is that it is an intentionally critical science. With the discovery of the real relations of capitalist production Marx discovers the material conditions which engender the ideology of the age, that is, the phenomenal categories which in everyday parlance account for the direct experience of life and labour and render innocuous what Marx shows to be unequal relations of exploitation. In Marx's science of society is his critique of capitalism. Second, Marx was not primarily a scientist, he was above all a revolutionary intellectual and leader of a European-wide labour movement. Marx's science was developed in the service of his revolutionary aspirations; in order to change the world he had to interpret it operatively, understand it scientifically. Thus one cannot say merely that Marx's work is scientific, it is a critical science which is an integral part of a wider revolutionary framework.

VI

The course of this chapter has ranged wide. Beginning with an examination of the epistemology of Marx's 1843 *Critique* and concluding with the scientific essentialism in *Capital*, the different conceptions of the conditions of knowledge held by Marx at different times in his writings have been discussed and summarised. By examining the different conceptions of essence employed in his writing of the 1830s on the one hand and of the 1860s on the other, it has been possible to show that Marx's epistemology in the former period is quite distinct from, indeed contradictory to that of the latter. An early idealist epistemology was replaced with a materialist epistemology; the one metaphysical, the other scientific. To conclude on a negative note it can be said that Marx's early writing does not provide the epistemological foundation of his mature thought; more positively, Marx's epistemology developed from an internal critique of German idealism to an expression of empirical science recruited to revolutionary ends.

Chapter Two

Feuerbach

By no means a forgotten thinker, it is largely for his influence on Marx's early intellectual development that Ludwig Feuerbach is remembered today. But it was Feuerbach's stature as the leading German philosopher during the late 1830s and early 1840s that is the real measure of his importance and that is responsible for the attraction he exerted on Marx at the time. Feuerbach's *The Essence of Christianity*, published in 1841, is still highly regarded as a pioneering contribution to the sociology of religion. Some recent scholarship, such as that of Michael Gagern and Marx Wartofsky,[1] has drawn attention to the original and enduring contribution Feuerbach has made to European philosophy.

Feuerbach's influence on the development of the Young or Left Hegelian movement began with the publication in 1839 of *Towards a Critique of Hegel's Philosophy*. This essay not only demonstrates that Hegel's philosophical system and method are contradictory and tautological, it also positively established the basic tenets of Feuerbach's own philosophy. The naturalism, sensualism and humanism of Feuerbach's thought are here clearly expressed for the first time. In the *Critique* Feuerbach argues that reality is the reality of nature, that the criterion of existence is sensory experience, and that as man is therefore the proper subject of philosophy, philosophy must be the study of man in his relation to nature. To these ideas are added in *The Essence of Christianity* the notion that man alienates the consciousness of his nature in religion. Man produces religion through his own emotional activity, Feuerbach reasons, and in being subjected to religious principles allows his own creations an independent existence. This leads to the religious domination and oppression of man, to religious alienation.

The new philosophy begun in the *Critique* and developed in the

Essence is given explicit formulation in subsequent writings. Of particular relevance for discussion in this chapter are the *Preliminary Theses on the Reform of Philosophy* and the *Principles of the Philosophy of the Future*, published in 1842 and 1843 respectively. The critique of Hegel's dialectic which is presented in the *Theses* reverses the speculative philosophy of Hegel, which functions through abstract concepts. Feuerbach establishes the concrete universal of natural, sensuous man as the basic axiom of philosophy. Material appearance is the starting point of philosophy, Feuerbach insists, so that the essence of man in nature rather than the abstracted Idea of Hegel, is the determinate factor of reality and knowledge of reality. The measure of truth in this ontology and epistemology, Feuerbach demonstrates in the *Principles*, is man's species existence. The communicative sociality of man, which defines man as both a self-conscious being and an essentially social being, is an attribute of all human individuals and therefore a necessary element of man's natural capacities. Man naturally possesses 'species-being' according to Feuerbach, and it is this faculty which distinguishes man from the rest of the natural order and a conceptualisation of this attribute which provides the basis of Feuerbach's account of the human subject.

The critique of Hegel's dialectic and the notion of species-being — first outlined in *The Essence of Christianity* — are the principle elements of Feuerbach's humanist and naturalist materialism which seem to have excited Marx's imagination in the 1840s. In considering the development of Marx's thought the ambiguous importance of Ludwig Feuerbach therefore presents itself. The Feuerbachian influence on Marx during the period 1843 to 1845 is self-evident. Its significance, however, is subject to different interpretations.

The importance to Marx of Feuerbach's 'transformative method' in the former's *Critique of Hegel's Philosophy of Right*, which was briefly mentioned in the preceding chapter, enjoys almost universal recognition in the critical literature. The Feuerbachism of the *Critique* is continued in the *Introduction* to that work published in 1844. There are also numerous acknowledgments by Marx and much secondary documentation of Feuerbach's importance to the terminology and formulations of the *Economic and Philosophic Manuscripts*.[2] The influence of Feuerbach on Marx's thought seems to end with *The German Ideology*, a work in which Marx and Engels subject Feuerbach to an extensive theoretical attack and develop their own revolutionary 'practical materialism' which is at once a critique of and an alternative to Feuerbach's 'contemplative materialism'.[3]

Several questions are posed by this sketch of Marx's relation to Feuerbach. Initially it must be asked whether Marx's use of Feuerbach is merely political, as claimed by Istvan Meszaros and Karl Korsch,[4] for instance, or theoretical. If Marx was in some sense a theoretical Feuerbachian his repudiation of Feuerbach in *The German Ideology* raises another question. Louis Althusser,[5] for instance, has argued that *The German Ideology* constitutes a significantly new theoretical departure in Marx's thought in contradistinction to a prior Feuerbachian position. David McLellan, on the other hand, says that it was through an adaptation of Feuerbach's materialism that Marx formulated his own historical materialism.[6] Similarly, Eugene Kamenka has said that throughout his life Marx employed a conception of man which is 'entirely in the Feuerbachian spirit and consciously derived from his work'.[7] On these accounts the critique of Feuerbach in *The German Ideology* can be interpreted as a quasi-political matter internal to the Young Hegelian movement which did not significantly affect an enduring theoretical influence of Feuerbach on Marx.

In addition to the Feuerbachian influence a further unifying feature of Marx's work up to 1845 is the continuing elaboration of a theory of alienation in the writings from the *Critique* up to *The Holy Family*. Although the term 'alienation' is not used in the *Critique*, the description of the dualism between the state and civil society, to which modern man is allegedly subjected, is clearly an account of the alienated condition. This is evocatively developed in *On the Jewish Question*, where it is explicitly described in terms of alienation. Marx's analysis of the alienated condition is elaborated further in the *Introduction*, and a more sophisticated version still is developed in the 1844 *Manuscripts*. Whether Marx continued to employ the theory of alienation after 1845 is a matter of dispute, but he does seem to disclaim it in *The German Ideology*.[8]

The question of alienation theory in Marx, indeed, the question of his theoretical development in the widest sense up to at least 1846, cannot be fully considered without reference to Feuerbach. Not only is Marx's concept of alienation and his Feuerbachism contemporaneously developed and then renounced, but a theoretical relation between Marx and Feuerbach is sufficiently apparent to invite exploration. Marx's critique of Hegel and his nascent materialism, which are developed in this period, as well as his theory of alienation, can be traced back to Feuerbach's writing on the same themes. His contact with Feuerbach and various acknowledgments of appreciation leave no doubt as to Feuerbach's influence on Marx. The present chapter will attempt to ascertain the nature of that influence and its significance in Marx's development.

It will be argued below that in his writing up to 1846 Marx finds Feuerbach to be an important political ally against those Young Hegelians who attempt to elaborate a 'left' Hegelian position. It will also be shown that Marx's own theorising during this period draws heavily on the intellectual content of Feuerbach's thought. In using Feuerbach's theories for his own purposes, it will be argued, Marx carries Feuerbachian thought to its limits, and in confronting it with tasks to which it is not equal, he is led to resolve certain tensions in Feuerbach's conception of man and nature in such a way as to construct a critique of Feuerbach and is led to the development of an alternative theory. In examining Marx's use of Feuerbach's materialism and related theory we will be able to trace the genesis and development of Marx's own theory of historical materialism.

I

The argument, that Marx's relation to Feuerbach is predominantly political rather than theoretical, has some currency. Karl Korsch, for instance, supports such a position when he says that Marx, unlike Engels, arrived at his materialism independently of Feuerbach's critique of philosophical and theological idealism 'by a much longer road through a study of Democritus and Epicurus, of the materialists of the 17th and 18th centuries, and finally through a detailed critical revision of the whole idealist philosophy of Hegel'.[9] On this account Marx's relation with Feuerbach could only have been political, for Marx's development of materialist theory had begun at a time prior to Feuerbach's influence on him. Whilst Korsch is mistaken in dating Marx's materialism from the period of his doctoral thesis, he does in effect correct Engels's suggestion that Marx fell under Feuerbach's spell in 1841 with the publication of the latter's *The Essence of Christianity*.[10] Although some writers[11] still claim that Feuerbach's influence on Marx began in that year or with that book, Franz Mehring's classic biography corrected 'the trick which Engels' memory played him',[12] and David McLellan has shown that it was Bruno Bauer rather than Feuerbach who exercised an intellectual influence on Marx during this period.[13] However, Korsch fails to acknowledge that Marx's 'detailed critical revision of the whole idealistic philosophy of Hegel' was not attempted until after he had read Feuerbach's *Preliminary Theses for the Reform of Philosophy*. Marx makes extensive use of this work in his *Critique of Hegel's Philosophy of Right*. It is also from about this time that Marx's political alliance with Feuerbach begins. The political and theoretical relations between Marx and Feuerbach are not so easily separated, as we will demonstrate below.

Marx's relation with Feuerbach has its pre-history in the relation between Marx and Bauer. Marx's career in political journalism began in early 1842 when the prospect of a university post was closed to him through Bauer's dismissal from Bonn University.[14] Marx had finished his doctorate on Bauer's insistence with the hope that he would join Bauer at Bonn University where they would collaborate on atheistic writing. After Bauer's dismissal the two did in fact work together briefly until Bauer moved to Berlin. From July 1842 Marx was drawn into the organisation of the *Rheinische Zeitung*, a journal of liberal reform, and was appointed its editor in mid-October. From the time of his first involvement with the paper Marx found himself to be in increasing disagreement with the Berlin Young Hegelians, known as the Freien, led by Bauer's brother, Edgar. And by the end of November Marx's break with the Berliners was complete. Marx's differences with the Bauer brothers and their group were both political and theoretical. The outlandish behaviour of the Berliners and their uncompromising attacks on liberal initiatives for reform were inimical to good relations with the progressive movement being mounted by the Rhineland bourgeoisie, which Marx supported. Theoretically, the Berliners were attempting to work out 'revolutionary' principles derived from Hegel, to further develop Hegel's ideas; Marx, on the other hand, regarded such projects poorly and was himself attempting to develop a total critique of Hegel. The articles which Marx wrote for the *Rheinische Zeitung* show no trace of Feuerbach's influence, and the unsigned article which appeared in the *Anekdota* proclaiming that 'there is no other road . . . to truth, and freedom except that leading through the stream of fire [the Feuer-bach]. Feuerbach is the purgatory of the present times,'[15] which has been widely attributed to Marx, was probably not written by him.[16]

The absence of Feuerbach's influence on Marx at this time does not mean that they had nothing in common. Marx shared with Feuerbach an interest in criticising Hegel and Hegelism. As early as 1839 Feuerbach published *Towards a Critique of Hegel's Philosophy* in the *Hallische Jahrbücher für Wissenschaft und Kunst*, which argued, among other things, that Hegel's philosophy is tautological to the extent that it assumes the conclusion it claims to prove, namely, an identity of ideality and reality, an identity which eliminates reality in favour of the ideal. Also, the hostility between Marx and the Berliners has its parallel in the hostility of the Berliners to Feuerbach's attack on speculative philosophy. This is all the more interesting for the fact that in 1841 Marx, Bauer and Feuerbach had together planned to found a theological-philosophical review. Feuerbach went through the same change in his relation with Bauer as did Marx. The basis for an alliance between Marx and Feuerbach, therefore, was well established during 1842. It was consolidated in early 1843. Marx had intended to write a systematic critique of Hegel's political philosophy for about a year before he drafted the *Critique* between March and August 1843, but it was not until he had read Feuerbach's *Preliminary Theses on the Reform of Philosophy*, published in February 1843, that he was able to do so. The lynch-pin of the *Critique* is the method developed in Feuerbach's *Preliminary Theses*.

Feuerbach's *Theses* can be summarised in four basic points which find expression in Marx's writing of that time. Firstly, Feuerbach corrects Hegel's speculative idealism by 'turn[ing] the predicate into the subject', thus establishing 'the true relationship of thought to being. . . . Being is the subject, thought the predicate.'[17] He advocates the negation or transcendence of philosophy, for the 'philosopher must take into the text of philosophy that aspect of man which does not philosophise, but, rather, is opposed to philosophy. . . . Philosophy has to begin . . . with its own antithesis; i.e., with non-philosophy.'[18] This second point is a necessary precondition to a third, which is an assertion of the primacy of man: 'All speculation . . . outside of or even above man, is speculation without unity, necessity, substance, ground, and reality.'[19] Finally, Feuerbach argues that the transcendence of philosophy and the realisation of man can be accomplished only through a Franco-German unity. 'The true philosopher who is identical with life and man must be of Franco-German parentage.'[20] While Marx's *Critique* emphasises only Feuerbach's method of criticising Hegel's logic, his *Introduction*, written but months later, proposes the entire Feuerbachian programme summarised in these four points.

The *Introduction* is not without its criticism of Feuerbach, as we shall see shortly, but in posing an alternative programme to the Berlin Young Hegelians and their attempts to propagate a 'revolutionary' elaboration of Hegel — they fail 'to realise that previous philosophy itself belongs to this world and is its complement'[21] — Marx mobilises a set of notions against them derived from Feuerbach. Marx's attack on Bauer and his group is repeated in *The Holy Family*. Here the themes of negating philosophy, Feuerbachian humanism and the need for a Franco-German unity, which first appeared in the *Introduction*,[22] are again asserted.[23] The Bauer group is subjected to criticism again in *The German Ideology*, but this time Feuerbach does not provide the battering rams; he is viewed from across the battlefield and counted as merely another representative of modern German philosophy along with Bauer and Max Stirner.[24] Marx's political use of Feuerbach, therefore, ranges from 1843 to 1845,[25] and abruptly ends with a theoretical critique of him the following year.

Actually, Marx's political and theoretical differences with Feuerbach pre-date the critique mounted in *The German Ideology*, but up to 1845 Marx's critical development of Feuerbach's theory forms the basis of his opposition to the Young Hegelians. While Marx was never a mere follower of Feuerbach, he did share with him a common starting point, utilised his critique of Hegel and adopted the programme outlined in the *Preliminary Theses*. The major difference between Marx's *Introduction* and Feuerbach's *Theses* is already suggested in an acclamatory letter Marx wrote immediately after his first reading of Feuerbach's essay:[26]

> I approve of Feuerbach's aphorisms, except for one point: he directs himself too much to nature and too little to politics. But it is politics which happens to be the only link through which contemporary philosophy can become true.

To Feuerbach's humanism, to his pleas for a transcendence of philosophy and a Franco-German alliance, Marx adds the political dimension when he identifies the proletariat as the agent of social revolution. Marx attempts to bring Feuerbach himself round to accept the necessity of a critique of politics, but fails to do so.[27] This did not lead Marx to believe that the Feuerbachian programme should be abandoned, however, for in the *Introduction* it is described as 'the prerequisite of all criticism',[28] and is similarly depicted in *The Holy Family*.[29]

While Marx and Feuerbach disagreed on the question of political action, Marx's political use of Feuerbach was premised on the assumption that in Feuerbach's writings are 'given — I do not know whether consciously or not — a philosophical foundation to socialism, and we communists at once have understood your works in this sense.'[30] It is, therefore, difficult to sustain the claim that in using Feuerbach in his struggle against the Bauer group Marx owed no intellectual debt to Feuerbach, for the political use of Feuerbach is based on an appreciation of the theoretical content of his thought. Marx's Feuerbachian references, then, cannot properly be summarised as no more than terminological, for the political weapons which Marx used against the Young Hegelians were at this time based on a particularly sympathetic understanding of Feuerbach's theory. Nor can the influence of Feuerbach's thought on Marx be said to end in 1844, when it was made clear to Marx that Feuerbach would not contribute to the *Deutsch-Französische Jahrbücher*,[31] for the main Feuerbachian elements of the *Introduction* are rehearsed in *The Holy Family* of 1845.

After recognising that Marx's political use of Feuerbach in his polemic against Bauer and his group entails an apprehension of Feuerbach's humanist programme, albeit supplemented with the political dimension of proletarian practice, it is crucial to also recognise that during this same period Marx develops some positive criticisms of Feuerbach. To avoid confusion and paradox in attempting to understand what is clearly a complex theoretical relationship between Marx and Feuerbach, it is essential that the precise nature of Marx's criticisms of Feuerbach be identified. Precision here is also important for an understanding of the development of historical materialism. The difficulty arises because Marx's criticisms of Feuerbach in the aphoristic *Theses on Feuerbach*, which draw together and summarise points made against Feuerbach during the period from 1843, are often regarded as the basis of the argument which when elaborated becomes the first part of *The German Ideology*. In this latter work Marx's full-length critique of Feuerbach is the obverse side of his theory of historical materialism.

If this view of the *Theses* is true it follows that the theory of historical materialism was merely enunciated in *The German Ideology* but developed in the writings of 1843 to 1845. This interpretation of the *Theses* generates a serious paradox, however. It maintains that Marx's historical materialist repudiation of Feuerbach, elaborated in *The German Ideology*, but already formulated in the *Theses* which draw on earlier criticisms of Feuerbach, was developed at the same time as and co-existed with Marx's incorporation of Feuerbach's theory when polemically engaging the Young Hegelians. This paradox is resolved when it is demonstrated that, firstly, Marx's critique of Feuerbach during the period of his accepting Feuerbach's programme, which is indeed summarised in the *Theses on Feuerbach*, is a critique of Feuerbach only in so far as it attempts to make Feuerbachism consistent with itself. Secondly, the main points against Feuerbach which when positively stated amount to the exposition of historical materialism found in *The German Ideology* are absent in the *Theses on Feuerbach*.[32]

II

The eleven *Theses on Feuerbach* make three broad criticisms of Feuerbach which can also be found variously in the *Introduction*, in the *Economic and Philosophic Manuscripts*, and, to a lesser degree, in *The Holy Family*. The first three *Theses* make the point that materialism up to and including Feuerbach has ignored the practical side of man. Marx very briefly indicates how materialism is better able to account for knowledge and historical change by incorporating into its system the concept of 'practice'. The second general point relates to the social nature of man. In the *Theses* IV to VII various aspects of Feuerbach's default in this area are noted. These two points, of practice and society, are brought together in a third criticism which faces materialism with the consequences of realising that social life is itself practical. The details and ramifications of this are rendered in the *Theses* VIII to XI. The particulars of these criticisms of Feuerbach can be made clear by examining Marx's comments on these matters in his writing up to and including the *Theses on Feuerbach*.

The factor of practice or *praxis*, which remained an essential part of Marx's mature theory of history, was noted to be crucial in itself and absent in Feuerbach by Marx when he first read the *Preliminary Theses on the Reform of Philosophy*.[33] The need for praxis is affirmed in the *Introduction*, man is described as essentially a consciously active being in the *Economic and Philosophic Manuscripts*, and in *The Holy Family* it is observed that ideas 'cannot carry out anything at all. In order to carry out ideas men are needed who can exert practical force.'[34] And yet, when Marx paraphrases Feuerbach in the *Introduction* by saying that 'Man makes religion, religion does not make man,'[35] he acknowledges that Feuerbach does indeed appreciate, in a sense, that man is not merely a product of circumstances but also active in making them. More significantly, Marx seems to suggest that Feuerbach's humanism, and especially his demand for the negation of philosophy, implies that man has an active side. Although Feuerbach is not specifically mentioned in this context in the *Introduction*, Marx's comments on what he ironically calls the 'practical political party' are pertinent. The practical party, says Marx, is 'right to demand the negation of philosophy', but such a demand can be achieved only when philosophy is first realised, and the realisation of philosophy is possible only 'through practice [Praxis]'.[36] Marx's criticism that Feuerbach's materialism is defective in failing to recognise that man's sensuousness exists as 'human sensuous activity, practice'[37] is not primarily concerned to chide him for ignoring practice. Marx's complaint, rather, is that Feuerbach has not sufficiently drawn out the implications of his theory of man as a sensuous being, a theory which leads, Marx claims, to the recognition that man is an active, practical being.

Marx's argument that Feuerbach's humanism, and especially the observation that man is a sensuous being, implies that man has a practical nature, takes three different but related forms or stages. One of these is that there is a practical imperative in intention. We have already seen Marx argue that the intention to negate philosophy can be approximated only through practice. Marx returns to this question in the *Economic and Philosophic Manuscripts* when he says that 'the resolution of the theoretical antitheses is only possible in a practical way.'[38] The view that Feuerbach's programme engenders or requires a practical imperative is not a consequence of Marx attempting to apply a moral and external principle to Feuerbach's humanism, such as one claiming that a person must act upon what he believes. On the contrary, it follows from a principle internal to Feuerbach's anthropology. The practical resolution of theoretical antitheses is possible, Marx continues, only 'by virtue of the practical energy of man'.[39] This is the second form of the argument that man is an active being, the sensuous nature of man anthropologically entails that man is by nature active.

The argument that it is in man's nature to be practical because it is in man's nature to be sensuous is taken directly from Feuerbach. Marx says that:[40]

Man as an objective, sensuous being is therefore a suffering being —
and because he feels what he suffers, a passionate being. Passion is
the essential force of man energetically bent on its object.

It is because man suffers that he is active. The idea that suffering is a middle link in a chain of sensuous man and his activeness had already been suggested in the *Introduction*, where religious suffering is discussed.[41] In the *Economic and Philosophic Manuscripts* the argument is much more general when it is explained that man's capacity for suffering is directly related to his sensuous nature.[42] 'To be sensuous is to suffer'[43] because the objects and forces external to man in nature which stimulate his senses also provide for the satisfaction of his needs. This sentiment is Feuerbach's: 'A being without suffering is nothing but a being without sensuousness, without matter.'[44] While suffering, and especially suffering through attempting to satisfy needs, somehow proves man's sensuousness, it is in the satisfaction of man's needs, and especially his species needs, that man is active.[45] Marx develops this point by rigorously applying Feuerbach's notion of man as an essentially natural and sensuous being.

The principle of praxis is not unknown to Feuerbach, and he argues that it is a consequence of sensuous existence when he says that all reality exists in space and time, 'the primary criteria of praxis'.[46] Feuerbach, however, does not so closely tie his concept of praxis to human sensuousness. Marx, on the other hand, holds that Feuerbach's conception of man's sensuousness entails human praxis, that a developed Feuerbachian anthropology is an anthropology of praxis.

There is a third form of argument employed by Marx which criticises Feuerbach for not developing the notion of man as a practical being but at the same time suggests that this notion is inherent in Feuerbachism. Marx's position is that it is in uniting the materialist doctrine of objective sensuousness with the idealist doctrine of man's mental activity that the concept of man as a sensuously active or practical being emerges. Marx's treatment of Feuerbach in relation to this issue is on the surface contradictory. In *The Holy Family* he says that 'the old antithesis between spiritualism and materialism has been ... overcome once and for all by Feuerbach,'[47] whereas it is denied in the first *Thesis on Feuerbach* that Feuerbach's materialism has incorporated idealism's discovery of man's 'active side'.[48] The resolution of this paradox is found in the *Economic and Philosophic Manuscripts* where Marx concludes that man 'is an active natural being' after developing the Feuerbachian themes of man as a species through his consciousness of others and of man as an objective sensuous being.[49] 'Here we see how *consistent* naturalism or humanism distinguishes itself both from idealism and materialism, constituting at the same time the unifying truth of both.'[50] It is 'consistent naturalism' which, in unifying the truth of materialism and idealism, shows man to be a practical being. Feuerbach himself is inconsistent, according to Marx. The neglect in Feuerbach of man's practical activity as a constituent part of sensuous reality is not merely criticised by Marx. He argues that it is only through the further development of the programme of humanist naturalism, which Feuerbach established, that such a concept can be advanced. Marx's comments, in effect, amount to the claim that while Feuerbach himself does not grasp the relevance of man's practical activity, the concept is nevertheless integral to Feuerbachian theory.

In his third *Thesis on Feuerbach* Marx employs what is the revised, corrected and consistent Feuerbachian principle of man as a practically active being to show that society is a unified whole rather than a dualist arrangement in which the source of historical change would be external to the circumstances of men.[51] This consideration raises the question of man's social nature, and this issue is central to Marx's second general criticism of Feuerbach.

The criticisms of Feuerbach in the *Theses* IV to VII are widely regarded as an attempt to confront Feuerbach's philosophical anthropology with a materialist sociology.[52] The evidence for this view in the *Theses* themselves is rather slender, however. Apart from the general impression created by the claims that Feuerbach's treatment of man is deficient in that it does not sufficiently recognise that he is a social being, there is little indication in the *Theses* of a 'sociological' vision of man. Marx does, of course, assert that man's human essence 'is the ensemble of social relations',[53] and that religious alienation must 'be explained by the self-cleavage and self-contradictoriness of [its] secular basis'.[54] It will become obvious, though, that these propositions are not equivalent to Marx's conception of social man developed in *The German Ideology*, where it is argued that man's social nature is explicable in terms of his material production.[55] This is a qualitatively different category from that of 'practical, human-sensuous activity',[56] announced in the fifth *Thesis on Feuerbach* and apparently invoked to serve the same function as the former, namely, to account for the basis of man's social relations. While the discussion in the fourth *Thesis*, of what is required to explain religion, can be regarded as parallel to the account in *The German Ideology*, stating that the 'phantoms formed in the human brain are also, necessarily, sublimates of [man's] material life-process, which is empirically verifiable and bound to material premises,'[57] the absence of anything but the general and non-empirical categories of self-cleavage and self-contradiction prevent us from seeing the two as anything like equivalents. The argument that the *Theses* do not comprise a summary of *The German Ideology* will be taken up later in the chapter; at this point it is intended to indicate no more than that the materialist sociology, first developed in the latter work, is not particularly indicated in the former.

The argument that Marx's discussion of man's social nature in his criticisms of Feuerbach in the *Theses* is devoid of a 'materialist' content does not itself deny that he develops a sociological critique of philosophical anthropology. But an ambiguity in the term 'society' and the special meaning Marx gives to the concept in his writings prior to *The German Ideology*, a discussion of which is developed more fully in the next chapter, does raise the question of whether there is anything that can be regarded as sociological in these *Theses*. What will be argued here is that Marx's criticisms of Feuerbach's conception of man do not constitute a radical departure from philosophical anthropology, but, like the criticisms of the first three *Theses*, attempt to make consistent and develop further an essentially Feuerbachian notion of man's 'social' essence.

A *prima facie* case contrary to the one to be outlined here, that Marx not only developed a sociological critique of Feuerbach in his *Theses*, but also that this critique was begun soon after his reading Feuerbach's *Preliminary Theses on the Reform of Philosophy*, could be argued by showing the similarity between Marx's seventh *Thesis* and certain passages in the *Introduction*. Marx claims in his *Theses* that Feuerbach 'does not see that the "religious sentiment" is itself a social product, and that the abstract individual whom he analyses belongs in reality to a particular form of society'.[58] A similar passage in the *Introduction* stating that 'man is no abstract being squatting outside the world. Man is the world of man, state, society,'[59] has also been regarded as a sociological critique of Feuerbach's anthropology of religion.[60] And yet it is probable that Marx was not criticising Feuerbach at all in this latter passage. A little later in the *Introduction*, when Marx returns to the question of abstracted treatments of man, his target is explicitly Hegel, not Feuerbach. The discussion there of 'the German conception of the modern state, which abstracts from the real man, was only possible because and in so far as the modern state itself abstracts from real man'[61] is reminiscent of the *Critique*. Before going further into Marx's criticisms in the *Critique* of Hegel's abstraction of man, in order to show its relevance for an understanding of the *Theses*, let us briefly consider the notion of 'society' as it is used by Marx in his writings of this period.

One meaning of the term 'society' is the anthropological notion of society as man's 'species-life itself',[62] as Marx expresses it in his essay *On the Jewish Question*, written just before the *Introduction* and published with it. This conception is not part of a sociological argument about man's condition, but one concerned with the question of the nature of man's human essence. It is precisely this anthropological meaning which is ascribed to Feuerbach when his great achievements are listed by Marx in the *Economic and Philosophic Manuscripts*: 'Feuerbach also makes the social relationship "of man to man" the basic principle of the theory.'[63] This social relationship is that derived from man's 'species-being' in which self-consciousness is the source of man's natural communicative sociality. It is possible, therefore, to see the assertion of the *Introduction*, that man is not an abstract being outside the world but a social being, as an affirmation of the Feuerbachian critique of Hegel's conception of man as a predicate of mind. There is no need to assume that Marx's consideration of society in the seventh *Thesis on Feuerbach* departs from this conception of man's social nature in the anthropological sense.

As we saw in Chapter 1 above, Marx criticises Hegel in the *Critique* for not regarding man as a being of essential sociality in an anthropological sense, for the social qualities of man's nature are expressed, even though in an alienated form, in the political state, according to Marx. Whereas Hegel regards the state as an entity quite external to man's nature, Marx contends that the political offices of the state, whilst not an expression of man's full universality, for the political state is not rational, are none the less a function of human sociality under particular conditions. It is this critique of Hegel which seems to inform the discussion in the *Introduction*, referred to above, of the abstraction of real man in the German conception of the modern state. A perfectly coherent interpretation of the seventh *Thesis on Feuerbach* can show that Marx is there directing comments against Feuerbach which are similar to those he made against Hegel in the *Critique*. While in the *Critique* the state is regarded as a 'mode of man's social existence as the realisation and objectification of his essence,'[64] the religious sentiment is analogously conceived as a social product in the *Theses*. This is to say that not only is religion an aspect of man's alienated condition, as Feuerbach correctly shows, but, as Marx maintains, that religion is a phenomenon which reveals something of the state of man's essential nature in a wider sense. Feuerbach, in seeing the alienation of individual men, ignores the fact, stressed by Marx, that the general condition of man's species-nature under religious alienation implies that all men 'belong in reality to a particular form of society',[65] or, as he more graphically puts it in the *Critique*, the 'modern age . . . isolates the objective essence of man, treating it as something purely external and material.'[66]

These comments of Marx relate to two points, namely that the alienation of essence is not a merely individual predicament and that in the alienation of essence man's species-nature is given a limited and particular expression. Feuerbach's conception of man's anthropologically social essence and its alienation is such that individuals may lose their essence under adverse circumstances. Marx's criticism of Feuerbach's individualised essentialism amounts to the assertion that as the social essence of man is a faculty of his species-being or species-nature — which is also Feuerbach's point of departure — any factor which interferes with the full expression of that nature, such as the state or religion, affects the species as a whole and determines a general condition of man, not merely the individual condition of particular men. For Marx man remains a species-being under religious or political alienation, even though his essential nature is without full expression. This is because Marx regards religion and the state as being themselves a consequence of man's species-being in a limited and incomplete sense. Feuerbach, on the other hand, sees religious alienation as a complete denial of man's species-being. These points are developed in the sixth *Thesis on Feuerbach* where Marx argues that 'the human essence is no abstraction inherent in each single individual. In its reality it is the ensemble of the social relations.'[67] In this Marx again attempts to introduce consistency into Feuerbachian thought.

Marx does not charge Feuerbach with denying that the human essence 'is the ensemble of the social relations', but with failing to 'enter upon a criticism of this real essence'.[68] Feuerbach's own general view, summarised in section 59 of *Principles of the Philosophy of the Future*, is remarkably similar to Marx's critical formulation:[69]

> The single man in isolation possesses in himself the essence of man
> neither as a moral nor as a thinking being. The essence of man is
> contained only in the community, in the unity of man with man.

However, in not criticising or understanding fully this real essence Feuerbach, according to Marx, perpetrates the double mistake of, firstly, abstracting from the historical process and thereby presupposes an abstract, isolated individual and, secondly, of assuming that the human essence naturally unites these individuals.[70] The introduction of 'history' as a counter to what appears to be a manifestation of methodological individualism on Feuerbach's part, and the condemnation of Feuerbach's alleged claim that man is united naturally, a condemnation usually associated with the sociological repudiation of the view that man has a pre-social nature, gives the impression that Marx is sociologically criticising Feuerbach's anthropologism. And yet these criticisms can be shown to be quite consistent with the anthropological concept of man outlined by Marx in his *Critique of Hegel's Philosophy of Right*.

According to Marx's early ontology, which was described in the previous chapter, man's essential nature of universal and rational sociality attains its full potential through an historical process of development. Prior to man's full apprehension of his essence, when man is isolated from the full sociality of his species-being, his essence is none the less immanent in his being and determinate in his institutions and their development. In these early stages of his human development man is isolated or alienated from the universal or rational form of his essence even though it exists empirically in a partial form as the political state or even as religion. The point that man exists as a species-being even in his alienation is very important to Marx's analysis and has too often been misunderstood;[71] it is crucial to Marx's argument that although man may be isolated from his objective essence, from his essence in its fully developed form, his essence exists empirically in the partial form of alienated institutions. The historical process of man's essential development described by Marx assumes that man's essence is ever present but in different forms at different times. It is in the culmination and conclusion of this historical process that man's full essence is realised 'in the community, in the unity of man with man', to use Feuerbach's words which Marx paraphrases throughout the *Economic and Philosophic Manuscripts*. It is probable that it is this historical process to which Marx refers in the sixth *Thesis on Feuerbach*. An interpretation based on this assumption shows that on the one hand Marx shares Feuerbach's notion of the human essence as the ensemble of social relations and, on the other, that he criticises Feuerbach's misunderstanding of this concept of social man.

Marx's argument is that Feuerbach abstracts from the historical process in two senses, in an ahistorical naturalism and in an individualisation of man. He posits the social essence of man's species-being ahistorically by considering that it unites men naturally without consideration of the historical development which leads to the full realisation of man's species-being in a universal form. For Feuerbach the datum of man's essential sociality, his species-being, is the self-consciousness of man which exists here and now. Marx implies that Feuerbach holds to a more or less idealised view of man's social essence in so far as Feuerbach suggests that essential species-being exists only in its full form as man's community with man, even though man is demonstrably without full community in religion and the political state. His conception of man's essence as species-being in communicative sociality has no regard for the fact, postulated by Marx, that its empirical rupture through religion is not a mere loss of essence, but itself an alienated form of man's essential nature which will be surmounted in man's historical development. Thus for Feuerbach the human essence is 'comprehended only as a "genus" '[72] whereas Marx comprehends it as a developing and evolutionary form. Because Feuerbach regards man's essence as an idealised reality of man rather than as an aspect of his historical development, he regards the loss of essence as a misery which befalls unfortunate individuals rather than as a general condition of the human species under specific conditions:[73]

> Only in human life does it happen, but even here only in abnormal and unfortunate cases, that being is separated from essence; only here does it happen that a man's essence is not where his being is.

This is the second sense in which Feuerbach abstracts from the historical process.

What Marx appears to be doing in those *Theses on Feuerbach* which argue his case for man's social nature is to reveal an inconsistency in Feuerbach's treatment of man and correct that inconsistency by developing the Feuerbachian presuppositions which he regards as fundamentally correct. His discussion in the *Theses* of man's practical nature and man's social nature is a criticism of Feuerbach's actual formulations from the point of view of Feuerbachian premises. Marx thereby develops a consistent Feuerbachism in a way that Feuerbach failed to do. We know that Marx at this time regarded Feuerbach as 'one who has made genuine discoveries' and as 'the representative of materialism coinciding with humanism in the theoretical domain.'[74] In breaking new ground for the first time it is quite explicable that Feuerbach would have retained vestiges of the old system of thought he overthrew and would not have been able to follow his original discoveries to all their ramifications. In those *Theses on Feuerbach* discussed above Marx attempts to complete the task Feuerbach began. This certainly constitutes a critique of Feuerbach, but the content of the critique is decidedly Feuerbachian.

The third general criticism which Marx raises in the *Theses on Feuerbach* VIII to XI, signifying that social life is itself practical and that in being practical it is subject to change, brings together his previous discussion of the practically active and the social nature of man. In this criticism of Feuerbach Marx again, in effect, attempts to strengthen the Feuerbachian programme but in doing so introduces into it an element of inconsistency which, when more fully developed, leads him to abandon Feuerbachism itself. In arguing that '[s]ocial life is essentially practical' and that 'the point . . . is to change' the world,[75] Marx introduces into his Feuerbachian anthropology a new

concept which it cannot bear. In developing a fully consistent Feuerbachism he paradoxically brings out a fundamental contradiction
internal to it.

The aphoristic nature of the *Theses* gives them a somewhat cryptic
quality, but we may be reasonably sure that when Marx refers to the
'human practice' which gives the 'rational solution' to all the 'mysteries
which mislead theory to mysticism'[76] he is discussing the practice which
is part of the historical process leading to the full sociality of man's
essence described above, the practice in which men engage in order to
overcome their mystifying alienation. This interpretation is borne out
in the tenth *Thesis* where the standpoint of Marx's new materialism
is said to be that of 'human society, or socialised humanity'.[77] 'Human
society' in this context can only be the condition of unalienated man,
the condition in which his fully social essence is completely realised,
especially as it is contrasted with the standpoint of 'contemplative
materialism' or the 'old materialism', which is that of 'civil society'.[78]
Civil society is the association of men who exist for each other through
their intrinsically individual needs and interests and is by its nature,
therefore, alienated society in which men cannot exist as full species-
beings. Human society or socialised humanity, then, is what Marx
elsewhere describes as communism.

Feuerbach, too, develops the notion that man is a species-being in
communism:[79]

> in essence what he is in the senses – he is Man or, rather – since
> Feuerbach transports the essence of Man only into his com-
> munity – he is social Man, communist.

We have already seen that Feuerbach's appreciation of man's essential
sociality is based on the assumption that there is an existing common
human condition of self-consciousness which constitutes this essence.
The condition of essential being, for Feuerbach, is achieved through
love, which is its content.[80] Feuerbach, therefore, sees the achievement of communism, the social unity of man with man, as coming
about through love. Marx, on the other hand, argues that it is achieved
with practice; an argument he develops from Feuerbachian premises.
This is the point of the eleventh *Thesis*, which requires that the world
be changed, and this itself is an extension of the postulation that man's
alienation is a condition of partial sociality suffered by the species as a
whole, an alienation which is within the spectrum of man's historical
evolution. Although Marx does not specify the class nature of practice
and change in the *Theses*, his introduction elsewhere in writings of the

period on political class action as the agent of change brings with it the political role of the proletariat as a class which is inevitably led to confront other classes in achieving change. From the point of view of Feuerbach's insistence that full species-being is achieved with love the class aspect of change is inhuman; it is also inconsistent with the Feuerbachian view of man as a species-being with a common and uniform nature, for class conflict is both unlovely and contrary to the concept of a shared and common human nature. It is at this point that the Feuerbachian system refined by Marx must begin to break down.

It would be a mistake, however, to gain the impression that in the last four *Theses* Marx undermines Feuerbachian thought while he attempts to elaborate and develop it in the others. The last four *Theses* really do no more than draw out the implications of those that went before them, and the contradiction inherent in his extended Feuerbachism is not here manifest. Neither do we want to suggest that Marx is aware of the contradiction in his development of Feuerbachian thought in the *Theses*. In *The Holy Family*, for instance, Marx says that the concept of man's consciousness in English and French materialism is one in which the development of consciousness is the result of forces external to it, and, therefore, is a concept of passive rather than of practical consciousness.[81] He then immediately goes on to argue that this form of materialism can be used to support the case for communism.[82] The first point of this argument is in the ninth *Thesis on Feuerbach*. What we have deduced of the meaning of the other *Theses* might suggest that the second part of the argument would still be acceptable to Marx at the time of his writing the *Theses* some five months later, namely, that although the position as stated by Feuerbach is inadequate there is in it a germ of truth accessible to a fuller development. Such a development is to be found in the tenth and eleventh *Theses*.

It is clear from writings of the period that Marx entertains both sides of the contradiction inherent in his extended Feuerbachism without being aware of the antagonism between them. With class political action coexist the principles of love and a common human nature. Although Marx does not elevate love to the determining position Feuerbach gives to it, love is listed with the five senses and other faculties as essentially 'human relations' in the *Economic and Philosophic Manuscripts*.[83] Similarly, his description of fully developed humanism and naturalism as communism in 'the *genuine* resolution of the conflict between man and nature and between man and man',[84] while wider than Feuerbach's notion of love, clearly contains this

Feuerbachian element.[85] To cite a third example, Marx's expression of distaste for the political economists who strip 'the individual . . . of all determinateness so as to class him as capitalist or worker',[86] while not a little odd in a book which discusses class and the class condition at some length, can be explained by the fact that Marx shares Feuerbach's disquiet at attempts to divide men and thereby obstruct the possibility of love between fellow men. Here we see the class concept and the concept of love coexisting none the less. Although class struggle is described in this work,[87] it is not yet conceived as the motor of communist revolution.[88]

In *The Holy Family* class struggle does appear as the mechanism for attaining communism, or at least as the means of abolishing private property, but even then Marx maintains the assumption of a common, a-class or non-class human nature. The proletariat and the so-called class of wealth suffer 'the same human self-estrangement', according to Marx, even though they experience it differently.[89] There is in this the notion of a singular, universal and essential human nature which is fundamental to the anthropological view of man. In *The German Ideology* and the writings thereafter, where communism is fully understood as a consequence of class upheaval, the concept of an essentialist human nature is removed. In these writings man is defined basically in terms of his relation to the production process and the means of production. In fact Marx now describes the class nature of man in a manner similar to that of the political economists who were criticised in the *Economic and Philosophic Manuscripts* for precisely this reason.[90] For it is largely unintelligible to talk of an essential human species-being common to all men in the context of a situation in which the individual condition is determined by one's class location and where the major classes are mutually antagonistic.[91]

III

The most complete statement of Marx's early alienation theory is to be found in his *Economic and Philosophic Manuscripts*, which fall in the middle of what might be described as his Feuerbachian period. A Feuerbachian influence is fairly self-evident in the *Manuscripts*; but as there are also in them concepts absent in Feuerbach's own writing, as Marx goes beyond Feuerbach's own formulations and as he outlines criticism of Feuerbach, some scholars regard the theoretical content of the work as non-Feuerbachian.[92] Such a position gains support in the fact that many of the themes discussed in the *Manuscripts* can be traced through all of Marx's writings subsequent to his theoretical repudiation of Feuerbach. A concern with the labour process, class relations, private property, political economy, the emancipation of labour and so on, which strongly emerges in the *Economic and Philosophic Manuscripts*, is both absent in Feuerbach and characteristic of Marx's later work.[93] It will be shown, however, that the Feuerbachian influence in the *Manuscripts* is not merely verbal and apparent but theoretical and central, and that while many of the themes discussed in the work are continuous with the content of Marx's later writing they are accounted for with significantly different theories.

It may appear precipitate to claim that the *Manuscripts* are Feuerbachian when the intellectual sources on which Marx drew in writing them are numerous and varied. The French economists Eugene Buret, Constantin Pecqueur and Jean Baptiste Say and the German economist Wilhelm Schulz contribute to Marx's discussion of the wretchedness of the workers' condition, for instance. The British classical economists Adam Smith and, to a lesser degree, David Ricardo are fundamental to Marx's account of the relation between capital and labour. The importance of Engels's *Outline of a Critique of Political Economy*[94] to Marx's own critique of political economy should not be forgotten. In his 'Preface' Marx describes Engels and Moses Hess as the authors of the 'only *original* German works of substance in this science'.[95] And yet Marx suggests that although he has used the ideas of many writers in drafting the *Manuscripts*, their theoretical core is largely Feuerbachian, for he goes on to say that 'positive criticism as a whole . . . owes its true foundation to the discoveries of Feuerbach.'[96] While Marx crossed out this line it was not because he wanted to revise his opinion, for the subsequent claim that it 'is only with Feuerbach that positive, humanistic and naturalistic criticism begins' is left intact,[97] and repeated in the body of the text.[98] Feuerbach is subjected to criticism in the *Economic and Philosophic Manuscripts* for the limited nature of his critique of Hegel,[99] but these are internal criticisms, similar in form to those of the *Theses on Feuerbach*, and do not interfere, as we will see, with Marx's appropriation of Feuerbach's theory of alienation in the *Manuscripts*.

The theory of alienation in Feuerbach is qualitatively different from Marx's theory in so far as one accounts for religious alienation and the other for the alienation of labour. But while Marx addresses himself to an area of life ignored by Feuerbach he nevertheless seems to regard the theory he develops in the *Economic and Philosophic Manuscripts* as an application of Feuerbach's theory. We have already seen Marx comment in the *Introduction* that the 'criticism of religion is the prerequisite of all criticism'; he goes on to say that:[100]

> It is the immediate task of philosophy . . . to unmask self-estrangement in its unholy forms once the holy form . . . has been unmasked. Thus the criticism of heaven turns into the criticism of earth, the criticism of religion into the criticism of law and the criticism of theology into the criticism of politics.

In the *Economic and Philosophic Manuscripts* this programme is extended, partly under Engels's influence, to include the criticism of the political economy, for Marx now regards alienated labour as the key to all human servitude.[101] This does not nullify Feuerbach's critique of religion, but builds upon it. Marx does argue that man's alienation in religion is different in content from his alienation in labour and that the latter is causally primary in so far as 'its transcendence . . . embraces both aspects'.[102] He also says, however, that formally they operate in much 'the same way'.[103] As religious and economic alienation are formally the same the same formal aspects of the theory which deals with each of them need not be different, the difference lies in the subject to which the theory is applied.

The Feuerbachian context of the *Manuscripts'* theory of alienation is evident in the particular nature of its philosophical framework. The *Economic and Philosophic Manuscripts* has been described as both a 'philosophical critique of the economy' and an 'empirically based criticism'.[104] Ernest Mandel argues that the work is neither one nor the other, but both.[105] While this is in a sense true it is also unsatisfactory, for it fails to make clear the function of empirical data in Marx's critique of political economy and the particular nature of that critique. Herbert Marcuse's formulation, quoted by Mandel, which states that:[106]

> all the philosophical concepts of Marxian theory are social and economic categories. . . . Even Marx's early writings are not philosophical. They express the negation of philosophy, though they will do so in philosophical language

offers a merely verbal solution to the question of the nature of the *Manuscripts*, even though it does appear to accord with Marx's own description of them as a negation of philosophy, 'the settling of accounts with Hegelian dialectic and Hegelian philosophy as a whole'.[107] Marx's claim that his 'results have been won by means of a wholly empirical analysis based on a conscientious critical study of political economy'[108] also seems to be a denial of philosophy. But it is in the details of his 'critical study' that Marx's Feuerbachian philosophy is to be found.

On one level Marx's analysis is fully empirical, indeed he begins with the facts analysed by political economy and says that he accepts its language and laws. He does not dispute the description of empirical reality presented by political economy, but argues that its explanation of these facts is inadequate.[109] As we saw in Chapter 1 above Marx later rejected outright the empiricism of political economy, but here he merely criticises it and explains its facts from the point of view of a 'science of man' which stresses man's 'true anthropological nature'.[110] Marx's empiricism and his naturalistic 'science' in the *Economic and Philosophical Manuscripts* are directly related in being equal parts of the Feuerbachian philosophical anthropology. For Feuerbach philosophy begins with an empirical reality indicated by the senses, its procedure is to organise that reality by subjecting it to 'criticism', a criticism or philosophy premised on the proposition that man is a natural being. The critique of political economy in the *Manuscripts*, like the critique of politics in the *Introduction*, is still a 'task of philosophy'. Not the speculative philosophy of Hegel, certainly, which is an autonomous and autonomously confirming reality, but rather the naturalistic philosophy of Ludwig Feuerbach.

To briefly recapitulate: In elaborating further the Feuerbachian notion of man as a species-being Marx was able to argue that man is an active and social being historically tending toward the full realisation of his essence in communism. The function of the theory of alienation in this schema is to account for the human condition in the pre-communist stage of the evolutionary unfolding of his essence. With Feuerbach's transformative method Marx is able to prove that man is the subject of history. With the Feuerbachian notion of species-being he is able to specify what is man's essential nature. The concept of 'alienation', for both Feuerbach and Marx, is a derivative of the concept 'species-being' in so far as the meaning of alienation can be understood only in terms of man's divested species-being. Feuerbach had shown that religion is an intellectual and emotional creation of man which comes to operate independently of its creators and stand over them as an oppressive force. Stated generally, it is in alienation that man's own products acquire an independence from him and become agents of his oppression.

Religious alienation, which became alienation *par excellence* for the

Young Hegelians, is the alienation of consciousness. Marx argues that man is not merely a conscious being but a practically active being. The basic form of alienation for Marx, therefore, is the alienation of his activity, of his labour. The difference between Marx and Feuerbach in this is parallel to the way they each differentiate man from the animals. In his 'Introduction' to *The Essence of Christianity* Feuerbach says that 'the essential difference between man and the animal . . . is consciousness.'[111] Although animals do possess consciousness in the sense that 'the animal experiences itself as an individual . . . it does not do so as a species.'[112] It is consciousness of species which Feuerbach regards as consciousness in the full sense, for '[w]here there is consciousness in this sense, there is also the capacity to produce systematic knowledge or science. Science is the consciousness of species.'[113] Marx accepts this view when he says in the *Economic and Philosophic Manuscripts* that it is 'in his knowing' that man proves himself to be 'not merely a natural being . . . [but] a *human* being'.[114] But Marx also adds to Feuerbach's position when he employs an extended Feuerbachism similar to that summarised in the *Theses on Feuerbach*. He says that:[115]

Conscious life-activity directly distinguishes man from animal life-activity. It is just because of this that he is a species-being.

As Feuerbach admits that animals in a sense possess consciousness Marx admits that they too produce, but they produce one-sidedly, under the compulsion of immediate physical need. Man, on the other hand, produces universally and in freedom, and it is in this type of production, directed by conscious life-activity, that man is proved to be a species-being, according to Marx.[116]

Using a Feuerbachism largely drawn from the *Preliminary Theses on the Reform of Philosophy* and the *Principles of the Philosophy of the Future* Marx develops an alternative to the definition of man outlined in Feuerbach's earlier *The Essence of Christianity* to show that production as conscious life-activity rather than mere consciousness is the essence of man's species-being. It is important to notice that in the *Economic and Philosophic Manuscripts* labour and production are equivalent to praxis in the full sense as it emerges in Marx's revised Feuerbachism and that the terms have a wider meaning than they do in Marx's later writing. In the *Manuscripts* Marx says that man's involvement in institutions such as religion, the family and the state and in cultural areas such as law, morality, science and art is each a manner of production, and even in being sensuous, in exercising the five senses, man labours.[117] While labour and production are not narrowly confined to material objectification in *Capital*, for instance, any more than they are in the *Manuscripts*, in the former work labour is specifically understood as an activity which augments capital.[118] In the *Economic and Philosophic Manuscripts* the concept 'labour' goes beyond this precise economic criterion in covering the exercise of all human faculties. Any activity engendering a consequence which may become independent of man and oppress him is a labour which may be alienated.

In the section of the first *Manuscripts*, however, where 'Estranged Labour' is most thoroughly and continuously dealt with, the labour with which Marx is concerned is the labour of material production.[119] For in his critique of political economy Marx must first confine himself to the industrial form of labour as that is the subject of political economy. Marx begins his discussion of alienated labour and his critique of political economy by stating that in certain circumstances, those dealt with by political economy, the realisation of labour takes the form of a loss of reality for the labourer. In production under these conditions 'the life which [the worker] has conferred on the object confronts him as something hostile and alien.'[120] Marx says that political economy does not explain this paradox and that it actually 'conceals the estrangement inherent in the nature of labour by not considering the direct relationship between the worker (labour) and production'.[121]

Marx identifies four basic aspects of the alienation of labour which indicate what he regards to be the content of the relationship between labour and production concealed by political economy. The first two aspects relate to the loss of labour as a product and as an activity.[122] From this statically conceived loss of objects and this dynamically conceived loss of activity in alienation Marx deduces a third aspect of estranged labour which he conceives as a total loss. In losing the object of his production and the freedom of his activity in production man is estranged from his own species-being, from his '*human* being'.[123] Finally, as a consequence of his loss of human essence in alienation, 'one man is estranged from the other,'[124] that is to say, each man regards every other by the criteria of his own alienation; man is alienated from his fellows who appear as mere means. In these different aspects of estranged labour is the source of man's alienation.

Marx argues that not only does political economy have no familiarity with the direct relationship between the worker and production, but that it is also incapable of revealing the source of estranged labour. The fact of estranged labour is known to political economy and Marx suggests that for political economy alienated labour has its basis in the movement of private property. Political economy is mistaken, however, for although 'private property appears . . . [as] the cause of alienated labour, it is really its consequence.'[125] In failing to perceive the division of labour as an expression of estranged labour – it sees it rather as the 'social character of labour', which for Marx it is not[126] – political economy fails to perceive the source of estranged labour. The key to the relationship of the worker to production, for Marx, is that it is an incomplete relationship; it is divided. It is in the division of labour that man's labour is estranged. It is in estranged labour that man is divided from nature and it is in this division of labour, which separates man from nature, that Marx finds the source of man's alienation.

The first and third aspects of alienation mentioned above account for man's alienation explicitly in terms of his separation from nature. The relation of the worker to the product of his labour is his 'relation to the sensuous external world, to the objects of nature as an alien world antagonistically opposed to him'.[127] And in being estranged from his species-life man's 'inorganic body, nature, is taken from him'.[128] Marx's argument for this general position moves through two stages. He universalises from the specific instance of the appropriation of some objects, those produced on the production line, to the appropriation of all objects, the universe of nature. He argues thus because he maintains that nothing can be created without the sensuous external world of nature; to have labour's products appropriated is to deprive man, therefore, of the sensuous external world.[129] In losing nature in this sense, in losing the natural objects with which man produces, man loses nature in a more fundamental sense. As man's own species-nature is free and universal activity in production, the appropriation of natural objects and the consequent loss of nature means that life is no longer a species-life, for production under such circumstances can be no more than a means to individual existence and species-life is turned, therefore, into individual life.[130] Man's estranged production 'transforms his advantage over animals into the disadvantage that his inorganic body, nature, is taken from him.'[131] In losing the product of his labour man loses his direct nexus with external nature and in losing his direct nexus with external nature man loses his species-nature.

In the *Economic and Philosophic Manuscripts* Marx understands the term 'nature' in three senses. External nature is the sensuous world external to man, nature as opposed to man, what Marx calls 'man's inorganic body'. There is also nature in the sense of human nature, man's 'species-being', his 'true anthropological nature'. The contents of nature in these two senses are connected in a third notion of nature, which is nature in general, external nature united with human nature, for Marx says that the link between man and nature 'means simply that nature is linked to itself, for man is a part of nature.'[132] Man and nature are consummated into a single unity, however, only when man exists as full species-being. It is in the breaking of this nexus with nature that man is alienated.

The notion of alienation in the *Economic and Philosophic Manuscripts* is dependent, therefore, upon a prior notion of man's fundamental unity with nature under the 'social' conditions obtaining in communism:[133]

> [The] human essence of nature first exists only for social man; for only here does nature exist for him as a bond with man . . . only here does nature exist as the foundation of his own human existence. Only here has what is to him his natural existence become his human existence, and nature become man for him. Thus society is the consummated oneness in substance of man and nature – the true resurrection of nature – the naturalism of man and the humanism of nature both brought to fulfilment.

Marx is encouraged by his analysis of man in nature and nature in man to comment that with communism the natural and human sciences will both subsume into a single unified science, 'there will be *one* science' only.[134] What is significant about this, apart from its bearing on Marx's theory of alienation, is its Feuerbachian origin.

Feuerbach's conception of man entails that man is a part of nature in a way which is similar to that described by Marx:[135]

> Nature is being that is not distinguished from existence; man is being that distinguishes itself from existence. The being that does not distinguish is the ground of the being that distinguishes; nature is, therefore, the ground of man . . . the thinking man [i.e., man at one with his essence] . . . knows himself as the self-conscious essence of nature.

Feuerbach also argues for a unified science 'grounded in nature'.[136] We might add that Marx follows Feuerbach in his criticism of Hegel's 'defective' appreciation of nature.[137] Typically Feuerbach's position is not as clearly worked out as Marx's, but equally typical is the obvious inspiration of Feuerbach in Marx. The parallels between the two are uncontestable. Not only is Marx's theory of alienation formally the same as Feuerbach's, Marx's explanation of the basis of alienation in the separation of man from nature derives from a Feuerbachian notion which holds that man in essence is a part of nature.

Earlier it was shown that Marx's development of the Feuerbachian conception of man as a practically active being led him to develop the notion of class struggle in opposition to Feuerbach's programme of human love. Marx's development of Feuerbach's notion of nature in terms of productive life activity similarly leads Marx to expose an inherent weakness and contradiction in Feuerbach's thought. From essentially Feuerbachian premises Marx initiates the formation of his own conception of historical materialism. An extension of Feuerbach's naturalism into the sphere of economic activity and the definition of nature in terms of production lead Marx to initiate the transition from a Feuerbachian materialism to his own historical materialism. We should be aware, however, that while the groundwork for this transition is prepared in the *Economic and Philosophic Manuscripts*, it is not yet completed. The theory of alienation in that work remains Feuerbachian rather than historical materialist.

IV

The assumption that in his objective essence man is united with nature, an assumption which permits Marx to explain alienation in the 1844 *Manuscripts* as a result of man's estrangement from nature, is rejected in 1846. In his criticism of Feuerbach's contemplative materialism in *The German Ideology* Marx illustrates his argument by saying that:[138]

the important question of the relation of man to nature . . . out of which all the 'unfathomably lofty works' on 'substance' and 'self-consciousness' were born, crumbles of itself when we understand that the celebrated 'unity of man with nature' has always existed in industry and has existed in varying forms in every epoch according to the lesser or greater development of industry.

These comments must be read as a criticism not only of Feuerbach but also of Marx's own earlier account of the celebrated unity of man with nature. According to the *Economic and Philosophic Manuscripts* man's nexus with nature is broken in industrial production, whereas according to *The German Ideology* there exists in industry a unity of man and nature, a unity which the *Manuscripts* claim is attained only when man returns to his objective essence in communism, when he is 'social man'. Two views could not be more opposed.

In his discussion in the *Economic and Philosophic Manuscripts* Marx says that industry 'is the actual, historical relation of nature . . . to man'.[139] But in man's alienation it is a relation of estrangement not unity, for:[140]

> the history of industry and the established objective existence of industry are the open book of man's essential powers

only in the sense that

> the objectified essential powers of man in the form of sensuous, alien, useful objects, in the form of estrangement, displayed in ordinary material industry . . . can be conceived as . . . activity estranged from itself.

The relation, then, between nature and man in industry under precommunist conditions is not one of unity, but the negation of unity, the relation is one in which man loses nature. Industry proves man's essential powers, his natural powers, but only by removing them from him. This is similar to Marx's earlier proof of man's essential being in the political state which exists as a partial, and, therefore, alienated expression of man's species-being. We saw in the *Critique of Hegel's Philosophy of Right* the historical development of man in the movement from the political to the rational state. In the *Economic and Philosophic Manuscripts* man's historical development in industry is the movement from man's relation of estrangement from nature to man's relation of unity with nature. But while industry is conducted with estranged labour man's relation to nature remains estranged.

The different relations in industry between man and nature, of separation and unity, which correlate with the alienated and 'social' conditions of man's species-being, have no place in *Capital*, for instance. The question of man being estranged from nature does not arise in that work any more than it does in *The German Ideology*. While man 'opposes himself to nature' in labour, he does so 'as one of her own forces'.[141] Labour's unity with nature in changing nature to 'a form adapted to his own wants' is 'not changed by the fact that the labourer works for the capitalist instead of for himself.'[142] Man's relation with nature in production is, therefore, unaffected by the form of man's own essential nature. Indeed, Marx says in *Capital* that by 'acting on the external world and changing it, [man] at the same time changes his own nature.'[143] The fundamental differences indicated here between the analysis of man's relationship with nature in industry found in the *Economic and Philosophic Manuscripts* on the one hand, and in *The German Ideology* and *Capital* on the other, must prevent us from accepting David McLellan's view that Marx's sketch of industry in the

Manuscripts 'anticipated his later and more detailed accounts of historical materialism'.[144] In fact the account of industry in historical materialism removes from the theory of alienation outlined in the *Manuscripts* Marx's explanation of alienation as the separation of man from nature in industrial production, removes from it its Feuerbachian content.

It is not only the Feuerbachian-inspired assumption concerning man's relation with nature that is undermined in *The German Ideology*. The largely Feuerbachian essentialist anthropological conception of man, which is correlative with the conception of nature outlined in the 1844 *Manuscripts*, is also repudiated in *The German Ideology*. Marx argues in the latter work that his approach methodologically entails the need to apprehend the empirical and factual reality of man's circumstances, and needs to posit the primacy of man's productive activities in shaping that reality. Marx says that he begins from the premise of men in their productive 'activity and the material conditions under which they live', premises which can be 'verified in a purely empirical way'.[145] This is not entirely new in Marx. The role of empiricism and the concept of 'praxis' in the consistent Feuerbachism he had developed earlier has already been discussed. What is new, and absent in the *Theses on Feuerbach*, is his outright rejection of any essentialist conception of man. Rather than refer to the 'species' of man Marx confines his discussion to 'the real individuals', to 'living human individuals'.[146] He says that it is 'definite individuals who are productively active in a definite way [who] enter into ... definite social and political relations', relations which are predominantly of a class nature.[147] Marx's point is that what the philosophers have mistakenly conceived as the 'essence of man' is really the 'sum of productive forces, capital funds and social forms of intercourse, which every individual and generation finds in existence as something given.'[148] These social forces are not here regarded as the consequence of man's alienation, as they are in Marx's Feuerbachian writings, but the cause of estrangement.[149] This reversal of the causal chain, more than anything else, indicates that Marx has abandoned his previous essentialist notion of man in *The German Ideology*, and replaced it with a materialist sociology.

The conception of 'history' in *The German Ideology* is also quite different from the one found in his writings prior to *The German Ideology*, including the *Theses on Feuerbach*. It was argued above that Marx had previously regarded history as an evolutionary unfolding or development of man's essential species-nature. In *The German Ideology* historical development is conceived as a process in which the development of productive forces shifts the social power held by one social class to another, previously subordinate social class.[150] The discussion of class action in historical change is completely absent of any account of an alliance between philosophy and the proletariat, the realisation of the philosophy of man or the transcendence of philosophy with its realisation.[151] In the *Theses on Feuerbach* and elsewhere Marx postulated the empirical social relations and their historical development within a framework of the development of man's essential nature, and social relations and history were categorially rather than materially conceived. In *The German Ideology* historical development is relative to the development of social forces. The social forces are not seen as expressions of the form of man's essential nature, as they are in Marx's Feuerbachian writing, but themselves determine the conditions of relations between men.

It has been shown in this chapter that Marx's early critique of Hegel and the importance he gave to the imperative for social change were derived from or sustained by the revised Feuerbachian programme he developed. What is not available in Feuerbachism, and what Marx's political interpretation of Feuerbach required, is a theory of social and historical change. The theory of social change in Feuerbachism, to the extent that one exists, affords no possibility of an approach which could develop a concrete and material analysis of social forces and factors which initiate and realise historical change. The notion of man as a species-being, while sufficient for the critique of Hegel, inhibits the development of a positive and programmatic theory of class action in historical change. The class reality, which Marx first began to conceptualise in his Feuerbachian writing, could have no genuinely positive explanatory role while it was part of a Feuerbachian theory of history. And while Feuerbachism entails a conception of social relations, it does not lend itself to empirical investigation.[152] It was only by developing a full critique of Feuerbachism, and therefore his own earlier position, a critique which fully repudiated its theoretical core, that Marx could begin to develop a theory of history and society which could be recruited to the service of a political programme of proletarian revolution. It is for this reason that Marx describes himself as a 'practical materialist'[153] in sharp contrast to Feuerbach and the theory of Feuerbach which Marx had adopted and then rejected.

Marx was initially attracted to Feuerbach's thought because of its political unity in criticising the Young Hegelians who attempted to develop the 'revolutionary' side of Hegelian philosophy and who depreciated the role of 'the masses' in political change. The strength of Feuerbachism was demonstrated to Marx through its critique of Hegel. In using Feuerbach for his own purposes Marx extended the competence of Feuerbachian thought, but in developing it to its limits its inadequacies were revealed to him. Marx's early acceptance of Feuerbach's programme, which he sympathetically developed, had an enduring influence upon his work in so far as it provided him with the concept 'praxis'. The notion of man as a practically active being was taken from Feuerbach. But the meaning the concept acquired in Marx's mature historical materialism, while deriving from Feuerbach and his own extended Feuerbachism of the 1840s, is not identical with nor does it operate in the same theoretical framework as that of the earlier materialism. Nevertheless, the importance of Marx's development of Feuerbachian materialism to the development of his own theory of historical materialism should be appreciated, although David McLellan's claim that historical materialism in general and the base/superstructure model in particular was directly derived from Feuerbach,[154] has been shown above to be true only in the sense of a literary allusion. The importance of Feuerbachism to Marx's theoretical development is partly in the form of a negative example to which he reacted and which provided him with the opportunity to resolve important questions of social analysis.

Marx's critical development of Feuerbachian theory during the period of 1843 to 1845, while of relatively short duration, amounts to a genuine intellectual accomplishment. His subsequent critique of 'consistent' Feuerbachism in *The German Ideology*, a critique which forms the basis of historical materialism, is a significant theoretical achievement. Our understanding of Marx's thought during this period can be adequate only when we appreciate the nature of his relationship to Feuerbachian thought.

Chapter Three
Society

European capitalist development has not only profoundly affected the human landscape of habitation and labour, it also provided the impetus for socialism and liberalism to emerge as movements of change. In sharing this common historical beginning both socialism and liberalism drew their inspiration and ideas from a common inheritance of the thought and experience of the Enlightenment, the Industrial Revolution and the French Revolution. To the extent that there is a common theme in the movements and their doctrines it can be said that each addresses itself to the problem of the relation of the individual to the wider society. This question necessarily arose with the collapse of stable and definite feudal relations wrought in the advance of capitalism. Socialism and liberalism diverge, as different reactions to political and economic change, in their quite different visions of man's place and role in the social world.

In its Marxist form socialism developed a thorough epistemological and theoretical alternative to the liberal conception of the relation between the individual and society. Society, according to liberal thought, is an aggregation of autonomous individual beings for whom 'the other' is essentially external. Society, for liberalism, therefore, exists as an abstraction external to the individual. Marx is generally seen to have rejected this liberal duality of the individual and society by arguing that the individual has no attributes which are independent of the social conditions of his existence. According to this view Marx claims that the individual is inseparable from society, he is both socially determined and in his activity generates social consequences. Marx's thought has been readily characterised, then, as a 'sociological' critique of liberal individualism.

The adequacy or otherwise of this summary statement of classical Marxism aside, it can be noted that a number of writers have recognised that a major component of Marx's thought is his sociological critique of atomistic liberalism. It is of particular interest that one passage frequently quoted in support of this observation is from the *Economic and Philosophic Manuscripts* and reads:[1]

> What is to be avoided above all is the re-establishing of 'Society' as an abstraction *vis-à-vis* the individual. The individual *is the social being*. His life, even if it may not appear in the direct form of a communal life carried out together with others — is therefore an expression and confirmation of *social life*. Man's individual and species life are not different, however much — and this is inevitable — the mode of existence of the individual is a more particular, or more general mode of life of the species, or the life of the species is a more particular or more general individual life.

Not every interpretation of this passage which assumes its sociological content sees it as a critique of liberalism. Irving Zeitlin, for instance, and also Tom Bottomore and Maximilien Rubel, suggest that this passage demonstrates that Marx's sociology is a critique of the Comtean or Durkheimian notion of society as a reality *sui generis* above the individual.[2] Another interpretation of the quotation, which conveys Marx's intended meaning, is advanced by Shlomo Avineri, who says it shows that Marx believed the full sociality of man is attainable only in communism.[3] Through this meaning the quotation is devoid of sociological content. But the frequency with which this passage is quoted for its sociological interpretation highlights the assumption held by many scholars that Marx had developed a sociological theory of civil society in his Paris Writings of the 1840s.

In his early critique of Hegel Marx implicitly challenges the liberal view of man when he argues that man is essentially a social being. This becomes explicit by 1844 when Marx criticises classical political economy, a discipline which founds the architecture of the liberal tradition by advancing the general doctrine that the relations between individuals are purely external relations, market relations. In his manuscript notes on James Mill's *Elements of Political Economy* Marx compares his own position with that of political economy. He says that economics conceives the relations between men as commercial relations. Adam Smith, for instance, sees '[s]ociety . . . [as] a commercial society. Each of its members is a merchant.' Man's essence, according to economics, says Marx, is conceived as 'the mutuality of men, in terms of exchange and trade', so that each man is distinguished from the other in his autonomy and they relate through an external medium of the market.[4] Against this Marx says that 'the essence of man is the true community of man' and that 'by activating their own esssence [men] produce, create this human community, this social being which is no abstract, universal power standing over against the solitary individual.'[5] In contrast to the liberal conception of man as an individual trader Marx postulates that man is essentially a social producer. In contrast to the liberal conception of society as a faculty external to the individual, which he enters for purposes of trade, Marx conceives society as the creation and community of men.

There are two possible responses to liberal doctrine. One is to argue that liberal theory fails to recognise that society cannot be reduced to its individual members and that the web of social relationships is greater than the market relations of individuals. This we call the sociological critique of liberal individualism. Another response might argue that liberal theory adequately describes civil society, but refuse to accept it as a description of a necessary situation. Things may be like this now, but need not always be thus, nor will they be. This we call the normative critique of liberal individualism. While the theory of historical materialism at least includes the first of these, it seems that Marx's early critique of liberalism is largely of the second type. Marx says in his notes on Mill, for instance, that political economy's conception of individual relations corresponds to 'the process of reality itself'.[6] He goes on to say that:[7]

> exchange or barter is the social species-activity, the community, social commerce and integration of man within *private* property, and for that reason it is external, *alienated* species-activity. . . . By the same token it is the very antithesis of a social relationship.

> Thus the more developed and important is the power of society within private property, the more man is egoistic, un-social and estranged from his own essence.

Thus Marx holds that in alienation man's relationships are not social and that the power of society, based on private property, confronts man as an external force with which he has no community save that of commerce. Marx therefore shares with liberal political economy the description of man in civil society as a being isolated from society.

It can be seen from the above comments that Marx's early notion of man as a social being is not a direct sociological challenge to the image of asocial man described by liberal political economy. Rather it assumes that given 'human' conditions, conditions in which man can realise his 'human, communal nature', man will live as a fully social being, but that in his alienation society is lost to man and in his individuality he exists in isolation from others.[8] In his writings after 1846, with the development of the theory of historical materialism, Marx broadens his critique of liberalism to include the sociological dimension. Familiarity with Marx's later sociological critique of liberal individualism and the superficially similar early assertion that man is essentially a social being has led some scholars to gloss over the dominantly normative nature of Marx's early discussion. The transposition of Marx's later sociological vision to his early writings amounts to a backward reading of Marx which prevents him from speaking for himself in his formative period. What he says is interpreted in terms of a pre-formed expectation of what he might mean based on a reading of his later work. The actual sense of his early writing is thereby misrepresented and misunderstood. The concept 'society' in Marx's 1844 writings is not equivalent to the concept 'society' employed in the theory of historical materialism, and the early meaning is particularly interesting for what it conveys of Marx's pre-sociological thought.

The content of Marx's early concept of 'society' will be examined in the present chapter. It will be shown that in 1844 Marx had not developed a theory of man which operates through purely social terms, but that he sees civil society as merely an aggregate of isolated individuals. It will be shown that Marx concurs with liberal political economy that the relations between individuals are basically exchange relations between isolated monads. There is no sociological alternative in the early writings to the liberal image of man in society. Marx's early critique of liberal atomism, it will be argued, operates through a philosophico-anthropological concept of 'society'. 'Society' in this sense is conceived as man's species-life, so that Marx regards society as an attribute of human nature, an attribute which is lost in the alienation of man's essence. This particular conception of society, therefore, functions as a normative principle against which civil society is measured. The truly social situation, according to Marx, is the human community of communism which is attained only when the power of private property, which determines the nature of civil society, ceases to estrange man from his real social essence. This early concept of 'society' will be contrasted in the discussion with the sociological concept developed in historical materialism by Marx after rejecting the earlier notion. The significantly different critiques of liberal individualism advanced by Marx at different times indicate the danger inherent in assuming that Marx's theoretical development followed a linear progression of elaboration and revision. Marx's writings of 1844 must be appreciated in their own terms to be fully understood.

I

In his writings of 1843-4 Marx develops an empirical account of civil society which largely corresponds to that developed by liberal writers. In his essay *On the Jewish Question* Marx says that the conditions of civil society and its constituent members are founded on the principles of juridical liberty and the right of property. These are described by Marx as the right of man to be separate from his fellows and the right of self-interest.[9] The implementation of these rights constitutes the full substance of civil society, according to Marx, in that through them civil society 'appears as a framework extraneous to the individuals'.[10] Marx, therefore, does not challenge the empirical description of man in civil society as a 'self-sufficient monad', and in fact agrees with political economy when he says that in civil society the 'only bond which holds [men] together is natural necessity, need and private interest, the conservation of their property and their egoistic persons.'[11] He differs with political economy, though, on the question of how civil society is to be regarded, and disagrees that the bonds of private interest are social bonds. Marx rejects the view, held by political economy, that man's individual existence in civil society is the condition of man's essential existence, for he maintains that it is in the alienation of his essentially social being that man's existence is individual,[12] for according to Marx man is unnaturally 'separated from his fellow men and from the community'[13] in civil society.

While man is regarded by both Marx and liberal writers as a private individual who confronts civil society externally Marx goes beyond liberal thought in arguing that commercial society is no society, it is the alienation of society from man. The liberal argument that individual relations in civil society are social relations is contested by Marx. Adam Smith, for instance, says that society exists in the social reciprocity of exchange and in the social bond of sympathy. In a passage from *The Wealth of Nations*, quoted by Marx in the *Economic and Philosophic Manuscripts*, Smith argues that self-interest, or self-love, as he calls it, is the basis of society, the basis of man's social reciprocity in exchange.[14] Marx argues that, on the contrary, Smith's claim is itself contradictory in that it attempts to establish 'society through unsocial, particular interests'.[15] This position is sustained by

Marx's argument that the means of exchange, money, is essentially the currency of self-interest, and is therefore inherently unsocial. Exchange itself cannot be other than an unsocial relationship. Marx's discussion of money as the agency of man's estrangement from society is developed in *On the Jewish Question*, in his notes on Mill's *Elements* and in the *Economic and Philosophic Manuscripts*.[16] He argues that money facilitates individual possession in such a way as to preclude the possibility of human social relations. Money, says Marx, actually creates a 'world of atomistic individuals confronting each other in enmity'.[17] Money, and through it exchange, is not the basis of society, but the basis of society's dissolution.

Smith's argument concerning the social bond of sympathy is not directly discussed by Marx. It is argued in the former's *The Theory of Moral Sentiments*, a work to which Marx does not refer. Sympathy is the social sentiment in man which is responsible for the fellow feeling between individuals.[18] Sympathy, at the core of liberal man's social morality, prevents injury to others in the pursuit of individual ends by subjecting such actions to social restraint, or at least the sanction of public opinion.[19] In his discussion of self-interest in civil society Marx implicitly reasons that self-interested action would be entirely corrosive of sentiments such as sympathy. For it is precisely the natural and human qualities, on which sympathy is based, which are confounded in the money relation.[20] Marx might argue academically that even if sympathy remained intact in civil society it would be irrelevant to and overruled by the relations of civil society. Money creates a situation in which individual relations operate 'beyond and above man',[21] man's sentiments are extraneous to his relations so that sympathy would be without a medium through which it could function. Marx does describe something like sympathy when he sketches a picture of communist workmen, who, in their association, acquire a need for society.[22] But the circumstances created in their common enterprise, where this social sentiment is exhibited, are so removed from the relations of civil society that it is an example of sympathy which is the exception proving Marx's rule of its impossibility in the atomistic relations of commercially dominated intercourse.

For Marx, as for liberal political economy, civil society is reducible to the relations of individuals, reducible to exchange relations between what are empirically egoistic individual beings. In his early writings, then, Marx completely endorsed the eighteenth-century view of civil society as a conglomeration of individuals defined by their particular and personal interests, by their 'needs'. Marx goes beyond classical liberalism in his contention that the relations of need are non-social relations which exclude social relations. There is no place for social man in the empirical world Marx describes, for the basis of civil society, individual self-interest, cannot be the foundation of society but is its negation. This theoretical proposition is given an historical dimension in the argument that the centralisation of the state, according to *On the Jewish Question*, and the growth of industry according to the *Economic and Philosophic Manuscripts*, in bringing about the collapse of feudalism, were responsible for the destruction of society.

In his writings of 1844 Marx developed separately these two different but related accounts of the historical emergence of the individual bereft of social bonds. In *On the Jewish Question* the dissolution of feudalism is described as a consequence of the political revolution in which the modern, centralised state comes to monopolise the authority and power which had been vested in the autonomous feudal institutions of estate, corporation and guild. Feudal society was itself 'directly political', says Marx, in that the relations of individuals were hierarchically structured on a system of authority and privilege which denoted directly social relationships.[23] The political revolution, by destroying the feudal institutions which supported these relations, allowed the 'political spirit' to be 'gathered together' into a single, central state structure.[24] Marx described the same process eight years later when he said that:[25]

> The seignoral privileges of the landowners and towns became transformed into so many attributes of the state power, the feudal dignitaries into paid officials and the motley pattern of conflicting mediaeval plenary powers into the regulated plan of a state authority.

The consequence of this political revolution was not merely to draw the political aspects of the separate feudal institutions into a single political institution of the modern state. The political revolution also dissolved feudal society 'into its foundation . . . into egoistic man'.[26] In destroying the political relationships of feudalism the political revolution had at the same time deprived the individual of the social bonds of the hierarchical relationships.

An economic event parallel to the political revolution, and which had the same consequence in the generation of asocial individuals, is described in the *Economic and Philosophic Manuscripts* where Marx says that in the historical development of the economy movable private property, or capital, came to replace the landed property which had dominated feudalism. The effect of this development, continues Marx, is that 'the slave of the soil' becomes the 'free worker', the hireling of capital.[27] In similar terms the abolition of the 'privileged exclusivity' of feudalism, through the development of trade and industry free of the feudal strictures, a process outlined in *The Holy Family*, is seen to be responsible for the fact that the individual is 'no longer bound to other men even by the *semblance* of a common bond'.[28] This general argument, that the directly social and dependent relations of feudal production become unstuck in the development of capitalism and that the individual emerged as a free, independent and isolated being, is central to Marx's later discussion of the transition from feudalism to capitalism. In Marx's mature writings, however, this argument does not carry the extra baggage of the claim that this process is one of social dissolution. We will return to this below. In his 1844 writings the demise of feudalism entailed that man's existence was to become individual and asocial in the strong sense. While the political revolution, the advent of the modern state, and the economic revolution, the preponderance of capital over land, are different causes they converge in their consequence – they dissolve society into a confusion of isolated individuals and simultaneously deprive the individual of any meaningful social contact.

Although we are arguing that Marx's Paris Writings maintain that in commercial society the individual is an asocial being – Marx insists on the 'asocial nature of civil life'[29] – and that historically this is the result of man's loss of feudal social relations, it is important for an understanding of Marx's early concept of 'society' to recognise that feudalism is not regarded as fully social in his early use of the term. He says in *On the Jewish Question* that property and labour are not elevated 'to the level of social elements' in the feudal order, rather they are compartmentalised into *'separate* societies within society'.[30] This separation of the individual of labour from the individual of property through relations of servility obstructs the full realisation of man's social nature. But while Marx says that the individual is not a fully social being in feudalism he makes it clear that the individual is not entirely without social determination. In contrast to the relations of commerce the feudal relations of individuals are social in being direct and close. What is important for Marx is that the relations of feudalism 'held in check the egoistic spirit of civil society'.[31] In so far as feudal relations prevent the dominance of self-interest in the intercourse of individuals they are social relations. The interdependence of rights and privilege and the functional relationship between political and economic factors which did not regard the individual interest as conclusive meant that for Marx the relations between feudal individuals were social relations. The feudal rein on self-interest was its social endowment, according to Marx, and when this went so too did society.

Marx's argument that the loosening of the feudal restraint on self-interest leads to the individual's loss of social relations is evident in the contrast he draws between the feudal character of labour, with its 'seemingly social significance', and free labour, which has the mark 'of indifference to its content, of complete being-for-itself'.[32] Feudal labour is directed by its significance for the community, labour for commerce has no determination but the individual end. With the eclipse of feudalism Marx saw that the individual's 'particular activity and situation in life sank to the level of a purely individual significance'.[33] Marx is quite explicit that the unfettered weight of individual interest and significance, made possible through the annulment of feudal restraints, extinguishes all meaningful social relations:[34]

> The relations of private property contain latent within them the relations of private property as labour, the same relations as capital, and the mutual relation of these two to one another. There is the production of human activity as labour . . . the abstract existence of man as a mere workman who may therefore daily fall from his filled void into the absolute void — into his *social, and therefore actual, non-existence*. On the other hand there is the production of the object of human activity as capital — in which all the natural and *social determinateness of the object is extinguished*; in which private property has *lost its natural and social quality*.

Here Marx claims that with the collapse of feudalism labour, capital and the relations between them become expressions of merely private interest and as such are devoid of social content and effect. Without communal significance labour and capital have no social quality. This assertion is particularly interesting because the same objective situation is described in the *Grundrisse*, but with a contrary evaluation. Marx says that 'private interest is itself already a socially determined interest, which can be achieved only within the condition laid down by society and with the means provided by society.'[35] Not only does private interest here have social determinateness, but the relations of self-interest are seen to take place in society. The objective situation described in these two quotations is the same, the meaning of the term 'society' is different.

When Marx says in the Paris Writings that the relations of individuals in civil society are unsocial and that the individual is without a social existence he is reserving the term 'society' to indicate a network of organic or communal relations which imply a reciprocal nexus of social partnership. This he contrasts to commercial relations in which the social bonds, in this sense, are absent. Historians might write in this fashion to differentiate pre-industrial from industrial societies.[36] Karl Polanyi, for instance, forcefully employs this usage when he says that the dominance of the 'market mechanism ... result[s] in the demolition of society', and complains that in the market economy man suffers a 'lethal injury to the institutions in which his social existence is embodied'.[37] Society in this sense is the community of human individuals whose relations are intentional, visible and reciprocal. It is certainly true, and this is Polanyi's point, that capitalist development does not take existing social organisation for granted, but subverts customary society by establishing the impersonal power of the market. If the term 'society' is confined to the description of what capitalism destroys, as with Polanyi, or of what capitalism denies, as with Marx in his early writing, then 'society' can be only a normative concept demonstrating that in a market environment man is alienated from society.

When describing market society or 'civil society' Marx regards society as a power which exists independently of the individual and outside him; society exists as an alien force to which the individual is subjected. The relations of individuals under the conditions of civil society are therefore non-social relations. Marx says in *On the Jewish Question* that 'in civil society ... [man] is active as a private individual, regards other men as means, [and] debases himself to a means'.[38] He goes on to say that man becomes a social being only when:[39]

> as an individual man has become a species-being in his empirical life, his individual work and his individual relationships, only when man has recognised and organised his *forces propres* as social forces so that social force is no longer separated from him.

Man has a social existence, according to this account, when he ceases to be separated from society, and this occurs only when man's species-being is empirically manifest, genuinely realised, rather than merely immanent in man's nature. Man as a species-being in this sense is man in free, reciprocal activity from others. It was noted above that Marx regarded the individual in feudal society as only a partially social being.

This is because the relations of feudalism are servile relations and therefore unfree, a point well made in the *Critique of Hegel's Philosophy of Right* where the Middle Ages are said to be 'a democracy of unfreedom'.[40] But in restraining private interest feudal relations retain for the individual a social dimension.

It can be seen that there are two distinct concepts of 'society' employed in Marx's early writing. One implies that society is external to the individual and that individual relations are therefore unsocial relations. The other meaning of the term 'society' is 'human society', implying that individual relations are social relations and that man is a social being. In Marx's early account the individual is a social being only when he has transcended his self-estrangement. On this criterion the social man of 'human society' is communist man.

This argument is most clearly expressed in the *Economic and Philosophic Manuscripts*. Alienation is conceived as the process through which the individual is divorced from society, the transcendence of alienation is 'the return of man . . . to his human, i.e., social mode of existence'.[41] The individual attains his social being in communism, for communism is:[42]

the positive transcendence of private property, or human self-estrangement . . . the complete return to himself as a social (i.e., human) being.

This postulation of man's social being is teleological rather than sociological, it assumes that the individual will ultimately become a social being after he has surpassed his non-social existence in civil society. It is based on the premise that social relations are attributable to human nature and explicable in philosophico-anthropological terms rather than in empirical sociological terms.

II

Marx's discussion of the individual's social relations in human society is conducted in the manuscript where he outlines the development of communist theory. After describing earlier and archaic conceptions of communism, which he criticises, Marx says that it is 'easy to see' that 'the entire revolutionary movement necessarily finds both its empirical and its theoretical basis in the movement of private property — in that of the economy, to be precise.'[43] The argument which follows this claim explains why it is so. It is mounted in decidedly non-economic and non-sociological terms.

The account of communism's empirical basis in the movement of private property is designed to show that early utopian conceptions of communism in the thought of Fourierist publicists and others such as Etienne Cabet and François Villegardelle are false. They argued that communism could be established by setting up communist settlements in opposition to an existing reign of private property. Marx criticises such programmes for attempting to '[tear] single phases from the historical process'.[44] Communism cannot be founded, contends Marx, on the formation of utopian pockets in the stream of history, as it were. He says that private property pervades an entire historical period of man's development as it is the material expression of alienated human life. Marx's point is that communism can be founded only after the transcendence of private property as an historical phase of man's development. The overcoming of private property through communism, therefore, has its empirical basis in the historical transendence of private property, not in the disengagement by particularly motivated individuals from existing private property. These 'empirical' comments are given significance and meaning in Marx's discussion of the theoretical basis of the 'revolutionary movement'.

Marx reminds us that in the non-alienated situation the basic and primary nature of production is in the social character of labour, for under these conditions a person's products are 'the direct embodiment of his individuality',[45] and hence man produces himself and his fellow man in being socially productive. While this is obscurely stated in the *Economic and Philosophic Manuscripts*, the same point is made with greater clarity in the notes on Mill's *Elements*.[46] The text of the *Manuscripts* goes on to say that:[47]

Likewise, however, both the material of labour and man as the subject, are the point of departure as well as the result of the movement (and precisely in this fact, that they must constitute the *point of departure*, lies the historical necessity of private property).

Again the sense of this statement is partly concealed, but it seems to indicate that although the social character of labour is realised in communism — it is 'the result of the movement' — it is also connected with the genesis of the movement — it is its 'point of departure'. To claim both that social labour is the achievement of the movement towards communism and that it is the point of departure of the movement is *prima facie* paradoxical. The corollary of the statement that social labour is realised in communism would seem to be that social labour is unavailable to the process of attaining communism. Indeed,

Marx says that in civil society, the historical stage prior to communism, labour is unsocial. However, the theoretical basis of the revolutionary movement developed by Marx contains an account of its logic and locomotion which shows that the paradox is merely apparent.

Firstly, the logic of the theory. Marx ties the claim that the social character of labour is the point of departure for the movement towards communism to the claim that private property is historically necessary to this movement. The necessity of private property to the attainment of communism lies in the fact that the latter is the transcendence of private property only. The sequence of stages in historical development assumed by Marx here is such that communism is the historical phase of man's human history which necessarily follows the historical phase of private property. It can logically follow no other historical stage. This is because in private property social labour is most fully alienated. Private property is the material expression of alienated human life; the alienation of man in religion, the state and so forth are merely particular aspects of the total alienation of man in material production. In the transcendence of private property, of alienated social labour, man has returned to him his social labour.[48] This is what Marx means when he says that communism is:[49]

> the negation of the negation, and is hence the actual phase neces-
> sary for the next stage of historical development in the process of
> human emancipation and recovery. Communism is the necessary
> pattern and the dynamic principle of the immediate future.

Logically, then, social labour is the point of departure for the movement towards communism because communism is the obverse of private property and private property is the denial of social labour. The negation of social labour as an empirical absence is the logical pre-requisite of communism and in this sense social labour as the negation of private property is the point of departure for the movement towards communism.

If social labour as a negative principle, as the alienation of social labour, is at the beginning of the historical movement towards communism, through what process is the negation negated? This is the question of locomotion, of dynamic. In his later writing Marx is explicit that communism is the consequence of a proletarian victory in the class struggle. The discussion of communism in the *Manuscripts*, however, is devoid of a reference to class struggle. When Marx does mention something like the victory of one class over another, as in his account of the 'victory of the capitalist over the landowner' in the movement from feudalism to capitalism, it is regarded as the result rather than the cause of the 'real course of development'. What Marx holds to be responsible for this historical movement is the suppression of a previously dominant form of property by another form of property.[50] We have already seen that in his explanation of the revolutionary movement towards communism the basic term is property, not class. Here too the historical movement is conceived as a consequence of the movement of property, the transcendence of private property, rather than as a consequence of the class struggle.

According to Marx's argument the importance of property, and the basis of its efficacy for historical change, is its relation to labour. It is important to remember that for Marx private property is alienated social labour. In his discussion of the theoretical basis of the movement towards communism Marx gives no more than a hint of this dynamic mechanism when he says that:[51]

> the *social* character [of human labour] is the general character of the whole movement [towards communism] : just as society [communism] itself produces man as man, so is society [communism] *produced* by him.

We interpret Marx to mean that man's social character, even when alienated in civil society, plays a dynamic and not a merely logical role in the revolutionary movement. The reference to 'the whole movement' is to the period which includes the historical phase of man's unsocial being in civil society as well as his social existence in communism. When Marx says that 'society [is] produced by' man he means that the social character of labour, although empirically absent in civil society, ultimately produces man as a social being, ultimately produces communism. Basically Marx is here claiming that man's social nature, his essential sociality, even when estranged from him, is the motor of the movement towards communism. There is slender basis for this elaboration of the above quotation in the passage itself, but such an interpretation is supported by various other comments made by Marx in the *Manuscripts*.

Marx opens his discussion of communism with an attempt to show that there is an internal relation of antithesis between labour and capital. He identifies labour as 'the subjective essence of private property as exclusion of property' and capital as 'objective labour as exclusion of labour'. On this basis private property is seen to be in a 'developed state of contradiction' and hence, the argument continues, there is a 'dynamic relationship moving inexorably to its resolution'.[52]

There are several things to notice here. Firstly, capital is defined in terms of labour and labour in terms of private property, so that the basic units of explanation are labour and private property. Secondly, the contradiction described here is not a class contradiction between labour and capital, but an ontological contradiction internal to private property. Thirdly, the dynamic relationship moving inexorably to its resolution is the dynamic of the contradiction within private property. As private property is estranged social labour the dynamic of the movement must derive from alienated social labour.

The picture becomes even clearer some pages later when Marx says that:[53]

> The nature which comes to be in human history — the genesis of human society — is man's *real* nature; hence nature as it comes to be through industry, even though in an *estranged* form, is true *anthropological* nature.

In other words, even when man's essential nature is alienated from him it is his true anthropological nature none the less. Earlier Marx had said that 'the history of industry and the established objective existence of industry are the open book of man's essential powers', and earlier still, that '[in] creating an objective world by his practical activity . . . man proves himself a conscious species-being.'[54] Industry, and *mutatis mutandis* property, demonstrate man's social nature even though it might take an unsocial form in them. Marx's statements that it 'takes actual communist [social] action to abolish actual private property' and that the process will be 'a very severe and protracted one',[55] which, from the perspective of his later thought, appear to be references to class struggle, are in this context references to man's productive activity as a species-being. Thus man's essential nature is productive of particular consequences in its estranged form as well as in its realised form. What is produced is human society, and this through the resolution of the contradiction inherent in labour's unsocial form as it exists in private property. For the contradiction within private property is fundamentally the contradiction of the unsocial form of man's essential sociality.

It should be noted that in certain passages of his mature works also Marx discusses the route to communism, or communist revolution at least, in the absence of class categories, as when he says in the 'Preface' to *A Contribution* that:[56]

> At a certain stage of development, the material productive forces

of society come into conflict with the existing relations of production or — this merely expresses the same thing in legal terms — with
the property relations within the framework of which they have
operated hitherto. From forms of development of the productive
forces these relations turn into their fetters. Then begins an era of
social revolution.

But here the contradiction which generates social transformation is not
internal to private property in an ontological sense, rather it is itself
fully explicable in social and class terms, as Marx suggests in *The
German Ideology*.[57] For the productive forces include such things
as the organisation of labour and the machinery and technology which
function as capital; and the relations of production are the class
relations in which the forces of production operate. This general
argument is quite unlike that of Marx's early discussion.

As Marx argues in the *Manuscripts* that the contradiction within
private property furnishes its own dynamic and resolution he envisages
a sort of entropic process in reverse in which the tendency of the
system is to attain a state of society. At the centre of the system is
man's social nature. The system is dynamic when labour takes an
unsocial form in private property. The *telos* of the system is man's
species existence as a social being. The movement toward this end is
a consequence of the inherent propensity in the nature of man's labour
to realise its social form.

In summary then, the concept of 'society' as human society in
Marx's early writings entails that social man is in a state of becoming in
civil society. Man is an unsocial individual in civil society and his
relationships are unsocial. Inherent in man's nature, though, is an
essential sociality. In its unsocial form the individual's labour is manifest in private property, but within private property the empirical
unsocial form of labour is in contradiction with its essentially social
form. The resolution of this contradiction is the realisation of man's
true anthropological nature as social man. Society and social relations
are, therefore, available to the individual at the end of an historical process and ultimately attributable to the essential faculty of human nature
postulated by Marx and explicable in philosophico-anthropological
terms. This conception of social man is clearly non-sociological. It does
function as a critical element in Marx's account of civil society and
provides a critique of the liberal conception of the relation between the
individual and society. But because it equates social man with communist man and argues that man's sociality is a function of human

nature it cannot be regarded as a sociological alternative to the liberal image of man in society.

III

What is perhaps surprising in Marx's early conception of society is the degree to which it shares a common formal ground with liberal thought, even in its critique of the latter. Social man as a conceptual entity is premised on a notion of human nature and a notion of harmonised community in both Marx's early thought and liberal theory. There is no need to restate Marx's position here as it has already been adequately outlined above. Adam Smith, as a typical representative of theoretical liberalism, argues that the structure of society has a pre-social origin when he accounts for the division of labour in terms of a disposition in human nature to truck, barter and exchange.[58] In a more general vein John Stuart Mill has written that '[h]uman beings in society have no properties but those which are derived from, and may be resolved into, the laws of the nature of individual men.'[59] This tendency of thought is inherent in the liberal conception of society as an aggregation of individuals, for if society is a conglomeration of individual beings it must be reducible to its individual members.[60] As society is deduced from the individual in liberal theory, the nature of society is deduced from human nature. Marx's own account of civil society is precisely in terms of the objective condition of human nature in its self-estrangement, and his account of human society is in terms of the full realisation of man's essential sociality.

Analogous to Marx's premise of the social nature of communism is the liberal premise of a harmonised community of social interest. According to Adam Smith, for example, human action is a consequence of self-love. The same concept, although under a range of different names, is found in all liberal writing where individual motivation derives from individual interests and needs. According to liberal theory the individual is the sole source and proprietor of his faculties and powers. As society is understood as an aggregation of such discrete units, the basis of human action in liberal theory is the endeavour of self to satisfy its needs. The social relations described by liberalism are, therefore, the set of external relations between the individual members of civil society. As these social relations are external to the social individuals they can be accounted for only in terms of metaphor, such as the 'invisible hand' of the market, or through natural law metaphysics or some other basically non-social factor. Marx writes with a measured irony in *Capital* that 'in accordance with the pre-established harmony of things, or under the auspices of an all-shrewd providence' the self-interested individuals of liberal theory 'work together to their mutual advantage, for the common weal and in the interest of all'.[61] As the social community of liberal theory is external to the allegedly social relations of individual interaction, it is actually a non-social phenomenon. The common interest of civil society is a hypothesised capacity standing above the relations of civil society which brings order to them. It is only by introducing the concept of a common interest into its model of society that the liberal image of social relations between self-interested individuals can be maintained; such a concept is no more than what has been called a 'communist fiction'.[62] The 'common interest' as a harmonised community of social interest functions in the liberal explanation of civil society in much the same way that Marx's 'social relations of communism' function to explain human society.

Marx, of course, argues against the claim in liberal political economy that self-interest gives rise to social relations by showing that, on the contrary, self-interest is responsible for the unsocial relations of antagonism between competitors.[63] Marx's critique of the liberal affirmation of the harmony of interests in civil society is contained in the statement, made in another context, that '[s]ociety is then conceived as an abstract capitalist'.[64] Marx's alternative to the liberal position is not, however, a sociology of conflict but an alternative conception of the harmonised community of social interest. The communist fiction of liberalism is replaced with Marx's communist fact, 'the first real coming-to-be, the realisation become real for man, of man's essence'.[65] The absence in liberal political economy of this type of dialectic appreciation of man's immanent social essence is criticised by Marx,[66] but his own 'communist fact' contains a 'social fiction' analogous to that in liberalism. Man's essential sociality, as it is conceived by Marx, does not derive from the individual's communal participation, it is merely precipitated in communism while remaining a factor inherent in the individual's human nature.[67] Marx's social community of communism is a conception of realised human nature, it describes the situation in which man 'submit[s] himself to his true essence'.[68] Thus human society is explicable in terms of the properties of human nature, of the human species and its individual members. Marx's account of human society therefore functions through a concept which is ontologically and methodologically prior to social relations.

From the sociological point of view Marx's communism, like liberalism's social interest, is non-social, for it is an attribute of the individual rather than of inter-individual social relations.

The model of social man developed in Marx's early writing is more consistent than the liberal model it criticises in so far as its premises of human nature and human society are conceptually related. The liberal premises of human nature and social harmony are not internally connected. The critique of the liberal position found in Marx's alternative vision of human nature and the community of social man acquires a compelling force in the fact of its consistency alone. But while Marx's version of social man is more successful than that of the political economists on one level, they both share a common flaw. There is developed in each a sub-social or pre-social conception of human nature; man's nature is prior to his social being and devolves on the individual essence. In liberal theory man's social nature is explained through the psychological concept of a propensity to truck, barter and exchange, whereas in Marx the philosophico-anthropological concept of an essential trans-subjective reciprocity in man's nature accounts for the individual's social being. Both of these concepts have a narrower range than the social concept of an ordered interaction of individual actors. Neither postulate the social faculty as something intrinsic to social relations themselves.

The conception of society in liberalism and in Marx's early writings, as they presuppose a human nature prior to social relations, a human nature which accounts for the social existence of the individual, must be regarded as defective from the sociological perspective. A more adequate depiction of society than that of either liberal theory or Marx's early writings would recognise that society exists in its own terms, as it were, and must be accounted for in something other than individual terms. The properties of society, as Marx demonstrated in his mature writings, are quite different from the properties of its individual members. Society is irreducible to its individual members, and must, therefore, be explained in social and not individual terms. The locus of society is in the ordered pattern of interaction between the individual members of society and the social relations thereby constituted. It has been argued by Alan Dawe, however, that our preferred conception of society is only one of two possible sociologies.[69] As well as the 'social system' perspective, in which society is ontologically and methodologically prior to its participants, there is the 'social action' perspective, in which the individual social actors create society and the operative element of social action is the subjective dimension of the participants. On this second conception of sociology it is arguable that the liberal and early Marxian concepts of society are indeed sociological and that Marx's early critique of liberalism is *mutatis mutandis* a sociological critique of liberalism and not, as it was suggested above, a merely philosophico-anthropological critique.

Indeed, Adam Smith, for instance, while arguing that society is ultimately reducible to the individual, goes on to show that the 'difference of natural talents in different individuals is not so much the cause as the effect of the division of labour.'[70] Thus in their interaction individuals create a social world which, in turn, has a causal effect on the individuals and their relationships. This constitutes an account of the individual condition in terms of social causation. A general statement of the sociology of social action derived from liberal premises is enunciated by John Stuart Mill:[71]

> In social phenomena the elementary facts are feelings and actions, and the laws of these are the laws of human nature, social facts being the results of human acts and situations. . . . The human beings themselves, on the laws of whose nature the facts of history depend, are not abstract or universal but historical human beings, already shaped, and made what they are, by human society.

A theory of society constituted along the lines suggested by Mill does not resolve the difficulties of developing a liberal sociology, which cannot be gone into here, but the pretensions of such a sociology are clearly set out.

Marx's early model of human society can similarly be seen as an instance of social action sociology in which the subjective and objective elements are mediated through action, the consequence of which is 'the social fabric':[72]

> my own existence is social activity, and therefore that which I make of myself, I make of myself for society and with the consciousness of myself as a social being.

> My general consciousness is only the theoretical shape of that of which the living shape is the real community, the social fabric.

Perhaps even more important to our discussion than an arguable social action sociology of human society is the concept of social causation which some scholars have found in Marx's early discussion of civil society.

Ernest Mandel has argued that in the *Economic and Philosophic Manu-*

scripts Marx explains alienated labour as 'the product of *a particular form of society*' namely class society in which the commodities produced by one class are appropriated by another.[73] He continues, however, that the manuscript then goes on to attribute the origin of alienated labour to human nature, and this, he says, is an 'anthropological concept of aliena- tion ... [which] remains largely philosophical and speculative'.[74] The conclusion which Mandel draws is that there is a 'contradiction within the *Economic and Philosophic Manuscripts*' in so far as Marx ascribes the cause of alienation to both social and philosophico- anthropological determination. This contradiction, Mandel continues, is resolved in *The German Ideology*, where the former mode of causa- tion only informs Marx's discussion.[75] The important point, though, is that a sociological account of alienation is already developed in the *Economic and Philosophic Manuscripts*, according to Mandel: Marx's argument that the class appropriation of the products of labour is generative of alienation is a sociological account of the alienation of labour.

Another facet of the supposed social cause of alienation is suggested by John Maguire when he says that the *Economic and Philosophic Manuscripts* show that the wealth created in industrial production is the product 'of human co-operation, of intelligent organisation of the capacity of the species, rather than of each individual acting in isola- tion'.[76] The causal role of the division of labour in man's alienation is also held to be an explanation of the individual's condition in social terms.[77] Even before writing the *Economic and Philosophic Manu- scripts* Marx had stated an apparently sociological proposition in *On the Jewish Question* with the claim that the unsocial aspect of the individual in civil society is a consequence of 'the entire organisation of our society'.[78] There is ample textual evidence, therefore, to support a sociological reading of Marx's early writings, even if it does run parallel to a philosophico-anthropological interpretation.

A sociological reading of Marx's early writings has been used to show not only that alienation is a consequence of social causes, but that the route to human society is also explained by Marx through the social interaction between alienated individuals. In his discussion of Marx's early naturalism Zbigniew Jordan, for instance, interprets 'the hypothesis that man "develops his true nature only in society" ' to mean that 'men acquire the means of cultivating their gifts in all direc- tions and of becoming ultimately free individuals' only in the social context.[79] In their social relations prior to the attainment of commun- ism men begin to develop the faculties which, when fully realised, constitute the advent of human society. This is similar to Maguire's claim that the operative capacity of the species for co-operation in production, under conditions of alienation, demonstrates the 'potential for the creation of new wealth', presumably in communism, which amounts to an argument for 'an empirical basis for the notion of species-being' in Marx's 1844 *Manuscripts*.[80]

Contrary to the argument of this chapter, then, the *Manuscripts* has been interpreted to provide a social explanation both of alienation and of the process leading to communism. While these interpretations seem to reinforce each other in proposing that Marx did indeed develop a sociology in the *Economic and Philosophic Manuscripts*, they are in fact inconsistent. As the alienated individual is man robbed of his social gifts, the argument that alienated labour is the consequence of social causes is one which proposes that there are social obstacles to the development of species capacities. Thus a sociological account of the movement to communism which focuses on the development of social capacities in man is inconsistent with a sociological account of aliena-tion, for the latter explains the impossibility of the former, not its veracity. A sociological account of the revolutionary movement, which Marx describes as the negation of the negation,[81] would have to inter-pret this dialectic in class terms such that communism was the outcome of class struggle rather than the incremental development of the capacity in individuals for free interaction between men. But this understanding of the movement towards communism does not furnish evidence, empirical or otherwise, of man's species-being. It does not necessarily deny the notion of a human-species-nature, it functions independently of such a notion or its denial, but it removes from the explanation of the movement towards communism any supposition concerning the development of social capacities in civil society.

In our earlier discussion of the movement towards communism we interpreted Marx's claims regarding the necessity for the transcendence of private property to imply that the contradiction which, when resolved, gave rise to human society, was a contradiction internal to private property itself, the content of which was the contradiction between alienated labour's empirical unsocial form and its essentially social nature. It was argued that Marx did not regard this contradic-tion as fundamentally one between labour and capital in a class sense, and that his argument constituted a philosophical rather than a social prognosis of man's movement towards communism. It is of interest that this philosophical interpretation is consistent with the 'socio-logical' explanation of alienation in so far as it proposes that alienated labour is labour which has become estranged through private property.

Rather than there being a contradiction in the *Economic and Philosophic Manuscripts* between the sociological and philosophico-anthropological explanations of alienation, the two are quite compatible. The basis of their consistency lies precisely in the fact that the sociological explanation in this particular instance is reducible to the explanation of alienation in philosophical terms. The passage in the *Manuscripts* which Mandel had quoted to show that alienation is a consequence of social causes, the consequence of the appropriation of the products of labour by the non-labourer, must be supplemented with Marx's comments a little later in the same manuscript that the relation between worker and capitalist is the result of alienated labour and that private property, which appears as the source of alienation, is really its consequence.[82] In anticipation of this point, and in answer to it, Mandel says that Marx 'is not dealing here with the problem of the historical origin of private property but rather with the problem of its nature, of how it reappears daily in a mode of production based on alienated labour.'[83] Actually the passage in question can be interpreted as a statement concerning both the historical and everyday genesis of private property. But the important thing, which renders Mandel's objection redundant, is that it is an account of alienation which is based on the assumption that what is alienated is human nature. The anthropological interpretation is reinforced by Marx's discussion of the division of labour. While the division of labour empirically functions as a social cause of alienation, it is primarily, Marx says, the alienated form of the social character of labour.[84] The social cause of alienated labour − in private property and the division of labour − is itself a consequence of human nature in its alienated form.

The apparent antinomy between Mandel's identification of two distinct explanations of alienation in the *Economic and Philosophic Manuscripts* and our argument that one reduces to the other, can be resolved by a few words about historical causation in general. It is important, in any causal explanation of historical or social events, to differentiate between what have been called 'internal' causes or 'pre-conditions' on the one hand, and 'external' causes or 'precipitants' on the other.[85] Roughly speaking precipitants or external causes are the agents which actually give rise to the empirical occurrence of an event or condition. The pre-conditions or internal causes, on the other hand, are responsible for the effect, for the precise nature of the event or condition. Applying this model of causation to Marx's explanation of alienation in the *Manuscripts* it can be seen that the references to a social cause of alienation are those which describe the precipitation of alienation. The effectivity of the social precipitant derives from the philosophico-anthropological pre-condition of man's species-nature. What Mandel has isolated are merely two levels of a single explanatory model. The social action sociology of the *Manuscripts* is the derivative of a philosophical anthropology. The identification of social causes in the *Manuscripts* which account for man's alienation should not lead us to depart from the view that Marx regards the individual in civil society as an unsocial being alienated from his social nature.

It has been argued, though, that in a description of civil society written some four or five months after the *Economic and Philosophic Manuscripts*, Marx did acknowledge that alienated individuals engage in social relations, and therefore that in this same period Marx disagreed with the liberal position that the individual was external to society. Zbigniew Jordan says that for Marx civil society is not merely an aggregation of unrelated individuals, but rather 'the totality of various social bonds, through which individuals mutually interrelate.[86] Jordan substantiates this with a quotation from *The Holy Family*:[87]

> it is natural necessity, the essential human properties however estranged they may seem to be, and interest that hold the members of civil society together.

The sentence immediately preceding the one quoted here shows, however, that Marx is actually reaffirming the liberal position rather than repudiating it, as Jordan maintains. It states that:[88]

> since the need of one individual has no self-evident meaning for another egoistic individual capable of satisfying that need, and therefore no direct connection with its satisfaction, each individual has to create this connection; it thus becomes the intermediary between the need of another and the objects of this need.

This passage, of course, does not deny that individuals relate to one another in civil society, but it does demonstrate that Marx believed that the relations were not the result of social bonds. It is a restatement of the liberal position that civil society is a net of relationships between individuals defined by their personal interests and particular needs. The point is, and Marx has not gone beyond it here, that the relations of civil society are entirely reducible to the relations of discrete individuals, exchange relations between egoistic individual beings. The passage can be read as a paraphrase of Adam Smith's discussion of the functional division of trades in the satisfaction of individual needs,[89] and certainly does not advance on the depiction of civil society in *On the Jewish Question* which argues that civil society:[90]

> appears as a framework extraneous to the individuals. . . . The only bond which holds them together is natural necessity, need and private interest.

What Marx is describing in both works is the unsocial nature of man's relations in civil society.

IV

The two concepts 'civil society' and 'human society' are coexistent in Marx's early writings. The latter is society in a condition of becoming, an as yet unrealised reality in which man's relations are fully social. The notion of human society is the critical measure against which is held the unsocial man of civil society. The anthropological essence of man's species-being, according to Marx's argument, is alienated from him in civil society, the corollary of which is that it is only through the transcendence of his alienation that man's species-nature is realised. Only then does the individual exist as the social being. Marx's account of man's anthropologically immanent social nature is absent from *The German Ideology*, where it is argued that the market economy is not the result of man's alienation, but that man's alienation is the consequence of the market economy.[91] Rather than an explanation of society based on an anthropology of species-being, we now find an account of the condition of man in terms of social structure.

Marx introduces a new meaning of the concept 'society' into his work when he says:[92]

> By social we understand the co-operation of several individuals, no matter under what conditions, in what manner and to what end. It follows from this that a certain mode of production, or industrial stage, is always combined with a certain mode of co-operation, or social stage, and this mode of co-operation is itself a 'productive force'. Further, that the multitude of productive forces accessible to men determines the nature of society.

According to this definition all relations between individuals which effect a common end are social relations. The relations between individuals who meet to satisfy merely their private interests and individual needs through exchange are thus also social relations. Secondly, this definition contains the proposition that the form of society is a consequence of the manner in which production is conducted. This entails that under all conditions of production, alienated or otherwise, the relations between individual operatives are social relations; although the form of the social relations will vary with the mode of production. Society in this sense, with the corresponding notion of the causal primacy on the nature of society of the mode of production, remains at the core of Marx's methodology in all of his research after *The German Ideology*. It stands in stark contrast to the earlier philosophico-anthropological conception of 'society'.

It was stated earlier in this chapter that historical materialism, and what has just been outlined is a summary statement of historical materialism, includes a sociological critique of liberal individualism. That is to say historical materialism demonstrates that society cannot be reduced to its individual members and that the web of social relationships is greater than the market relations of individuals. The question of whether the theory of historical materialism can be regarded as a sociological theory is in many ways controversial. Not all post-classical Marxism, i.e. self-designated Marxist interpretations of Marxism, concedes that historical materialism contains a sociological theory.[93] However, that which does, more or less follows the perspective of Lenin's statement that:[94]

> Marx put an end to the view that society is a mechanical aggregation of individuals ... and was the first to put sociology on a scientific basis by establishing the concept of the economic formation of society as the sum-total of given relations of production.

The principle distinguishing feature of Marx's sociology is the emphasis it places on the fundamental role of the production process for an understanding of the structure, and, one might add, dynamic, of society. The process of production for Marx is fundamentally the labour process:[95]

> It is always the direct relationship of the owners of the conditions of production to the direct producers — a relation always naturally corresponding to a definite stage in the development of the methods of labour and thereby its social productivity — which reveals the innermost secret, the hidden basis of the entire social structure.

The social structure, therefore, is understood through the relations of production, and these are essentially value relations in capitalism, the relations of the creation and appropriation of value. It is on this foundation that Marx, in his mature writings, differentiates between feudalism and capitalism, explains the emergence of individualistic society and develops a sociological critique of liberal individualism. He shows that the individual of commercial or capitalist society is a social being whose social bonds are not in the relations of the market place, in human sympathy or in species-being, but in the social relations of social production.

It was shown above that in his early writings Marx conceived the difference between feudal and capitalist labour as a difference between labour which was directed by its significance for the community and labour which was directed by its significance for the individual. In capitalism labour and capital were held to be devoid of social content and meaning, and the relations between individuals were regarded as unsocial relations. The asociality of civil society was explained in terms of the individual's untrammelled egoism, and this was seen as a consequence of the alienation of man's social species-being. In his later writings Marx differentiates between feudalism and capitalism in terms of the nature of social production, and rather than regarding the relations of man in civil society as unsocial, he now says that they are merely a particular form of social relation, different in content from the relations of feudal society. The difference between these two types of society, Marx argues, is the difference between a society in which production is predominantly for use and a society in which production is for exchange. In Marx's later work the relationship of individuals is explained in terms of the social structure within which production takes place, rather than through a teleological concept of human nature. Human nature and the individual's social relations are now seen as dependent upon the structure of social production, whereas in the early writings human nature is an independent variable, itself consequential upon the relations between individuals.

The distinction between feudal and capitalist society is succinctly expressed in the *Grundrisse* when Marx says that 'the dissolution of the servile relationship which binds the labourer to the soil, and to the lord of the soil' is essentially the dissolution of 'relations of production in which use-value predominates'.[96] Under feudal conditions the labour of the serf and its products is divided into that which is directly provided to the lord of the land, and that consumed by the serf and his family.[97] In neither case is production separated from consumption by a commercial intervention and labour, therefore, produces only use-values. Such production requires that labour be combined with the means of labour, 'the instrument of labour is . . . intimately merged with living labour,'[98] and that the social relations through which it operates be close and direct. The dissolution of labour relations productive of use-value is therefore firstly 'the historical process of divorcing the producer from the means of production'.[99] The labourer is thus freed from the close and servile relations of manor and guild and from his means of production: he emerges as the free individual of capitalist society.[100] The newly free labourer is available to be freely hired and set to work for a wage by an independent owner of means of production. What is produced under these new conditions is physically the same as what had previously been produced, but, Marx says, 'a new social soul has popped into its body,'[101] for it is a commodity, produced not for immediate consumption by either the labourer or the owner of the means of labour, but a product which exists solely to be placed on the market for sale. What is produced by free labour is not a use-value but an exchange-value.

As the basis of capitalist production is the production of exchange-values rather than use-values,[102] so its relations are spatial rather than direct. The production of an exchange-value or commodity is separated from its use or consumption by the exchange relation. Exchange is a relation between private and mutually independent proprietors who meet solely to fulfil a particular transaction.[103] Production for exchange is similarly conducted between mutually independent persons.[104] Not only is exchange itself an interaction between independent individuals, but it 'is a major agent of this individualisation',[105] so that the process is self-reinforcing. Thus the image of the isolated atom of commercial society, the individual bereft of social relations, does appear to be an apposite description. But in his 'Introduction' of 1857 Marx criticises such a suggestion in liberal political economy, and, incidentally, his own former view, when he says that:[106]

the epoch which produces this standpoint, namely that of the solitary individual, is precisely the epoch of the (as yet) most highly developed social . . . relations. Man is . . . not only a social animal, but an animal that can be individualised only within society.

Marx argues, therefore, for a very strong correspondence between the degree of individualisation and the advanced state of capitalist social relations. The connection between the two is implicit in the nature of exchange-value.

Before looking at the social context let us begin with the individual particle. The basic unit of the capitalist mode of production is not the individual labourer, according to Marx, but the single commodity.[107] The commodity is both a private thing, in so far as it is always in the possession of a particular individual; and a social thing, it is produced for another's consumption. Private labour, in the production of commodities, bestows upon them an exchange-value. In the realisation of that value in the market place, in the sale of the commodity, the social character of private labour is confirmed. Engels catches these complex interrelations nicely:[108]

What are commodities? Products made in a society of more or less separate private producers, and therefore in the first place private products. These private products, however, become commodities only when they are made, not for consumption by their producers, but for consumption by others, that is, for social consumption; they enter into social consumption through exchange. The private producers are therefore socially interconnected, constitute a society.

Thus the private production of commodities by individual labourers is the social production of exchange-values for social consumption.

The social character of exchange-value lies in the fact that it registers the quantity of social labour allocated to the production of a commodity. The value relation is not a natural property pertaining to material objects, but 'something purely social'.[109] As Marx explains in his pamphlet on *Wages, Price and Profit*, the production of a commodity is not merely the production of 'an article satisfying some *social* want', for the labour expended in the production of commodities 'must form part and parcel of the total sum of labour expended by society'.[110] And herein is the advanced nature of the social relations of society based on exchange-value, for the social relations of exchange-value function independently of the will of the social actors themselves. Marx comments that 'the behaviour of men in the social process of [commodity] production is purely atomic,' and goes on to say that 'their relations to each other in production assume a material character independent of their control and conscious individual action.'[111] Thus exchange-value 'develops a whole network of social relations spontaneous in their growth and entirely beyond the control of the actors'.[112] This spatial society contrasts sharply with the directness of feudal social relations in which individual labour is the consciously applied labour of the community in the production of use-values. While commodity society is individualised it 'does not consist of individuals, but expresses the sum of interrelations, the relations within which these individuals stand'.[113] The structure of production corresponds to a particular form of interrelations, which are essentially and wholly social relations, even though they are not relationships willed by the individuals themselves. Here is Marx's sociological analysis of individualised society. What of his critique of liberal individualism in social terms?

A crucial feature of commodity production, and a consequence of the separation of production from consumption through exchange, is that commodities exist independently of men and assume a life of their own. Exchange-values, Marx says, 'vary continually, independently of the will, foresight and action of the producers. To them, their own social action takes the form of the action of objects.'[114] Thus 'production relations are converted into entities and rendered independent in relation to the agents of production.'[115] A phenomenal effect of commodity production, therefore, is that 'the relations connecting the labour of one individual with that of the rest appear, not as direct social relations between individuals at work, but as ... material relations between persons.'[116] Thus the commodity form is not only the basis of individualised society, it is also at the root of the view that the individual is without social relations. Marx calls this the fetishism of commodities, which was discussed briefly in Chapter 1 above.

It is through the fallacy of commodity fetishism that the liberal political economists, and Marx in his early writings, reduce the social relations of individuals to the external relations of independent and unsocial beings. With his theory of commodity fetishism Marx sociologically demonstrates that social relations only appear as things under the conditions of commodity production, in the production of exchange-values.

Chapter Four

Capitalism

The present chapter focuses on the economic aspects of alienation. Two broad and mutually exclusive positions on the concept of alienation in Marx can be identified within the critical literature. Some have argued that although Marx developed the concept of alienation in his early works, he abandoned it in his mature writings.[1] Others have held that the concept of alienation is not only developed in the early writings, but is also central to Marx's later thought, and hence constitutes the common thread which unifies his work.[2] This chapter will attempt to resolve the controversy of whether Marx abandoned or continued to employ the concept of alienation. It will show that the concept of alienation, while employed by Marx throughout his writings, is part of a theoretical framework in his early writings which is significantly different from the one in which it functions in his mature thought.

It will also be shown in this chapter that the theory of alienation in the *Economic and Philosophic Manuscripts* is empirically verifiable for a particular stage of capitalist development, but inadequate – indeed implausible – as a theory of capitalism in general. Marx's own mature analysis of the differences in the conditions of labour and the division of labour for different phases of capitalist development shows the limitations of his early theory of alienation as an empirical theory of capitalism.

Although Marx began to advance his early theory of alienation in the *Critique of Hegel's Philosophy of Right* it is most highly developed and most clearly outlined in the 1844 *Manuscripts*. Unlike other early writings the statement of the theory of alienation in the *Economic and Philosophic Manuscripts* is more directly commensurate with the mature theory of alienation as it provides an account of the alienation of labour. Thus in the discussion below the *Manuscripts* will be taken as representative of Marx's early theory of alienation. Representative of the mature theory of alienation will be that found in *Capital*. Most accounts of Marx's mature theory of alienation have focused on the *Grundrisse*, where the term 'alienation' appears with much frequency.[3] The reasons for virtually ignoring the *Grundrisse* in our argument are two-fold. Firstly, whatever is of interest in the *Grundrisse* can be found in *Capital*;[4] secondly, it is clearly more important to show that the theory of alienation appears in a work which Marx wrote for publication, rather than in working notes which he left in a drawer.

Four basic propositions will be advanced below. It will be shown that the concept of alienation is current throughout the entirety of Marx's thought. Secondly, it will be shown that the concept of alienation in the *Economic and Philosophic Manuscripts* is part of a theory which is quite different from the theory of alienation developed in *Capital*. Thus the argument of theoretical continuity errs in failing to notice that there are at least two theories of alienation in Marx's writings, one of which supersedes the other. Thirdly, it will be shown that the empirical content of the early theory of alienation is limited to a particular phase of capitalist development. The theory of the *Manuscripts* is not a general theory of capitalism. Finally, it will be shown that from the perspective of the mature theory of alienation the early theory is false.

I

Not only is Marx's interest in the theme of alienation manifest throughout his intellectual career, he also continued to employ the term 'alienation' after writing the *Manuscripts*. It appears in the *Grundrisse*, as we have already noted, and also in *The Poverty of Philosophy*, in *A Contribution to the Critique of Political Economy*, in *Capital* and in the *Theories of Surplus Value*.[5] It is used in all of these works as part of Marx's explanation of the conditions of labour in commodity production.

Two basic facets of alienation can be differentiated in Marx's mature usage, what Daniel Bell calls 'dehumanisation' and 'exploitation'.[6] Bell believes that Marx 'glossed over' the first of these in *Capital* because he was concerned with the consequence of capitalist social relations, and therefore exploitation, rather than with technology in general, which Bell says Marx saw as the basis of dehumanisation. Actually, Marx regards the capitalist application of technology rather than technology neutrally conceived to be the cause of dehumanisation,[7] and his treatment of the problem in the rather lengthy chapter on 'Machinery and Modern Industry' in *Capital* indicates that he accorded the matter some importance. Perhaps mindful of this fact Fredy Perlman distinguishes in Marx not dehumanisation and exploitation, but qualitative and quantitative aspects of exploitation:[8]

> Thus when Marx speaks of the capitalist's appropriation of 'surplus value' or 'surplus labour', he refers to the quantitative aspect of exploitation, not the qualitative aspect. Qualitatively, the labourer alienates the entirety of his creative power, his power to participate consciously in shaping his material environment.

This conveys the sense of Marx's explanation, lost in Bell's account, of both dehumanisation and exploitation in terms of capitalist production, rather than in terms of technological development on the one hand and capitalist development on the other.

It is convenient to deal here with the general question of the distinction between 'alienation' and 'exploitation', as the comments above may have been read to suggest that the two can be treated as equivalents, which they cannot. According to Marx alienation occurs in commodity production only. Under such conditions the exchange relations of market society separate production from consumption, and the product acquires a life of its own, independent of the producer, and comes to oppress him as an alien force. Exploitation, on the other hand, is not confined to situations of commodity production, in Marx's account. The serf is exploited by the feudal lord, even though he produces only use-values. Similarly, the slave owner exploits his slave and the oriental despot his peasants when no commodity is appropriated. Exploitation, for Marx, is the appropriation of the surplus labour of one class by another class. Only in commodity production does surplus labour take the value form.[9] Thus exploitation is a category with a wider scope than the category of alienation. All alienating relations are relations of exploitation, but not all exploitation is alienating. A description of the relations of commodity production — which is a description of the alienating relationship — is found in both the *Manuscripts* and *Capital*, as was shown in the previous chapter.

In *Capital* Marx seldom uses the term — although he clearly employs the concept — 'alienation' when referring to man's dehumanisation, to his loss of creative power, to the situation in which man is mutilated, crippled, becomes a mere appendage to the machine.[10] The use of the word is generally confined in the mature writing to refer to the situation in which things, including the many attributes of labour, become objects of exchange.[11] But when he describes the 'sine qua non of capitalist production'[12] Marx shows how these two aspects of alienation, that of capitalist exploitation and dehumanisation, are related to a single process. Marx says that before entering the production process the worker's 'own labour has already been alienated' in the sale of his labour-power to the capitalist.[13] The labour power thus appropriated by the capitalist is realised in a product belonging to the capitalist, not the labourer. Here is the process of quantitative alienation. But, Marx continues, not only is the product of labour consumed by the capitalist converted into commodities, it is also converted into capital, 'into means of production that command the producers'.[14] Here is the alienation of the worker's creative powers, for the 'labourer therefore constantly produces material, objective wealth, but in the form of capital, of an alien power that dominates and exploits him.'[15] In making available his labour power to the capitalist, in alienating his labour power, the worker creates the means of his further alienation by creating a force which does not belong to him but which, by taking from him his power to control production, becomes an agent in his exploitation. For capital is not merely a physical and technical relation, according to Marx, it is a coercive social relation which dictates the regularity, intensity and magnitude of labour.[16] Here in *Capital* is described the condition of alienation first outlined by Marx in the *Economic and Philosophic Manuscripts* which corresponds to Feuerbach's account of alienation, discussed in Chapter 2 above, in which alienation is the consequence of man producing an effect which, in becoming independent of him, comes to be a force in his oppression.

Two things have been established so far: that Marx uses the term 'alienation' in *Capital* as well as in the *Economic and Philosophic Manuscripts*, and furthermore, that he uses it to describe those processes to which he refers when applying the same term in the *Manuscripts*. However, the appearance of the concept 'alienation' in a description of labour's objectification as hostile phenomena cannot itself prove that the theory of alienation developed in the *Manuscripts* is continued in *Capital*. There is no doubt that the idea of alienation is enduring in Marx's thought. But the mere statement of a common theme in the two works and the fact that they share a description of man's condition as alienated, does not entail nor constitute the statement of a single theory. What this shows, rather, is that they both account for a common empirical situation. The question which remains is whether there is a theoretical explanation of alienation which is common to both works. In order to prove theoretical continuity it must be shown that the concept of alienation is part of a common system of concepts in the two works, and that the role of the concept of alienation in the structure of explanation has not changed between the *Economic and Philosophic Manuscripts* and *Capital*.

II

There is, in fact, a large disjuncture between the theoretical accounts of alienation in the two works. There are significantly different conceptions in the *Manuscripts* on the one hand, and in *Capital* on the other, of the workers' impoverishment in alienation, of the nature of the loss incurred in alienation and of the process by which alienation is transcended. These differences indicate that there are two quite different theories of alienation in Marx's work.

The first of these differences between the two works relates to the quantitative aspect of alienation. The theory of alienation in *Capital* is derived from the labour theory of value and the concomitant theory of surplus value. In summary, these claim, firstly, that the value of all commodities, including labour power, is determined by the socially necessary labour time required for their production; secondly, that the worker is paid the full value of his labour power when he sells it to the capitalist; and thirdly, that when the already purchased labour power is consumed in production by the capitalist it creates, in addition to its own value, a surplus value which constitutes a nett gain to the capitalist. While Marx had explicitly rejected the classical labour theory of value at about the time he wrote the *Economic and Philosophic Manuscripts*,[17] it has been claimed that a germ of the labour theory of value is in the alienation theory of the *Manuscripts*.[18] Nevertheless, it should be recognised that Marx's explanation of quantitative alienation in the *Manuscripts* is based on a different theoretical foundation than that of *Capital*, and it carries with it different implications.

On the assumptions of the labour theory of value, that labour power, like all commodities, is sold at its value, and that its value is determined by the labour time required for its production, it follows that an increase in labour productivity, that is, a decrease in the labour time necessary to produce a commodity, decreases the share of income going to labour and increases the part appropriated by the capitalist. In other words the labour theory of value implies a relative impoverishment of the working class. Relative impoverishment is a decrease in the share of the national income going to the working class as opposed to an absolute decrease in the income of labour. Relative impoverishment may occur when the real income of labour rises. Marx had already arrived at this conclusion by 1847.[19] The proposition that under conditions of capitalist development the working class suffers a relative impoverishment is assimilated into Marx's 'General Law of Capitalist Accumulation' in *Capital*.[20] The concept of alienation in its quantitative form in *Capital* implies the concept of the relative impoverishment of labour.

The alienation theory of the *Manuscripts* entails not a relative but an absolute impoverishment of labour. Marx argues here that an increasing appropriation of labour's products requires an increasing absolute loss to labour, for:[21]

> the greater this [productive] activity, the greater is the worker's lack of objects. Whatever the product of his labour is, he is not. . . . Therefore the greater the product, the less is he himself

and,

> The worker becomes all the poorer the more wealth he produces, the more his production increases in power and range. . . . With the increasing value of the world of things proceeds in direct proportion the devaluation of the world of men.

Marx arrives at this general conclusion through two routes. The early alienation theory has no conception of an increase in labour productivity which results from an application of less labour time to more technology.[22] An increase of productivity is seen in the *Manuscripts* only as a consequence of more labour being consumed in production. Marx says that:[23]

> The product of labour is labour which has been congealed in an object. . . . So much does labour's realisation appear as loss of reality that the worker loses reality to the point of starving to death . . . the more objects the worker produces the fewer can he possess. . . . [These] consequences are contained in the definition that the worker is related to the product of his labour as to an alien object.

As the product of labour is congealed labour, it follows that an increase in the volume of products created increases the loss of labour to the labourer himself. This is an absolute, not a relative loss of labour and, therefore, an absolute loss of the products of labour.

The second route to the concept of absolute impoverishment is in an explanation of the price of labour. Whereas in *Capital* wages are more or less equivalent to the value of labour power expressed in the money form, in the *Economic and Philosophic Manuscripts* the price of labour is accounted for purely in terms of the laws of supply and demand. This comes out in Marx's discussion of the conditions which he says give rise to the growth of capital and revenue. The first condition states that as capital is accumulated labour the growth of capital is in 'the accumulation of much labour'.[24] This is the argument claiming that the greater the product the less the labourer. The other two conditions of capital accumulation are an increase in the division of labour and an increase in the concentration of capital, both of which are held to result in an increase in the size of the working class.[25] What is important for our argument in all of this is that Marx says that an increase in the size of the working class intensifies the competition between workers and this has the effect of depressing wages — which is tantamount to an absolute impoverishment of the working class.

The general thrust of the discussion of capital accumulation in the *Economic and Philosophic Manuscripts* is clearly biased toward the view that an absolute impoverishment of the working class is a necessary consequence of the accumulation process. This is quite contrary to the view expressed in *Capital*. The relation between the theory of wages and the theory of alienation in the *Manuscripts* is not direct. But given that all wage labour is estranged labour and that 'the more objects the [estranged labourer] produces the fewer he can possess',[26] it seems quite conclusive that the *Manuscripts* in general and the theory of alienation in particular imply the concept of an absolute impoverishment of labour.

Related to different treatments of the quantitative aspect of alienation in the two works is a fundamentally different conception of its qualitative aspect, the loss of labour's creative power in alienated production. A dual consequence of capitalist exploitation, according to Marx in *Capital*, is the advent of an authority function of capital itself and the fact that in increasing the efficiency of labour, the capitalist division of labour and industrial form robs labour of its creativity. Marx argues that the organisation of labour within a factory context has its precondition in the capitalist property relation of private ownership. Labour is necessarily subjected to the authority and rule of capital, which dictates the actions of labour in production. That this is a direct effect of capitalist exploitation is made quite clear by Marx when he says that:[27]

The control exercised by the capitalist is not only a special function, due to the nature of the social labour-process, and peculiar to that process, but is, at the same time, a function of the exploitation of a social labour-process, and is consequently rooted in the unavoidable antagonism between the exploiter and the living and labouring raw material he exploits.

Under this 'autocracy'[28] of capital the labourer is prevented from exercising any control over his productive tasks. The loss of power in labour activity is intensified by virtue of the industrial division of labour which, in increasing the labourer's efficiency, removes totally the creativity of his labour and deforms him into a mere adjunct of the machine.[29] Thus in *Capital* the qualitative alienation of labour is the loss of labour's power for creative activity, the exercise of which the labourer is capable but prevented by social restraints. This concept of qualitative alienation therefore implies the alienation or loss of labour's potential for creative activity.

In the *Economic and Philosophic Manuscripts* qualitative alienation is also conceived as a loss of potential for creative activity. In alienated production man loses his capacity for creative activity, for it 'does not develop freely his physical and mental energy but mortifies his body and ruins his mind'.[30] The more the needs of wealth are satisfied the more must life and human needs be denied.[31] Daniel Bell is perfectly correct, therefore, to say that alienation in the *Manuscripts* is the 'failure to realise one's potential *as a self*'.[32] While the *Economic and Philosophic Manuscripts* share with *Capital* the view that in alienation man loses his potential for creative activity, there is in the former a further dimension of qualitative alienation which has no part of the conception of the latter. In the *Manuscripts* Marx argues that man's loss in alienation is not only a loss of potential creativity but also an ontological loss of self.[33]

Marx says that the object of labour is:[34]

the objectification of man's species life: for he duplicates himself not only, as in consciousness, intellectually, but also actively, in reality. . . . In tearing away from man the object of his production, therefore, estranged labour tears from him his species life, his real species objectivity.

The alienation of labour, in being the alienation of man's 'real species objectivity', is therefore an objective loss rather than merely a loss of the potential for creative activity. It is true that there is a sense in

which this objective alienation relates to the question of man's potential, for even in alienation man has the potential to attain his full
species being in the historical development of his essential nature. But
against this merely 'potentialist' interpretation Marx suggests that the
condition in which man's full essence is only a potential (rather than an
actual) reality is the condition in which the alienation of labour
'appears as a loss of reality for the workers'.[35] Under these circumstances man's objective essence itself is lost to him. It is not the
potential for creativity which man especially loses in alienation, but
rather that in alienation man has the historical possibility or potential
of acquiring his objective nature which is lost in alienation. Ernest
Mandel accepts this interpretation of the concept of alienation in the
Manuscripts, but adds that it is contradicted by another conception
developed by Marx in the same work.[36] Rather than being contradictory on this point the *Manuscripts* are quite consistent in so far as the
concept of qualitative alienation, which entails the concept of an
objective loss to man's anthropological nature, is implied by the notion
of quantitative alienation developed at the same time by Marx.

We have already seen that the theory of exploitation or quantitative
alienation in the *Economic and Philosophic Manuscripts* postulates
that the appropriation of products is the appropriation of objectified
labour. The more man produces the less he has. The alienation of
labour in exploitation is, therefore, a devastation of the labourer
because the 'product of labour is labour which has been congealed in an
object, which has become material: it is the objectification of labour.'[37]
As labour is 'congealed' in the product of labour the labourer and his
product are objectively, indeed, ontologically linked. Marx says that the
'worker puts his life into the object; but now his life no longer belongs
to him but to the object.'[38] The appropriation of the fruits of labour is,
therefore, the appropriation of the labourer's life, that is, his objective
species-life. It is for this reason that Marx says that the labourer's
products are torn from him when they are appropriated. It is in the
argument concerning the exploitation of labour, therefore, that Marx
first demonstrates that the concept of alienation in the *Manuscripts*
implies a concept of objective loss rather than a loss of potential.

The theory of exploitation which is part of Marx's mature theory of
alienation has a conception of appropriation which is different from the
one of the *Manuscripts* and which implies an entirely different conception of what is lost to labour in qualitative estrangement. The value
theory of exploitation maintains that in production the labourer does
not merely congeal his labour in the product appropriated by the

capitalist, but rather sells his labour power, his capacity for labour, to the capitalist. As Marx says in *Wages, Price and Profit*:[39]

> What the working man sells is not directly his labour, but his labouring power, the temporary disposal of which he makes over to the capitalist.

This account is similar to the one of the *Manuscripts* in so far as both maintain that the product of labour is appropriated from the worker and that labour goes into the production of objects, or commodities. The labourer loses control over his activity and time and is subjected to the rule of capital in both Marx's account of the worker selling his labour power to the capitalist, as in *Wages, Price and Profit*, and in the account of the capitalist appropriating labour, as in the *Manuscripts*. According to both accounts work is not a means of self-expression and it does not directly satisfy the labourer's needs. But here the similarity ends. For in conceiving the worker's relation to production as a temporary disposal of his capacity for labour to the capitalist, as in Marx's later statement, it follows that the labourer has forsaken not his labour, which is inextricably connected with the labourer, but only his potentialities for human development. There is no ontological loss implied here, as there is in the *Manuscripts*.

It is through their different conceptions of the worker's relation to production that the 1844 theory of alienation and the mature theory differently conceive the nature of the qualitative loss to labour in alienation. According to the *Manuscripts* man's creative capacity is inherent in his objective nature, and in production man objectifies his species life. Appropriation of the product is therefore the estrangement of his 'real species objectivity'. His loss is ontological. According to *Capital* and other mature writings, on the other hand, man's capacity for labour is alienated in appropriation and what he loses, therefore, is his potential for free creative development. The basic theoretical difference between the two works in this is that whereas in the *Manuscripts* the 'worker ... [is] a commodity,'[40] in *Capital* it is labour power which is the commodity.[41] The appropriation of the commodity in the former is the objective loss of the worker himself rather than the loss of his capacity or potential for labour.

All theories of alienation entail a concept of the transcendence of alienation, of the negation of alienation, for all theories contain negatable propositions. The concept of alienation's transcendence, or communism, implied by the theory of the *Economic and Philosophic Manuscripts* is again quite different from that contained in Marx's mature theory of alienation. In the *Manuscripts* Marx describes communism as 'the real appropriation of the human essence by and for man'. He goes on to say that communism is 'the complete return of man to himself as a social (i.e. human) being', and that it is:[42]

> the true resolution of the strife between existence and essence, between objectification and self-confirmation, between freedom and necessity, between the individual and the species.

In overcoming alienation man's nature or species character, which, after all, is what he is alienated from, is fully and objectively realised; he is returned to his own free and conscious activity.[43] Communism is 'the first real coming-to-be, the realisation become real for man, of man's essence'.[44] Thus the concept of objective loss in qualitative alienation implies a concept of a resurrectionary transcendence of alienation in the realisation of man's true essence.

In his mature writings Marx is, regrettably, reticent in describing communist society as it might be. As he quips in *Capital*, he prefers to confine himself to 'critical analysis of actual facts, instead of writing receipts (Comtist ones?) for the cook-shops of the future'.[45] But as the concept of the transcendence of alienation is the concept of the negation of alienation, the one can be inferred from the other and checked against the *obiter dicta* on communism in the mature writings. Marx's mature theory of alienation holds that a surplus created in production is appropriated from the labourer and that the conditions of production dominate labour and detract from the freedom and creativity of which the labourer is potentially capable. In the transcendence of alienation, therefore, labour controls the surplus it creates and controls the conditions under which it produces it. This is roughly Marx's meaning in the *Communist Manifesto* when he says that:[46]

> In bourgeois society, living labour is but a means to increase accumulated labour. In Communist society, accumulated labour is but a means to widen, to enrich, to promote the existence of the labourer. In bourgeois society, therefore, the past dominates the present; in Communist society, the present dominates the past.

Under communism labour's control of the surplus it produces and of its conditions of production is attained by 'socialised man, the associated producers, rationally regulating their interchange with nature, bringing it under their common control, instead of being ruled by it'.[47] This is similar to Marx's depiction of communism in the *Manuscripts*. But whereas man attains total freedom in his attainment of essence in the early conception of transcended alienation, here the strife between freedom and necessity is not truly resolved, for socialised production 'nonetheless still remains a realm of necessity'.[48] While man is able to realise his potential in creative activity after transcending his alienation, according to *Capital*, his freedom is not complete in the manner of the *Manuscripts*.

The mature conception of transcended alienation does not imply a total freedom, the full termination of necessity. The realisation of man's full potential, in his control of the surplus he produces and the conditions of production, is a diminution of necessity, the minimisation of its domination over man. But it is not a situation of entirely 'free conscious activity' in production, as it is in the *Manuscripts*,[49] it is rather 'a greater reduction of time devoted to material labour in general'.[50] According to *Capital* the transcendence of alienation is not itself the negation of necessity, but it is the necessary condition of such a negation. Marx says that 'the true realm of freedom . . . can blossom forth only with this realm of necessity as its basis.'[51] Whereas in the *Manuscripts* the act of transcending alienation is itself the negation of necessity and the realisation of freedom, in *Capital* total freedom is not realised through the mere transcendence of alienation, although the material basis for the attainment of total freedom is achieved with the transcendence of alienation. The difference between the two works is not merely in the different conceptions of the transcendence of alienation, but also in their different accounts of the process of attaining total freedom. In the *Manuscripts* the attainment of total freedom is identical with the transcendence of alienation. It is only the drastic reduction of necessity rather than its negation which is equivalent to the transcendence of alienation according to *Capital*, although the transcendence of alienation is seen as the basis of the process through which 'the true realm of freedom' can be obtained.

The mature concept of alienation implies, therefore, a concept of transcended alienation which is a large increment of freedom, but not the total abrogation of necessity. This latter, according to Marx's mature theory, is a goal attained by a process which can be set in motion only after the transcendence of alienation has itself occurred. The early concept of alienation, on the other hand, as it postulates an alienation of man's essence, entails a concept of transcended alienation which, in being the return of man to his essential nature, is a full reversal of his loss of freedom in alienation.

The foregoing discussion has shown that Marx's early concept of alienation belongs to a system of concepts which is markedly different from the system of concepts entailed by the mature theory of alienation. We saw that the concept of quantitative alienation in the *Economic and Philosophic Manuscripts* implies a conception of workers' impoverishment in alienation which is contrary to that developed in *Capital*.[52] Similarly, the concepts of qualitative estrangement and transcended alienation entailed by the early concept of alienation are contrary to the analogous concepts entailed by the mature concept of alienation. Not only does the concept of alienation belong to different systems of concepts which explain the alienated condition differently, but the role of the concept of alienation in the structure of explanation is also different in the two theories.

In the *Manuscripts* private property and the division of labour are seen as a consequence of man's alienation,[53] whereas in Marx's mature theory of alienation they are the causes of alienation.[54] This reversal of the chain of causation is strictly deducible from differences in the conception of alienation. In the *Manuscripts* the division of labour and private property, as partial expression of man's essence, as expressions of the alienation of his essence, are necessarily the result of alienation. In the mature account of alienation man's loss of his capacities results from dominating social relations, which when absent allow man to realise his full potential. We must conclude, then, that while Marx's early and mature writings both make use of a theory of alienation, the same theory is not found throughout his work. There are, in fact, two different and contrary theories of alienation in Marx's writing, the basic contours of which have been outlined above.

III

The theory of alienation developed in the *Economic and Philosophic Manuscripts* was displaced by a different theory of alienation in Marx's mature writings, most completely elaborated in *Capital*, although not in a compact and easily discernible form in the manner of the *Manuscripts*. The reason for Marx's theoretical change of course can be traced to various sources. In Chapter 2 above the Feuerbachian background of the early theory and Marx's repudiation of Feuerbach in *The German Ideology* was examined. These factors provide part of the explanation. Another important consideration which led to the development of a second theory of alienation is in the empirical limitations of the early theory as a theory of capitalism.

Marx identifies the historical advent of capitalism with the process of 'primitive accumulation', 'an accumulation not the result of the capitalist mode of production, but its starting point'.[55] This development began, he says, with the usurpation of feudal property by the feudal lord and the expropriation of the serf from the soil, thus giving rise to private property and free labour.[56] The historical starting point of this is the fourteenth and fifteenth centuries.[57] By the sixteenth century, with 'the creation ... of a world-embracing commerce and a world-embracing market', Marx says that the 'modern history of capital' had begun.[58] The capitalistic labour process, which is uniform for the entire capitalist epoch, has two basic characteristics; firstly, 'the labourer works under the control of the capitalist' and secondly, 'the product is the property of the capitalist and not that of the labourer, its immediate producer.'[59] This model of the labour process is assimilated into the early theory of alienation as well as into the mature theory, the only differences being that in the *Manuscripts* Marx splits the first of these characteristics into two aspects, the externality of labour and its forced nature.[60] While these characteristics of the labour process are uniform for the whole of capitalism, Marx says in *Capital* that the method of production, of which the labour process is only a single part, is historically variable within the capitalist mode of production. The theory of the *Manuscripts* has no such conception.

Marx divided capitalism into the historical periods of manufacture, on the one hand, and machinofacture or modern industry, on the other; the watershed separating them is the Industrial Revolution. Marx says that the first period, 'roughly speaking, extends from the middle of the sixteenth to the last third of the eighteenth century',[61] while the second became established 'only during the decade preceding 1866'.[62] Although this may appear to be an all too precise periodisation, Marx does say that manufacture and machinofacture are '[not] separated from each other by hard and fast lines of demarcation'.[63] What is important, though, is that the method of production in the two periods is qualitatively different. 'In manufacture, the revolution in the mode of production begins with the labour-power, in modern industry it begins with the instruments of labour.'[64] According to Marx's own periodisation he wrote *Capital*, published in 1867, just inside the period of modern industry, a theory of which is developed in that work. The theory of the *Manuscripts*, on the other hand, takes no cognisance of modern industry. Three elements of the early theory of alienation are the claims of an absolute impoverishment of labour, that labour is the essence of the historical subject and that labour productivity is increased through an intensification of the social division of labour. Each of these propositions constitute an economic claim, or imply another proposition which amounts to an economic claim,[65] which indicates that the object of inquiry can only be the period of manufacture. None are applicable to the period of modern industry, as Marx's discussion in *Capital* demonstrates. In what follows the three elements of the early theory of alienation will be dealt with in turn.

The majority of accounts dealing with Marx's early writings explain his theoretical development in terms of his reaction to and relations with other theorists, most notably Hegel and Feuerbach. The theoretical climate in which he worked obviously has some importance for the content of Marx's own theoretical development. But the empirical nature of Marx's theorising must also be given an important place in any explanation of his intellectual development. Running throughout Marx's early writings is an attempt to explain poverty theoretically, and the philosophical aspects of his theoretical apprenticeship must be tempered, therefore, with the recognition that Marx's initial problematic was the problem of poverty, as Heinz Lubasz's important paper argues.[66] As well as the articles from the *Rheinische Zeitung*, discussed by Lubasz, Marx's Paris Writings largely concern themselves with the problem of poverty. The entire thrust of the *Economic and Philosophic Manuscripts*, as we saw in discussion above, is in its attempt to explain the absolute poverty of capitalist labour.

The discussion of alienation in the *Manuscripts* begins with the contradiction between the growing wealth of society and the growing poverty of the immediate producers of this wealth.[67] In the *Manuscripts* Marx explicitly rejects arguments pointing to external causes of labour's poverty – such as the growth of population – when he says that the 'demand for men necessarily governs the production of men, as of every other commodity.'[68] Rather, he identifies the source of industrial poverty as one internal to the industrial system:[69]

> when society is in a state of progress, the ruin and impoverishment
> of the worker is the product of his labour and of the wealth
> produced by him. The misery results, therefore, from the essence of
> present-day labour itself.

This is different from the diagnosis proposed in the *Introduction to the Critique of Hegel's Philosophy of Right*, written just a few months before the *Manuscripts*, where the poverty of the proletariat is seen as a result, not of the structure of society, but of its 'acute disintegration'.[70]

In the *Manuscripts* the proletariat's poverty is a result of the method of labour employed by society in creating its wealth.

The issue of poverty is related to a number of different factors. In stating that there is a direct relationship between the ruin, impoverishment and misery of the worker and 'the essence of present-day labour', Marx confines his argument to the nature of the labour process. Thus the poverty of labour discussed in the *Manuscripts* is conceived as a result of the capitalist labour process. We have already seen that the role of labour in the production of private property is regarded by Marx as the key to human alienation, and the labourer's misery is seen as a direct consequence of his alienation. It is particularly interesting that Marx's discussion of the labour process in the *Manuscripts* which is used to account for the labourer's absolute impoverishment, indicates that his analysis is relevant for the period of manufacture, but inadequate for the period of modern industry. That is, irrespective of the accuracy or otherwise of Marx's argument in the *Manuscripts* of labour's absolute poverty, the manner in which the argument is developed demonstrates that the theory from which it arises could only refer to a particular and early phase of capitalist development, a point which will be substantiated in what follows.

The major premise of the theory of alienation in the *Economic and Philosophic Manuscripts* is the proposition that labour is the essence of the historical subject, man. Marx celebrates Adam Smith as the Luther of political economy for bringing man 'within the orbit of private property, just as in Luther he is brought within the orbit of religion';[71] political economy does this by 'elevating *labour* to the position of its *sole* principle'.[72] Hegel is praised for accepting the standpoint of modern political economy, for he too 'grasps *labour* as the *essence* of man − as man's essence in the act of proving itself'.[73] Marx's apprehension of the idea that man is not merely a conscious being but a consciously active being in production allowed him to make more profound the Feuerbachian conception of alienation, by arguing that the alienation of man's essence is the alienation of his activity, of his labour. Man's estrangement in production, therefore, 'is that of real life', and when it is transcended man's alienation in religion, in the state and so forth, is also remedied.[74] Thus labour and the alienation of labour are at the centre of Marx's analysis of man's condition in capitalism. By incorporating the concept of labour as the 'sole principle' into his philosophical anthropology, Marx also took from Smith a particular model of the labour process.

In *Capital* Marx says that the basic factors of the labour process are three-fold: man's labour itself, the subject of labour on which he works, and the instruments of labour with which he works.[75] The importance of the last of these is that they 'not only supply a standard of the degree of development to which human labour has attained, but they are also indicators of the social conditions under which that labour is carried on.'[76] According to the *Manuscripts* man's alienation in production has its basis in 'the essential relationship of labour', which is 'the relationship of the *worker* to production'.[77] This is a depiction of the alienating labour process: 'The direct relationship of labour to its produce is the relationship of the worker to the objects of his production'.[78] It is significant that Marx here reduces the labour process to an application of labour to the subject of labour, there is no mention of the instruments of labour. Actually, this omission is not terribly serious if what is described is taken to be a summary of production within the context of manufacture, for there the workman is predominant in the labour process, the instruments of labour are subject to the labourer and production is 'dependent on the strength, skill, quickness and sureness of the individual workman in handling his tools'.[79] In this sense labour is the 'sole principle' of production, for the labourer is the dominant factor in the production process. Under different social conditions, however, the instruments of labour assume a different role and the labour process takes on a different configuration. In machino-facture the instruments of labour dominate the labourer,[80] and the Smithian model of the labour process as it is understood by Marx in his early theory of alienation is thereby shown to have no application for this stage of capitalist development.

The economic component of Marx's philosophical anthropology which relates to the labour process indicates that Marx, following Smith — whom he later describes as 'the political economist par excellence of the period of Manufacture'[81] — was working from an empirical assumption valid for the stage of capitalist development in which variable capital — or living labour — was significantly dominant over constant capital — or the instruments of production — in the labour process.[82] The predominance of labour over its instruments in production is a consequence of the organisation of labour typical of the formative period of capitalist development, prior to the introduction of machinery as the instrument of labour. Marx says in *Capital* that the organisation of co-operating labour 'is the machinery specially characteristic of the manufacturing period'.[83] Any mention of machinery in the description of the labour process in the *Manuscripts* would have been redundant, therefore, if we understand Marx to have been discussing the manufacturing labour process. In the period of modern industry, on the other hand, the machine 'supersedes the workman' in the labour process,[84] and its productiveness is 'measured by the human labour-power it replaces'.[85] Under these conditions 'machinery really plays a far more important part in the business of production than the labour and skill of the operative.'[86] In failing to include the instruments of labour as a separate category in his model of the labour process in the *Manuscripts*, and by insisting on the primacy of labour in the process of production, Marx's account of production in the early theory of alienation is too narrow to adequately explain the capitalist process of labour as such. Basing his analysis on the experience of an early stage of capitalist development Marx fallaciously reduces production to labour and fails to develop a theoretical comprehension of the instruments of labour and the historical variability of their importance in the labour process. These flaws of the early theory are corrected in the later writings.

Marx does not entirely ignore machinery in the *Manuscripts*, however. He observes that machines replace workers, but the confrontation between labour and the machine is here described as a function of the division of labour,[87] a topic to which we shall move shortly. Marx also refers to machinery when describing the degradation of life in the early industrial towns. Again, this is not a general account of machinery in the labour process of capitalist production, but a description of the introduction of machinery for the employment of child labour in the early phase of the Industrial Revolution.[88] It is likely that a reading of Wilhelm Schulz, *Die Bewegung der Produktion*, and other literature informed Marx of this English practice, for a description of it quoted from Schulz is included in the first of the *Manuscripts*.[89]

IV

While Marx says in the *Manuscripts* that 'the worker has sunk to the level of the machine,'[90] the reduction of the worker is explained primarily in terms of the appropriation of labour under conditions of private property, rather than in terms of machine production. The theoretical account of the worker's impoverishment through production of wealth by his labour is here devoid of a reference to machinery. It is relevant to mention, though, that when discussing the theory of the political economists Marx says that the '[d]ivision of labour and use of machinery promote wealth of production.'[91] It is not clear from the context whether Marx accepts this idea as his own or whether he is merely paraphrasing James Mill. On the same page, in a paraphrase of Jean Baptiste Say, Marx drops the reference to machinery when he says that '[w]ealth – production – is explained by division of labour and exchange.' What is interesting in this is that here and elsewhere in the *Manuscripts* Marx accepts the view of early political economy that the production of wealth and increases in productivity can be accounted for strictly in terms of the division of labour. It is evident from this that Marx's economic model of 1844 is strictly confined to the period of manufacture rather than to the capitalist mode of production in general.

The concept 'division of labour' has an extremely important function in the theory of alienation in the *Manuscripts*. Basically Marx argues that man is alienated through the production of wealth which is appropriated from him. As it is the alienation of man's labour which produces private wealth, human labour is therefore the essence of private property. Once this has been recognised, says Marx, 'the division of labour had to be conceived as a major driving force in the production of wealth,' for the 'division of labour is the expression in political economy of the social character of labour within the estrangement.'[92] Here the philosophico-anthropological notion of man's alienation and the economic notion of labour productivity are united in the concept 'division of labour'. An increase in the division of labour increases man's alienation by increasing the wealth he produces:[93]

Whilst the division of labour raises the productive power of labour and increases the wealth and refinement of society, it impoverishes the worker and reduces him to a machine.

It can be seen from this that the concept of the division of labour is central to Marx's account of the mechanism of alienation and also his analysis of the productivity of labour. The two are directly related in that an intensification of the division of labour, which raises the productive power of labour and therefore the quantity of wealth appropriated from it, intensifies labour's alienation.

The theory of alienation in the *Manuscripts* entails, therefore, the economic proposition that labour productivity is raised through an intensification of the division of labour. The economic argument is not original to Marx, of course, and he acknowledges Adam Smith as its source.[94] But Marx's analysis is not merely taken over from political economy as such, it is drawn from classical economy's explanation of manufacture.[95] Marx says in *Capital* that the division of labour is 'the distinguishing principle of manufacture'.[96] He explains that this is because in manufacture:[97]

> [t]he quantity of [raw material] consumed in a given time, by a given amount of labour, increases in the same ratio as does the productive power of that labour in consequence of its division.

The productive consumption of raw material, and, therefore, the volume of production, is proportionate to the intensity of the division of labour. While this is true for manufacture, when the organisation of labour is the 'machinery' of production,[98] it does not hold for production under the conditions of modern industry. When machinery is introduced into the labour process it 'sweeps away by technical means the manufacturing division of labour'.[99] The manufacturing division of labour becomes redundant under these new conditions because machinery itself is the 'most powerful means for increasing the productiveness of labour'.[100] The theory of alienation advanced in the *Economic and Philosophic Manuscripts*, which is incompetent to deal with modern industry, is unable to explain labour's productivity and alienation for the stage of capitalist development subsequent to the period of manufacture.

In proclaiming the demise of the manufacturing division of labour with the advent of modern industry Marx does not propose that the division of labour disappears, for 'the capitalist form of that industry reproduces this same division of labour in a still more monstrous shape.'[101] But the function of the division of labour is now altered. Rather than directly affecting the productivity of labour, the division of labour in modern industry merely deploys the operatives within the factory, where they are subjected to the machines which increase their productivity.[102] The division of labour remains, in Marx's analysis, an important feature of the social structure. In fact Marx develops in *Capital* a characterisation of the division of labour which corrects a confusion he finds in Adam Smith's writings on the subject and implicitly demonstrates the implausibility of his own early theory of alienation.

Marx differentiates between the division of labour in general, or the social division of labour on the one hand, and the division of labour in particular, or the detail division of labour on the other.[103] While the former 'arises from the exchange between spheres of production',[104] the latter results from the organisation within the workshop which distributes the operatives to their separate tasks in production.[105] Marx says that the two forms of the division of labour, while practically linked and similar in many ways, are nevertheless different 'not only in degree, but also in kind'.[106] The differences which Marx identifies are many-fold, relating to the nature of the object exchanged, the deployment of the means of production, and the authority relations of exchange, each of which presents itself differently in the different types of division of labour.[107] Adam Smith's discussion of the division of labour does not recognise the differences in kind between its social and detail forms. Marx points out that this is quite plausible. During the period of manufacture the detail division of labour does appear to be a replication, in miniature and within one location, of the social division of labour which occurs between the various industries in society at large. While Smith was mistaken to regard the differences between the social and the detail division of labour as subjective, in the mind of the observer rather than in reality, Marx says that this is an understandable mistake.[108] The plausibility of an error is no corrective, however, and a failure to be aware of the distinction he makes in *Capital* has serious ramifications for Marx's early theory of alienation.

In the *Manuscripts* Marx follows Smith to a fault when he too fails to distinguish between the social and detail divisions of labour. In his discussion of the concept 'division of labour' in the writings of political economists Marx moves from a consideration of the social division of labour, in which the products of divided labour are exchanged socially in the market, to a consideration of the division of labour within production, which impoverishes the labourer, without being aware that he is dealing with two different kinds of divisions of labour.[109] The fault primarily lies with political economy, of course, and Marx had not yet picked it up in 1844. But in duplicating Smith's lack of discrimination in this matter the early theory of alienation is nullified from the point of view of Marx's later correction of Smith on the division of labour.

In the *Manuscripts* Marx discusses the class experience in terms of its individual members: alienating production is 'the relationship of the *worker* to production', 'the product of labour . . . belongs to some *other man than the worker*'.[110] So that when he says that the worker produces commodities and himself as a commodity,[111] Marx is referring to the individual activity of labour under the conditions of alienation. It has already been shown above that at the centre of the *Manuscripts'* argument is the claim that each worker, in producing a commodity with his labour, is alienated from his labour through the appropriation of the commodity. This is the claim that in the

manufacturing division of labour the individual's alienation is a consequence of the appropriation of a commodity he has produced with his
labour. The difference between the social division of labour and the
detail division of labour described in *Capital* is primarily in the fact that
while products of the former are commodities, in the latter 'the detail
labourer produces no commodities.'[112] Thus according to Marx's
position in *Capital*, the explanation of alienation provided in the
Manuscripts is meaningless.

As we saw above, in *Capital* the worker's alienation is a consequence
of the sale of his labour-power to the capitalist, rather than a result of
his labour – in the form of a commodity – being appropriated by the
capitalist, as it is in the *Manuscripts*. By focusing on the alienation of
labour-power as opposed to congealed labour the theory of alienation
in *Capital* is concerned with commodities only at a second remove.
Labour's alienation is the alienation of the capacity to labour, it is not
directly the alienation of labour itself. This is not to say that Marx's
mature theory of alienation is unconcerned with commodity production, but that the process is much more complex than the theory of
the *Manuscripts* assumes. In his discussion of the detail division of
labour in manufacture Marx says that:[113]

> the connexion between the detail operators in a workshop is due to
> the sale of the labour-power of several workmen to one capitalist,
> who applies it as combined labour-power.

Here is the process of alienation. It is posterior to the labourer's initial
alienation that commodities are produced. For it is 'the common
product of all the detail labourers that become a commodity.'[114]
While the individual's alienation is a consequence of commodity
production, according to *Capital*, it is not the individual's own production of commodities which accounts for his alienation, for the
individual labourer does not produce commodities. The individual's
alienation is located in the alienation of his labour-power. This latter,
in conjunction with the labour-power of others in manufacture, is
productive of commodities.

The proposition that labour's productivity is raised by an intensification of the division of labour, which Marx adapts from Smith and
incorporates into his early theory of alienation, demonstrates that the
Manuscripts contains a theory relevant for the period of manufacture
only, which is inadequate for an analysis of the capitalist mode of
production as such. In failing to differentiate between the social and
detail divisions of labour, and erroneously accepting that the latter is

merely a version of the former, Marx operates from an assumption concerning the manufacturing labour process which he shows in *Capital* is without foundation. The function of the division of labour in labour productivity aside, this last point raises a further question concerning the theory of alienation in the *Manuscripts*.

The argument of *Capital*, that the individual labourer is not himself the producer of commodities, but that commodities are the product of a collective labour power, does not relate to the question of whether the theory of alienation in the *Manuscripts* is empirically valid for one phase of capitalist development but not another. It shows, rather, that from the perspective of Marx's later theory the early theory of alienation is formally false, irrespective of any historical difference between the stages of capitalist development.

It has been shown in this chapter that although the concept of alienation is current throughout Marx's writings his mature account of alienation can be regarded as belonging to a theoretical framework which is different from that of the *Economic and Philosophic Manuscripts*. The theory of alienation presented in *Capital* superseded the early theory for basically two reasons. Not only is the alienation theory of the 1844 *Manuscripts* limited in the scope of its empirical explanation, but from the perspective of the mature theory its formal content is false. The conclusion to be drawn from the argument of this chapter is that while Marx is engaged in a continuing endeavour from the 1840s to the 1860s to explain alienation empirically, he does so through two utterly different theories of alienation, one in the *Economic and Philosophic Manuscripts*, the other in *Capital*.

Chapter Five

Human emancipation

In the *Critique of Hegel's Philosophy of Right* Marx first clearly formulated the view that man is alienated in civil society and that his alienated social power constitutes the political state. Marx's discussion of the political state in all of his writings prior to 1845 is largely a reaffirmation of this position first outlined in the *Critique* of 1843. This fact is perhaps responsible for the tendency on the part of some scholars to ignore or underplay significant differences in other aspects of Marx's political theory which emerge between the works of the period 1843 to 1845. A number of writers[1] have regarded the *Critique* as a work which furnished Marx with a political theory which continued to be the stable core of his later reflections on political matters. Such a position ignores the exploratory and tentative nature of Marx's thought at the time. During this early period Marx's ideas were held with some uncertainty, and his research should be seen as the endeavour to discover an adequate theoretical foundation on which he could build a critical and revolutionary analysis of society and politics.

It will be shown in what follows that despite some verbal similarities between certain passages of the *Critique of Hegel's Philosophy of Right* and formulations in Marx's subsequent works, in a number of respects the *Critique* is a far from reliable guide to the political theory which emerges in Marx's writings immediately after the *Critique*. The analysis of democracy, for instance, and also the means and process of emancipation from alienation presented in the *Critique* are immediately revised in *On the Jewish Question* and the *Introduction to the Critique of Hegel's Philosophy of Right*. Similarly, different accounts of the cause of alienation are offered in the different works of the period 1843 to 1845. At the same time, however, the theory of the state as alienated social power is continuous in all of the writings of the same period, as we shall see in the next chapter.

After discussing the development of Marx's political theory of alienation in the writings from the *Critique* to the *Economic and Philosophic Manuscripts*, the chapter presents an argument concerning the different treatments by Marx of the concept 'proletariat' as the class agent of revolution in the 1843 *Introduction* on the one hand and the *Communist Manifesto* on the other.

I

The *Critique* can be differentiated from the works which follow it in a number of ways, some more insightful than others. It has been said, for instance, that whereas the *Critique* attempts to 'refute philosophy with philosophy', Marx's later writings bring out that 'the main question is not how to understand reality, but how to bring it to its own perfection.'[2] While it is true that the *Critique*, as an internal discussion of Hegelian philosophy, is in that sense philosophical, Marx's other writings up to and including *The German Ideology* could similarly be described as philosophical. For they too lack the detailed concrete analysis of, say, *The Poverty of Philosophy*, *Wage-Labour and Capital* and the *Communist Manifesto*. The distinction between understanding reality, which is the alleged focus of the *Critique*, and changing reality, is also less than a satisfactory summary of the difference between the *Critique* and what followed.

While the subsequently written *Introduction* is a strongly programmatic work, it should not be forgotten that the *Critique* also offers a programme for change in its advocacy of true democracy as a means to realise human freedom. It should be added that when Marx wrote in 1845 that the point is to change the world, whereas philosophers have only interpreted it,[3] he was not committing himself to the view that interpretation should cease. The necessity of an adequate and correct interpretation of the social world is the basic premise of Marx's injunction that the world be changed. The works after the *Critique*, such as the essay *On the Jewish Question*, the *Economic and Philosophic Manuscripts* and especially *Capital*, would be seriously misunderstood if it is not recognised that they are before all else attempts to understand reality. It is Marx's later estimation of the inadequacy of the *Critique's* understanding of reality which led him to abandon the idea of publishing it.

Rather than a difference of intention it is a difference in theoretical content which separates the *Critique* from Marx's later writings.

As a pre-communist statement the *Critique* advocates neither the abolition of the state nor of private property; the rejection of both is at the basis of Marx's later normative politics. It has been suggested, though, that while the abolition of the state and private property are 'explicitly formulated in subsequent writings', the groundwork for this position is 'prepared in the *Critique*'.[4] The *Critique* can be interpreted in this way, but such a backward reading of Marx interrupts any serious comprehension of the development of his political thought and tends to misconstrue the theoretical importance of the *Critique* to his later thought. Before turning to a discussion of the differences in Marx's political thought between the *Critique* and the works which directly follow it, the status of the *Critique* in Marx's intellectual development will be briefly outlined.

The intellectual autobiography sketched in the 'Preface' to *A Contribution to the Critique of Political Economy* explains that as a result of the collapse of the *Rheinische Zeitung*, of which he was editor, Marx took the opportunity provided by unemployment to return to the study. The *Critique* is clearly identified as the 'first work which I undertook to dispel the doubts assailing me.'[5] Its importance to Marx therefore lies in the fact that it was the chronological beginning of his systematic criticism of prevailing contemporary doctrine. The manuscript available to us today is a very rough first draft in which passages from Hegel's *Philosophy of Right* are followed by Marx's commentary.

Marx had originally intended immediately to redraft the manuscript for publication, but this did not occur. Instead, he used some ideas of the draft for his essay *On the Jewish Question* and wrote an *Introduction* to the proposed revised draft. These were both published in the *Deutsch-Französische Jahrbücher* in 1844 after Marx had moved from Kreuznach, where he wrote the *Critique*, to Paris. In many respects these essays do summarise parts of the earlier work. However, as we shall see below, aspects of *On the Jewish Question* are quite different from the rough manuscript from which it was drawn, and the tenor of the *Introduction* is totally different from that of the *Critique*. Marx explains in his 'Preface' to the *Economic and Philosophic Manuscripts* that the style of the draft *Critique of Hegel's Philosophy of Right* made it 'utterly unsuitable' for publication.[6] He goes on to say that he intended to issue instead a series of pamphlets on the critique of law, ethics, politics and so forth. The series was to conclude with a work which drew the threads of the earlier pieces together and presented an overview of all the material.[7] This project, too, lapsed. It is likely that with his residence in Paris, where he moved in socialist circles and read a literature largely new to him — including Engels's *Outlines of a Critique of Political Economy*, published in the *Jahrbücher* — Marx began to settle some of the uncertainty which had initially led him to write the *Critique* and he began to rethink various positions stated in that work. This suggests that Marx did not publish a version of the *Critique* because his ideas took a new turn of development almost immediately after he had drafted it. This rendered the *Critique* an inadequate, indeed, an impossible basis for the elaboration of his later ideas.

The tentative nature of Marx's thought during the period 1843 to 1845 is indicated in his reluctance to publish his research. In early 1845, before moving to Brussels in February, Marx signed a publisher's contract and received an advance of 1,500 francs to produce a book entitled *A Critique of Economics and Politics*, for which the *Economic and Philosophic Manuscripts* were a first draft.[8] At about the same time he drew up a 'Draft Plan for a Work on the Modern State'[9] which suggests that he intended to rework the themes of the *Critique of Hegel's Philosophy of Right* and *On the Jewish Question*. Neither project was carried out. In spite of strong encouragement from Engels, Marx abandoned the contracted book because of his dissatisfaction with the proposed rewritten *Manuscripts* of 1844.[10] Instead of completing work already begun he embarked upon an entirely new project with Engels which was, he explained in a letter to his publisher, 'to prepare the public for the point of view of my *Economics* which is diametrically opposed to the previous German intellectual approach'.[11]

Whereas he had deemed his earlier writings, for one reason or another, to be inadequate foundations on which to develop his ideas, Marx believed that he had found his intellectual feet with *The German Ideology*. When recalling this work some years later he cavalierly dismissed the fact that it remained unpublished with the remark that he had willingly 'abandoned the manuscript to the gnawing criticisms of the mice' as its main purpose — 'self-clarification' — had been achieved.[12] But in fact Marx and Engels tried very hard to get the book to press. They recruited friends to negotiate on their behalf and sent the manuscript to at least eight publishers, but fear of the censor and of financial risk prevented any of them from publishing it.[13] Marx's keenness to have *The German Ideology* published clearly distinguishes it from the *Critique* of 1843 and the *Economic and Philosophic Manuscripts*. It also reveals something of the respective status of each work in his theoretical development.

It has been argued above that Marx did not publish the *Critique of*

Hegel's Philosophy of Right because his ideas continued to develop immediately after it had been drafted. It could be said that the *Critique*, more than *The German Ideology*, was written for its author's self-clarification, for it showed Marx what he had yet to do. The value of the *Critique* is that it allowed Marx to develop for the first time the Feuerbachian insight that man is the subject rather than the predicate of history. In his elaboration of this notion Marx saw that the history of the state must be understood in terms of the history of man. This is a remarkable discovery which became, as Marx said in another context, 'the guiding principle' of his later studies. Marx's apprehension of this insight and the particular interpretation he gave to it was without precedent in the Hegelian context from which it emerged. The implications of the discovery made in the *Critique* could be expected, therefore, to be quite different from the other ideas which surrounded it at the time of its first statement. The many changes which Marx's thought underwent during this early period between 1843 and 1845 can be seen, therefore, as his endeavour to remove the heritage of old conceptions from his new formulation, to develop an original idea into an entirely new theory of history and politics.

II

The theory of alienation in Marx's early writings has been discussed in previous chapters above. In Chapter 2 the Feuerbachian background to the theory was indicated and in Chapter 4 its economic dimension and the differences between it and the mature theory of alienation were discussed. It may have been assumed from a reading of these accounts that Marx took over the Feuerbachian conception of alienation and merely elaborated it to serve his own polemical and theoretical purposes. What emerges from a close study of Marx's thought of the period 1843 to 1845 is that the theory of alienation, which is the critical core of these writings, undergoes significant development in the short period of time between the *Critique of Hegel's Philosophy of Right* and the *Economic and Philosophic Manuscripts*. As the theory of alienation changes in these writings so does Marx's evaluation both of the state's potential as a liberating factor and of the nature of democracy. Marx's understanding of the agency and process of human emancipation also changes significantly during this period.

(a)

Although the concept of alienation is seldom referred to by name in the *Critique*, the work constitutes Marx's first full treatment of the problem of estrangement. The question of man's alienation pervades the work as a whole, is fully defined in it, and a proposal is outlined for the rectification of the alienated condition. According to the *Critique* man's alienation is a consequence of the division between the state and civil society:[14]

> Civil society is separated from the state. It follows, therefore, that the citizen of the state is separated from the citizen as a member of civil society. He must therefore *divide up his own essence*. . . . The separation of civil and political society appears *necessarily* as the separation of the political citizen, the citizen of the state, from civil society and from his own empirical reality.

Marx argues against Hegel's claim that there is no tension between the private sphere of civil society and the public or social sphere of the state by maintaining that man is indeed estranged from the state in his private or individual life. The substance of the individual's alienation is constituted in political representation, according to Marx, in the representation of the legislative function by particular bodies, for:[15]

> the fact that civil society takes part in the political state through its *deputies* is the expression of the separation and of the merely dualistic unity.

On this basis Marx is able to propose that alienation can be overcome through the abolition of the representative function, in the institution of full or direct democracy in which 'all as individuals . . . take part in the legislature'.[16] Marx differentiates, therefore, between the political state, in which man is alienated, and the democratic state, in which he is not.

Marx's basic complaint against the political state in the *Critique* is concerned with its failure to allow man to achieve his full nature. The political state is not able to carry its social or communal content beyond the merely political sphere and cannot infuse itself through the whole of society and of man's life.[17] The individual is deserted by the political state, and left to an atomistic existence in civil society.[18] On the other hand the democratic state, according to Marx's argument in the *Critique*, is the condition of man's fully human existence. Democracy, Marx says, is founded on 'real human beings and the real people; not merely implicitly and in essence, but in existence and in reality'.[19] Rather than suffer a divided life and a divided essence, as with the political state, all of man's aspects are realised in unity within the democratic state. The democratic state embraces all spheres of life. Marx warns against confusing the Republican state, in which democracy is merely formal, with the democratic state, in which the form and content of democracy are unified.[20] Only in the democratic state is man's alienation overcome.

Marx argues, therefore, that the attainment of full human freedom ultimately rests on the development of the state. The division between the political state and civil society, and the alienating division in man's own essence, is overcome only through the radical democratisation of the political state, in which all of the separate spheres of civil society are absorbed into a single rational organism. In the *Critique*, then, Marx offers a political solution to the problem of alienation, and the mechanism of this solution is electoral reform:[21]

> Only when civil society has achieved *unrestricted* active and passive *suffrage* has it *really* raised itself to the point of abstraction from itself, to the *political* existence which constitutes its true, universal, essential existence. But the perfection of this abstraction is also its transcendence. By really establishing its *political* existence as its authentic existence, civil society ensures that its civil existence, in so far as it is distinct from its political existence, is *inessential*. And with the demise of the one, the other, its opposite, collapses also. Therefore, *electoral reform* in the *abstract political state* is the equivalent to a demand for its *dissolution* and this in turn implies the *dissolution of civil society*.

The politicisation of civil society, through electoral reform – the universal suffrage, breaks down the separation of political and civil life. In so doing both civil society and the political state are transcended and the differences between them become united into a single whole which is the democratic state.

It will be clear from the above discussion that in the *Critique* Marx conceives of alienation primarily as political rather than economic alienation, as in the *Economic and Philosophic Manuscripts*. The resolution to man's alienation, as we have seen, is in the democratic state, which comes into being through the democratisation and therefore politicisation of civil society. It was shown in the first chapter above that Marx's arguments in the *Critique*, regarding man's de-alienation, bear some resemblance to Hegel's position. Both Marx and Hegel regard the state as the agency of human emancipation. This is not to say that their positions are identical, of course. Hegel sees the state as subject to the moving force of universality in the Idea, whereas Marx maintains that the rational state, in achieving its true social nature, brings man to the perfection of his essence. But Marx's insistence upon a political solution to alienation is unique to the *Critique*. Two features of Marx's consideration in the *Critique* which distinguish that work from those immediately following it are that while he is opposed to the separation of politics from the rest of life,[22] he is not opposed to politics as such. In the later works he is. Secondly, unlike his later writings the *Critique* does not argue for the abolition of the state, but only for the abolition of the non-democratic state. Marx regards the democratic state to be very much a state.

In the *Critique* Marx understands the concept 'the state', like Hegel, to refer to an organic state; the state in this sense is politically organised society. The claim that 'Marx's call for democracy and universal suffrage ... is equivalent to his demand for the abolition of the state'[23] fails to appreciate that democracy in Marx's sense is not the abolition of the state as such, but the universalisation of the state. The political state, although claiming universality for itself — it 'assumes the significance of the universal'[24] — exists as a particular institution separate from civil society. Man's existence in the political state is divided from his existence in civil society, and his essence is therefore similarly divided. This is the basis of man's alienation, according to the *Critique*. Democracy, on the other hand, says Marx, 'is the first true unity of the particular and the universal'. He goes on to say that:[25]

In democracy the state as particular is only particular, and as universal it is really universal; i.e. it is not something determinate set off against other contents.

That is, in democracy the state is the whole, it is really universal, embracing all of society and therefore all of man.

It is not even clear that Marx saw the advent of the democratic state as implying the abolition of the political state. When commenting on the French revolutionary view that the universality of democracy means that the political state disappears he says that '[this] is correct in the sense that the political state, the constitution, is no longer equivalent to the whole.'[26] When this is taken in conjunction with the statement quoted above, that '[in] democracy the state as particular is only particular,' Marx appears to be saying that while the political state is no longer the whole of the state in democracy, it may remain as a particular institution.[27] In so being, of course, it is no longer the political state that it was. We saw Marx argue above that unrestricted suffrage, in politicising civil society, leads to the dissolution of both civil society and the political state. But the dissolution of the political state seems to imply, in this context, no more than the abolition of its pretension to a false universality, not its institutional abolition. The reference is obscure, however, and Marx does not return to this theme again. But what is clear is that Marx's call for democracy is a call for the democratic state, which he considers to be the real state.

The political solution to alienation, in the call for universal suffrage, assumes that man's essential nature is realised in the full development of the state. Immediately after writing this in the *Critique* the notion is rejected in the *Introduction*, where Marx describes as a 'utopian dream . . . the partial, merely political revolution, the revolution which leaves the pillars of the house standing.'[28] The rejection of the position of the *Critique* is even more thorough in Marx's 1844 polemic against Arnold Ruge, 'Critical Notes on "The King of Prussia and Social Reform"'', published in *Vorwärts!*. In this piece Marx describes the organic conception of the state, in which 'the state and the organisation of society are not two different things. The state is the organisation of society', as 'a political point of view.'[29] He goes on to assert the epistemological and practical limitations of politics when he says that 'political understanding is [inadequate] to the task of discovering the source of social need,'[30] and that:[31]

[the] more developed and the more comprehensive is the political understanding of a nation, the more the proletariat will squander its energies . . . in senseless, futile uprisings that will be drowned in blood.

Marx's break with the solution of universal suffrage after the *Critique* is total. After 1843 he saw it only as a Republican and not a revolutionary instrument.[32] Marx's attitude to politics in his later thought is more complex, though. In the *Communist Manifesto* his major criticism of utopian socialists is their rejection of political action.[33] In the *Inaugural Address of the Workingmen's International Association* Marx says that 'the great duty of the working classes' is to 'conquer political power'.[34] But the proletariat's engagement in legal politics is important for its educative value, it raises the class to a social force. Marx never again proposes a political solution to the liberation of the proletariat. Even the educative role of political action has the dangerous possibility of leading to opportunism and reformism.[35] In the *Critique* Marx not only begins a new search for revolutionary theory, he concludes an earlier development to which he does not return.

The difference between the democratic road to de-alienation described in the *Critique*, and the communist road first fully outlined in the *Economic and Philosophic Manuscripts*, is far-reaching.[36] The differences between the two can be simply enumerated: democracy overcomes political alienation, communism overcomes economic alienation; democracy is the realisation of the authentic state, communism is not the full universalisation of the state but its negation; democracy amounts to the citizenry, as opposed to the bureaucracy, becoming the universal class, in communism the proletariat is the universal class which liberates mankind through its transcendence of economic alienation. But Marx's later position is not reached in a quantum leap. While still in Kreuznach he wrote a criticism of Bruno Bauer's articles on Jewish emancipation and published it in the *Jahrbücher* as *On the Jewish Question*. This work can be seen as a summary of the *Critique*, for it restates the discussion of the dichotomy between state and civil society, and carries the argument further. However, to say this alone inadequately describes the relation between the two works.

(b)

The ideas elaborated in *On the Jewish Question* which are taken from the *Critique* are easily traced. Marx explores the abstract nature of the political state and the consequent dualism which it generates in the lives of its citizens in a way that is clearly a development of the analysis begun in the *Critique*.[37] The historical beginning of the political state is in the political revolution, according to Marx, a revolution which led to the dissolution of feudalism, an 'organisation of the life of the people ... [in which] property [and] labour ... [were separated] from the state as a whole and constituted ... as separate societies within society.'[38] The political state was to restore a unity denied in feudalism by gathering up 'the political spirit which had, as it were, been dissolved, dissected and dispersed in the various cul-de-sacs of feudal society ... and constitute it as the sphere of the community.'[39] But the political revolution which brought about the political community of the state also freed 'egoistic man', who is without community, from the fetters of feudalism, and made him the foundation of the civil society on which the political state rested: 'The constitution of the political state and the dissolution of civil society into independent individuals ... are achieved in one and the same act.'[40]

Because the political state is separated from civil society it in fact failed to unify society, and its universality remained a merely theoretical phenomenon: 'Political emancipation was at the same time the emancipation of civil society from politics, from even the *appearance* of a universal content.'[41] All of this can be found in one form or another in the *Critique*,[42] but the implications Marx now draws are new ones.

The politicisation of civil society in the movement from the political to the democratic state, which in the *Critique* is seen to lead to the emancipation of man from his alienation, is regarded as impossible in *On the Jewish Question*. Marx's reasons for this are three-fold: the politicisation of civil society is unable to lead to its dissolution, there is no difference between the political and democratic states, and political emancipation is a limited form of emancipation, which is not able to overcome man's alienation. It will be seen that each of these propositions logically follows from the preceding one. In *On the Jewish Question* Marx says that the equality of man in the political state derives from the fact that each person 'is an equal participant in popular sovereignty'.[43] It is on this basis that the political state can lay claim to its supposed universality, for it is an equal community of all citizens. But Marx points out that the political state creates the equality between citizens by declaring the real inequalities of civil society 'to be non-political distinctions'; indeed, its existence presupposes them.[44] The universalisation of the suffrage is not sufficient to abolish private property, and therefore private interest, on which civil inequality and the political state rest. Marx does cite a situation in which 'political life attempts to suppress its presupposition, civil society and its elements, and to constitute itself as the real, harmonious species-life of man.'[45] But it does so 'in violent contradiction to the conditions of its own existence' and 'the political drama necessarily ends up with the restoration of religion, private property and all the elements of civil society.'[46] Marx holds this view because in recognising that 'the political annulment of private property does not mean the abolition of private property,'[47] he recognises that an extension of politics into civil society could not lead to the dissolution of civil society, it must remain essentially the realm of private interest. It follows from this that the political state and the democratic state are not fundamentally different.

In the *Critique* the democratic state is the organic unified state in which man's essence is whole rather than divided, as it is in the political state. In *On the Jewish Question* Marx continues to describe the democratic state as 'the true state',[48] but he also says that it is 'the state which relegates religion to the level of other elements of civil society',[49] which is to say that it recognises religion as non-political, but has no interest in abolishing it any more than it has an interest in abolishing private interest. Thus the democratic state is the political state. In the *Critique* Marx differentiates between the form and the content of democracy. The republic, for instance, has a democratic form, but in lacking the democratic content it remains a political state, and on this basis is distinguished from the true democratic state. In *On the Jewish Question* the democratic content of the state is the same as its democratic form, both are merely political and founded upon the dualism of civil society and political life.[50] Thus according to *On the Jewish Question*, and in contradistinction to the *Critique*, political emancipation in democracy is not able to overcome man's alienation, which is the third point.

The key to the political theory of the *Critique* is the proposition that man attains his freedom in political emancipation through the full development of the democratic state. In *On the Jewish Question* Marx argues that human freedom is not identified with the fully developed state, and that political emancipation is an incomplete form of liberation for man:[51]

> The limitations of political emancipation are immediately apparent from the fact that the state can liberate itself from a restriction without man himself being truly free of it, that a state can be a free state without man himself being a free man.

Marx does not deny the importance of political emancipation, for he says that it 'is certainly a big step forward',[52] but he does argue that it is of an intrinsically limited nature. It is especially relevant to his later thought that Marx regards political emancipation as 'the last form of human emancipation within the prevailing scheme of things',[53] for this implies that full human emancipation requires the overthrow of 'the prevailing scheme of things', the overthrow of an order partly characterised by the existence of the state itself.

Marx makes it clear in *On the Jewish Question* that nothing less than a fundamental re-organisation of civil society is the necessary precondition of human emancipation, and that the full abolition of the state is part of such a re-organisation. In calling for '[an] organisation of society that abolishes the basis' upon which money and commerce exist,[54] Marx calls for an abolition of the preconditions of egoistic man, the individual dominated by his private needs and by private interest. As the state finds its own precondition in egoistic man, human emancipation requires the abolition of the state:[55]

> Only when real, individual man resumes the abstract citizen into himself and as an individual has become a species-being in his empirical life, his individual work and his individual relationships, only when man has recognised and organised his *forces propres* as social forces so that social force is no longer separated from him in the form of political force, only then will human emancipation be completed.

This is precisely the reverse of the process described in the *Critique*. It is not the democratic state's absorption of civil society, but rather the absorption of the state by society. It is the resumption of the abstract citizen into the individual person, rather than an extension of citizenship to all areas of civil society. The liberation of man is realised in the annulment of the state; it is not a consequence of the highest form of the state, as it is in the *Critique*, but the abolition of the highest form of the state. But it is not the abolition of the state itself which liberates man.

In the *Economic and Philosophic Manuscripts*, when describing early theories of communism, Marx criticises communism 'of a political nature still — democratic or despotic' and communism based upon 'the annulment of the state'.[56] *On the Jewish Question* repudiates the first of these and avoids the second, for although it assumes that in his liberation man must abolish the state, as Marx does in the *Manuscripts*,[57] man's emancipation is not the result of the state's abolition, but a consequence of social emancipation. It is this latter which leads to the abolition of the state. Marx's first full account of the agency of social emancipation is to be found in the *Introduction* rather than in *On the Jewish Question*, but the need for social emancipation as opposed to political emancipation is sufficiently clear in *On the Jewish Question* to distinguish the theory of alienation outlined in that work from the one of the *Critique*.

(c)

It has been shown above that in the *Critique* Marx explains that man's alienation is a result of the division between state and civil society. The programme for de-alienation in the *Critique* is based on this diagnosis. As well as arguing that the democratisation of civil society leads to its ultimate dissolution, he also says that a mere politicisation of civil society cannot achieve democracy. Marx says that for civil society to

be politicised in order that it be receptive to democracy, it is necessary
that it first be changed. But Marx only vaguely points to the need for
changes in civil society without saying specifically what they might
be.[58] Overall, and irrespective of changes in civil society prior to its
politicisation, the *Critique* maintains that the full universalisation of
the state is fundamentally responsible for the emancipation of man
from his alienation. The dichotomy between state and civil society is
central to the discussion of *On the Jewish Question* also, but this does
not mean that Marx proposes in this work that man's alienation is a
result of the bifurcation between civil and political life.[59] Marx now
takes the argument that the state is a consequence of civil society to
imply that the agency of man's alienation is in the nature of civil
society itself. In *On the Jewish Question* the dualism of state and
civil society is regarded as a consequence or manifestation of man's
alienation, rather than its cause, as it is in the *Critique*.

According to *On the Jewish Question* man's alienation is a consequence of the nature of civil society, and emancipation from alienation
therefore requires the total transformation of civil society, which its
democratisation is incapable of achieving. *On the Jewish Question*
differs from the *Critique* in the way that it identifies specific features
of civil society in its explication of the alienating condition. In the
Critique man is alienated in his particular existence and emancipated
when his essential nature becomes universal. The philosophical categories 'particular' and 'universal', while not wholly absent from *On the
Jewish Question*, are replaced in the explanation of alienation by
concrete categories. Marx says that '[m]oney is the estranged essence
of man's work and existence; this alien essence dominates him and he
worships it.'[60] It follows, therefore, that '[e]mancipation from haggling
[commerce] and from money . . . would be the self-emancipation of
our age.'[61] The identification of money as the cause of alienation is,
in a sense, a refinement of the position adopted in the *Critique*. It
could be argued that the root of alienation identified by each work
is the same, only the language has changed in becoming more concrete.

While the basis of alienation in each work bears some relation to the
other, the difference between the *Critique* and *On the Jewish Question*
is greater than their similarity in so far as the account of emancipation,
based on the conception of alienation, is in *On the Jewish Question*
contrary to that of the *Critique*. The similarities in the concept of
alienation do not prevent the theory of alienation, which includes
propositions concerning man's emancipation from alienation, from
being significantly different in the two works. This is analogous to the

differences between the theory of alienation in the *Economic and Philosophic Manuscripts* and that of *Capital*, discussed in Chapter 4 above. It was shown there that although the concept of alienation in each work is similar, the system of concepts in which it operates is quite different in each work.

Marx's account of the basis of alienation in the *Critique*, which is generally similar to, but not specifically the same as that of *On the Jewish Question*, changes again, but more significantly, in the *Economic and Philosophic Manuscripts*. In a manner similar to *On the Jewish Question*, Marx points to the need to appreciate 'the connection between this whole estrangement and the money-system'.[62] In the third *Manuscript* he says that 'money transforms the real essential powers of man and nature into what are merely abstract conceits',[63] for what a person is 'is by no means determined by [his] individuality',[64] but by his possession of money. In man's alienation money becomes the universal bond of civil society, and it alone possesses 'truly creative power'.[65] In its operation money supersedes man's own faculties, and becomes for him 'the other person'.[66] Marx shows, then, that in his alienation man is dominated by money, which substitutes for him. All of this has previously been stated in *On the Jewish Question*.[67]

The difference between the two works is that whereas in *On the Jewish Question* money is the cause of alienation, in the *Economic and Philosophic Manuscripts* it is the phenomenal form of alienation. While money is the 'object of eminent possession',[68] and exalted by man in his alienation when he himself is humbled, it is itself a consequence of alienation. In the *Manuscripts* the basis of man's alienation is not in commerce, but in labour. 'Private property is thus *the product, the result, the necessary consequence*, of alienated labour, of the external relation of the worker to nature and to himself.'[69] Thus the causal relation of alienation described in *On the Jewish Question* is reversed in the *Manuscripts*.[70] The discussion of money is similar in the two works, but its role in the explanation of man's alienation is quite different.

It can be seen that during a short period of time Marx advanced in the *Critique*, *On the Jewish Question* and the *Economic and Philosophic Manuscripts* three different specific causes of alienation; the division of man's essence between the state and civil society, money, and labour, respectively. In a sense each explanation is a refinement of the one which precedes it, but it is also clear that with each modification in the account of the basis of alienation, the theoretical formulation of the alienated condition also changes significantly. The different conception of the root of alienation in each work is designed to not merely strengthen the preceding conception, but to replace it with another. This indicates the degree to which Marx was dissatisfied with the conclusions of his inquiries during this period and the relentless nature of his research in attempting to develop the foundation of an explanation of the human condition and of a programme of emancipation from alienation.

It has been shown above that in the *Introduction* to the proposed redrafted *Critique* Marx forcefully rejects the political solution to alienation proposed in the *Critique*. He introduces the proletariat into a theory of human emancipation for the first time in the *Introduction*, and gives it a key role in bringing about the emancipating social revolution intimated in *On the Jewish Question*. Some writers have argued that apart from the new emphasis on the proletariat, all of the elements of the *Introduction* 'are already contained' in the *Critique*.[71] Others have seen the formulations of the *Introduction* as demonstrating that Marx's ideas have evolved in a new direction.[72] Certain features of the *Introduction* can be found in the *Critique*, but the new emphasis on the proletariat carries with it a political theory which is fundamentally different from that of the earlier work.

(d)

There is a brief discussion in the *Critique* which has been identified by a number of writers as an anticipation in Marx's thought of the 'proletariat' as the class of historical transformation. It will be shown here, though, that while in the *Critique* Marx introduces the concept of the proletariat, although not the word, its function in the political theory of the *Critique* is quite unlike that of the *Introduction*.

In the *Critique* the concept of the proletariat appears in a critical discussion of Hegel's class analysis. In an endeavour to show that there is full harmony and no disparity between political and civil reality 'Hegel wishes to demonstrate', as Marx says, 'that the classes of civil society are the political Estates.'[73] Marx entirely rejects this view for the position that there is a fundamental 'separation of political life and civil society',[74] and argues for this proposition, in part, by claiming that since the French Revolution the Estates have been 'transformed into social classes, i.e. the class distinctions in civil society became merely social differences in private life of no significance in political life.'[75] Marx, then, rejects the archaic content of Hegel's class analysis in saying that the essentially Medieval Estate is breaking down into merely apolitical classes of civil society.[76] The former, he says, are characterised by their political significance, whereas the latter are distinguished by the 'criteria . . . of money and education'.[77] A person's civil and political positions do not coincide in modern society, therefore, as they do in feudalism, save for members of the executive.[78]

The principle underlying civil society, and the division of society into classes, is fundamentally arbitrary.[79] The only determinate factor which Marx can identify is that the class which satisfies the material needs of society is constituted through its absence of property:[80]

> The only noteworthy feature [of the fluid division of masses] is that the absence of property and the class of immediate labour, of concrete labour, do not so much constitute a class of civil society as provide the ground on which the circles of civil society move and have their being.

Marx's discussion of 'the class of immediate labour' can be seen to foreshadow the discussion of the proletariat in the *Introduction*, written just after the *Critique*, and also in Marx's later work. It should be emphasised though that the concept of the class of immediate labour does not refer to the proletariat in the sense that Marx later came to understand the term, for it can be more readily seen as a category employed to merely demonstrate the legalistic limitations of Hegel's class analysis.

Shlomo Avineri[81] has said that Marx's discussion of the class of immediate labour follows the *Philosophy of Right*, section 243, in which Hegel points out that the amassing of social wealth through demographic and industrial expansion results in the poverty and distress of factory labour.[82] In the next paragraph Hegel goes on to argue that an intensification of poverty results in 'the creation of a rabble',[83] of the pobel or proletariat. In Prussia during the 1840s 'proletariat' was a term used to signify not merely industrial workers, but a much larger social grouping in which dispossessed peasants and landless agricultural labourers predominated. This group was a numerically significant section of the population and largely 'unincorporated', that is, without membership of an estate and therefore outside the established order of civil society.

Marx's class of immediate labour most probably refers to the large mass of dispossessed agricultural labourers who supported the grain export industry, Germany's main economic activity during the period. It could thus be said that the propertyless agricultural labourers ultimately supported German society, but because largely unincorporated they were themselves outside civil society and did not constitute a class in the Hegelian sense. Marx's reference to the class of immediate labour, therefore, flies in the face of Hegel's class model and contradicts Hegel's description of the agricultural class as the 'immediate' class which 'has its capital in the natural products of the soil which it cultivates'.[84] The significance of Marx's comments is in the fact that they point to a social development for which the traditional legalistic concept of class is inadequate, and specifically indicates the archaic analysis of class in Hegel. So that while in the *Critique* Marx for the first time identifies the proletariat, it is not here integrated into his prognosis of full human emancipation. The anticipated emancipation of man has a very different agency in the *Critique*, as was indicated above.

In the *Introduction* the concept 'proletariat' takes on the Hegelian identity of the universal class, as Avineri and others have indicated.[85] The proletariat is the class which in overcoming its particular sufferings represents the general interests of society by abolishing suffering *per se* and *in toto*. This is a position quite dissimilar to the one adopted in the *Critique*, where Marx identifies the whole of civil society as the class of private citizens which has the capacity to become the universal class in the democratic state. Marx's argument is directed against Hegel's assumption that 'the universal class is the class of civil servants'.[86] The civil service, which Marx perjoratively calls the bureaucracy, is shown in the *Critique* to be a particular class with particular interests which uses the state as its own private property.[87] Thus the universal class must be found elsewhere. As the state and civil society are separate and as the individual's civil and political positions are distinct, in order to attain political significance in the political state the individual 'must discard his class, civil society, the class of private citizens; for it is precisely this class that stands between the individual and the political state.'[88] This highlights the absence of universality in the political state, but in the democratic state it is precisely in the class of citizens that universality resides. 'What is crucial in the true state is ... the capacity of the universal class to be really universal, i.e. to be the class of every citizen.'[89] In place of Hegel's bureaucracy, Marx identifies in the *Critique* the democratic state's real universality in the class of the citizenry, not in the proletariat as he does in the *Introduction*.

The notion of the universality of the class of citizens described in the *Critique* does not appear in any of Marx's later works. First, the claim that the citizenry constitutes a class, which is uncritically taken from Hegel, is quite foreign to Marx's later usage of the term 'class'. Second, it is a wholly different class, the proletariat, which is the universal class in the *Introduction*. But much more important still is the fact that the universality of the citizenry is meaningful only in an etatist solution to alienation, in which the development of the state is responsible for man's emancipation. The alienation suffered by the proletariat described in the *Introduction* cannot be comprehended by an account of alienation in terms of the division between state and civil society, between citizen and bourgeois, for the proletariat is outside of this systematic division. Marx hints at this last point in the *Critique* when he says that the class of labour 'do[es] not so much constitute a class of civil society', but it has no place in his explanation of man's alienation and emancipation. In the *Introduction* the revolutionary nature of the proletariat derives from the fact that it is not a class of civil society and is a class without even political citizenship. Its universality cannot be a consequence of the universalisation of civil society nor of the state. It is the exclusion of the proletariat from civil society and the political state which gives the proletariat its insurrectionary potential. The proletariat strives neither to enter civil society nor democratise the state, but to emancipate man from both. The difference between the *Critique* and the *Introduction* is not merely that the universal class is different in each. The whole approach of the *Critique* to the foundation of universality in the analysis of alienation and emancipation is replaced by a significantly different series of generalisations in the *Introduction*.

The notion of a universal class of citizens loses all meaning for Marx when in *On the Jewish Question* he realises that the democratic state is still the state and that a political solution to alienation is no solution at all. But while the universality of citizenship is no more than an illusion after the *Critique of Hegel's Philosophy of Right*, Marx remains aware of the political importance of citizenship and of its denial. During the nineteenth century much political writing was motivated by the dual fear that exclusion from the political community of the state would lead the proletariat to rise up, and that an extension of the suffrage to the working class would destroy liberal democracy. What was a frightful dilemma for liberal writers was cause for Marx's optimism. He accepted that the proletariat would 'strive to obtain' citizenship where it did not have it, and use it to advantage where it did.[90] In the *Vorwärts!* article Marx says that isolation from the community is the root of all rebellions,[91] and in the draft plan for a work on the modern state, written a few months later, he identifies the suffrage with 'the fight for the abolition of the state and of bourgeois society'.[92] But Marx also maintains that such a fight would not lead to the emancipation of the proletariat. In the *Vorwärts!* article he says that the community from which the proletariat is isolated, and toward which it is led in revolution − in attaining its emancipation − is not the political community, but the community of human nature.[93] The attainment of citizenship, according to Marx, can provide no more than membership of the political state. In achieving citizenship man does not achieve emancipation from alienation, for citizenship is itself a manifestation of alienation, of political alienation. After the *Critique* Marx rejected the notion that alienation results from the representative function of political suffrage, but he continued to argue in subsequent writings that political alienation is manifest in citizenship. This forms the basis of the conception of the state as alienated social power, to which we will turn in the next chapter.

III

It has been shown above that although the concept 'proletariat' appears in both the *Critique* and the *Introduction*, its content and its place in the theory of the agency and process of human emancipation is different in each. In the brief discussion above it was shown that in the *Introduction* Marx introduces for the first time the notion of proletarian revolution as the means to human emancipation and identifies the proletariat as the class of revolutionary transformation. This has encouraged Jean Hyppolite,[94] for instance, to say that the *Introduction* is 'the germ' of the *Communist Manifesto*, the work through which Marx's theory of proletarian revolution has been given its widest currency. Hyppolite's statement both acknowledges any superficial differences between the *Introduction* and the *Communist Manifesto* while emphasising their essential unity as proclamations of Marx's revolutionary theory.

It is appropriate to show here that Marx's political theory of the *Introduction*, although not of the *Communist Manifesto*, is based upon an idealist expectation that revolutionary change could be achieved through the realisation of philosophy in its Feuerbachian form, and upon a social analysis premised upon the supposition that abject poverty and degradation are necessary conditions for the insurrectionary mobilisation of the proletariat. Marx came to abandon these and related notions in his attempt to elaborate a theory of capitalist society, spelled out in the *Communist Manifesto*, which identified in a very different manner the operative variables of social dynamics, and the social processes which provided levers of action to the agents of social revolution.

In both the *Introduction* and the *Communist Manifesto*, the proletariat is identified as the revolutionary class, as the human agency of social transformation. Marx's conception of the proletariat in the *Introduction*, however, is not the same as the one developed in the *Communist Manifesto*. The basis of revolutionary emancipation is also differently conceived in each work: it results from the realisation of philosophy in the *Introduction*, while it follows from the proletariat's place in the production process according to the *Communist Manifesto*. Finally, Marx argues in the *Communist Manifesto* that proletarian revolution is to overthrow capitalism, whereas in the *Introduction* it is argued that revolution is to overcome Germanic backwardness only. The theoretical significance of these differences between the two works is of major importance in the development of Marx's thought.

The proletariat of the *Introduction*, the 'class with radical chains', while seen as the result of industrialisation by Marx — it is the class 'of the emergent industrial movement' — is defined by him in moral terms: the proletariat is a class 'which is the dissolution of all classes, a sphere which has a universal character because of its universal suffering . . . which is, in a word, the *total loss* of humanity.'[95] According to the *Communist Manifesto*, on the other hand, the proletariat is understood strictly in terms of its place in the capitalist production process and through its relation to the bourgeoisie.[96] The *Communist Manifesto*, of course, does not deny the degradation of the proletariat, which is so crucial to the analysis of the *Introduction*; but neither does it depict such degradation as total, nor does it account for the proletariat's 'universal character' — its ability to effect human liberation — in terms of its suffering. These different conceptions of the proletariat have generally been noted in the secondary literature. What has been largely overlooked, however, is the significance of these differences and their implications for the development of Marx's theoretical system.

The different definitions of the proletariat, one stressing its abject poverty and loss of humanity, the other its place in the production process and class system, has usually been seen as a difference of focus and empirical content. Marx's discussion in the *Introduction* is concerned with the small and immature German proletariat of the early 1840s, whereas his account in the *Communist Manifesto* is based on an examination of the English and French proletariats up to the middle 1840s. In this way changes between the two works in the presentation of the concept 'proletariat' have been seen as the result of differences of fact; differences of little or minor theoretical substance and consequence.[97] While the empirical content of the *Introduction* is indeed less detailed than that of the *Communist Manifesto*, the difference between the two works runs much deeper than the level of fact. It will be shown that they are different in significant theoretical ways as well.

What is most striking in a comparison of the two works is that the proletariat of the *Introduction* bears less resemblance to the proletariat of the *Communist Manifesto* than it does to what Marx identified in the latter work as the 'lumpenproletariat'. This is not merely because of the total nature of the destitution of both the proletariat of the *Introduction* and the lumpenproletariat of the *Communist Manifesto*, but also their passivity.

In the *Introduction* Marx makes it clear that the origins of the proletariat and its total poverty both result from social dislocation:[98]

the proletariat is not formed by natural poverty but by artificially produced poverty; it is formed not from the mass of people mechanically oppressed by the weight of society but from the mass of people issuing from society's acute disintegration and in particular from the dissolution of the middle class.

In the *Communist Manifesto* the proletariat's origins are partly the result of the break-up of the old society effected by the growth of modern industry, but more importantly, its life conditions of oppression and poverty are determined by the exploitative nature of the ongoing economic systems rather than the disintegration of the prior social system.[99] While the proletariat of the *Communist Manifesto* is deprived through economic exploitation, a concept absent in the *Introduction*, the degree of deprivation is not at its social lowest in that class, as it is in the proletariat of the *Introduction*. Below the proletariat of the *Communist Manifesto* is the sub-class of the lumpenproletariat, whose members suffer abject degradation in the manner of the proletariat of the *Introduction*, and, again like the proletariat of the *Introduction*, the abject degradation of the lumpenproletariat results primarily from social dislocation and disintegration.[100]

The notion that the pauperisation of the proletariat is absolute, indicated in the claim that it suffers 'the total loss of humanity', is maintained not only in the *Introduction* at a descriptive level, but repeated and theoretically elaborated in the *Economic and Philosophic*

Manuscripts. In *The German Ideology*, however, Marx draws a distinction between the proletariat as such and the abjectly pauperised proletariat, the lumpenproletariat of his later writings. In a polemic against the Young Hegelian Max Stirner, who 'is constant ... in identifying the proletariat with pauperism', Marx says that:[101]

> pauperism is the position only of the impoverished proletariat,
> the lowest level to which the proletariat sinks who has become
> incapable of resisting the pressure of the bourgeoisie, and it is
> only the proletarian whose whole energy has been sapped who
> becomes a pauper.

Although loosely and somewhat crudely outlined here, this is an important development in Marx's class analysis which already mentions the two essential characteristics of the lumpenproletariat, differentiating it from the proletariat as it is described in Marx's mature writings. Not only does *The German Ideology* distinguish between the economic profiles of the proletariat and the lumpenproletariat, Marx also clarifies a discerning political point which serves to clearly distinguish the concept of the proletariat in the *Introduction* from that of the *Communist Manifesto*. Because its 'whole energy has been sapped' the lumpenproletariat is necessarily a passive class, available for action only on behalf of other classes and as an instrument of other classes and social forces.[102] In the *Introduction* Marx describes the proletariat as a passive element of revolution, as the material weapon in the praxis of philosophy. The passivity of the proletariat here is the direct political correlate of its total pauperisation. This is contrary to Marx's account of the proletariat in the *Communist Manifesto*, which is not only cushioned from the floor of economic destitution by the lumpenproletariat, but achieves its revolutionary potential through its own practice and struggle; it realises its own interest through its own revolutionary efforts.[103]

Like the lumpenproletariat of Marx's mature thought the proletariat of the *Introduction* is a totally pauperised class, passive in itself and activated by an agency external to it, whose objective it serves. The major difference between the early depiction of the proletariat and the lumpenproletariat of Marx's later writings, is that in the *Introduction* the former is described as serving a revolutionary rather than a counter-revolutionary role, as it is in *The Eighteenth Brumaire*, and is activated by philosophy rather than by a directly social force. It is the discussion in the *Introduction* of the role of philosophy in proletarian revolution which both highlights the difference between the *Introduction* and the

Communist Manifesto and also substantiates the claim that in the earlier work Marx saw the proletariat as an essentially passive class.

It has been suggested by George Lichtheim, for instance, against the tenor of assessment developed here, that the account of the relation between philosophy and the proletariat in the *Introduction* remains implicit in Marx's mature work and that its theoretical content 'was never repudiated, nor could it have been, for it is precisely what he meant by the "union of theory and practice" '.[104] Briefly, then, how is the unity of theory and practice in Marx generally understood? This notion is usually taken to mean that in the proletariat's practical discourse with adversity, a theory of the social world is evolved which has an instrumental value to the class in guiding future actions and evaluating its present practices. These actions and practices, in their turn, affect the continuing development of revolutionary theory. The relation between theory and practice, therefore, is reciprocal. There is one qualification, however; as the end of theory is practice and as the end of practice is emancipation of labour, practice has an ultimate primacy over theory. This does not undermine their reciprocity, though, for while revolutionary theory is epistemologically dependent upon revolutionary practice in this account, theory and practice nevertheless exist in a state of strong mutual reliance in so far as the power of one depends upon the potency of the other. This is quite unlike the relation between philosophy and the proletariat developed in the *Introduction*.

The revolutionary potential ascribed to philosophy in the *Introduction* derives from a particular faculty of philosophy *per se*, rather than from the practice of the proletariat. It should also be noted that the mutual reliance of theory on practice in their unity relates to the application only of revolutionary philosophy in proletarian revolution, and not to its development.[105] Indeed, in the *Introduction*, philosophy is fully external to the proletariat in its development, which removes it entirely from the concept of the unity of theory and practice as it is understood in the description quoted from Lichtheim above. The application of philosophy to proletarian revolution, according to the *Introduction*, is a demonstration of the unity of the theory and practice of philosophy itself.[106] Marx's argument rests basically on the quasi-Hegelian view that history is a rational process which unfolds through the development of philosophy, for philosophy 'is in the service of history'.[107] The revolutionary significance of philosophy is internal to philosophy, rather than operative through some other faculty. The point is emphasised by Marx when he claims that in contradistinction to theology, it is through philosophy alone that human emancipation will ensue.[108]

With the advent of human liberation through philosophy, Marx argues, philosophy itself will be transcended.[109] The revolutionary role of the proletariat is introduced into Marx's discussion with the qualification that for philosophy to transcend itself, and for man to be thereby liberated from his oppression, the practice of philosophy requires a material element, a material instrument, for 'material force must be overthrown by material force.'[110] Theory becomes such a force 'once it has gripped the masses.'[111] The masses, then, are subordinate to theory, even though necessary for its realisation and transcendence. For, as Marx says in the *Introduction*, 'revolutions need a passive element, a material basis,'[112] and it is at this juncture that he begins to refer to the proletariat, the passive element of revolution which is gripped by philosophy and used in its revolutionary practice as a material force. While Marx says that 'the proletariat finds its intellectual weapons in philosophy,' this is secondary to the central point that 'philosophy finds its material weapons in the proletariat.'[113] It is as an instrument of philosophy that the proletariat is a revolutionary force, according to the *Introduction*, and human emancipation is achieved through the realisation and transcendence of philosophy. This is a progression on Marx's thought prior to the *Introduction*, in which the instrument of philosophy was conceived as criticism, and criticism through journalism,[114] but it is nevertheless quite distinct from his later conception of proletarian revolution.

It can be seen, then, that Marx's German revolution of the *Introduction*, unlike the proletarian revolution of the *Communist Manifesto*, does not result from the development of the proletariat, beginning in 'its struggle with the bourgeoisie' and accelerated by 'the development of industry'.[115] Indeed, according to the *Introduction* revolution is to overthrow German backwardness rather than capitalism. Revolution must occur because it is needed — it is 'a pressing need of the German nation'[116] — and it is needed because of the German state's inability to bring about social reform. Revolution is precipitated in the 'struggle against the German political present [which] is the struggle against the past of modern nations.'[117] In the *Communist Manifesto*, on the other hand, the necessary condition of the proletarian revolution is a preceding bourgeois revolution, and the basis of revolutionary emancipation is the full development of capitalism. The industrial growth which gives rise to the proletariat also means that the 'productive forces at the disposal of society no longer tend to the further development of conditions of bourgeois property . . . they are fettered . . . [and] endanger the existence of bourgeois property'.[118] The revolution described in the *Introduction*, on the other hand, is merely against 'an anachronism'[119] and has a teleological if not a metaphysical basis.

Whilst elements of Marx's mature theory of proletarian revolution, as developed in the *Communist Manifesto*, such as class and the growth of modern industry, are present in the *Introduction*, the role they play in the early theory is quite unlike that given to them by the later theory. While there is class polarisation in the *Introduction*,[120] there is no class struggle; while there is industrial development it is seen to be responsible for the disintegration of the old society rather than providing the basis for the development of the new social order. Marx's comments on industrialisation in the *Introduction* are hardly complete, but there is some suggestion of a causal link between the 'emergent industrial movement' and 'society's acute disintegration'.[121] There is no mention here, as there is in the *Communist Manifesto*, of the role of the development of industry in the organisation of a revolutionary proletariat, nor of the development of industry giving rise to the socialisation of the process of production as the objective groundwork of socialist revolution. In any event, the discussion of industrialisation in the *Introduction* has more in common with the account given in Marx's correspondence of 1843[122] than with the theory outlined in the *Communist Manifesto*. The absence of the positive revolutionary role of industrialisation in these works is compensated by the revolutionary role given to philosophy.

Indeed, the place of philosophy in proletarian revolution outlined in the *Introduction* strongly resembles the credo of critical philosophy given in a letter to the Young Hegelian Arnold Ruge. Marx first made his revolutionary sympathies clear as a series of letters written to Ruge, which were published in the *Deutsch-Französische Jahrbücher*. The third and last letter, dated September 1843, concludes:[123]

Our programme must be: the reform of consciousness . . . by analysing mystical consciousness obscure to itself. . . . [T]he world has long since dreamed of something of which it needs only to become conscious for it to possess it in reality. . . . [O]ur task is not to draw a sharp mental line between past and future but to complete the thought of the past . . .

We . . . sum up the credo of our journal in a single word: the self-clarification (critical philosophy) of the struggles and wishes of the age.... What is needed above all is a confession, and nothing more than that. To obtain forgiveness for its sins mankind needs only to declare them for what they are.

Not only is this form of Marx's revolutionism 'very idealistic', as David McLellan[124] says, it is also rejected by Marx in 1845. In *The German Ideology* he writes that:[125]

> Since the Young Hegelians consider . . . all the products of consciousness, to which they attribute an independent existence, as the real chains of men . . . it is evident that the Young Hegelians have to fight only against these illusions of the consciousness. . . Th[e] demand to change consciousness amounts to a demand to interpret reality in another way, i.e., to recognise it by means of another interpretation.

Although Marx here mentions the Young Hegelians without referring to his own development, the position he rejects is precisely the one outlined in his letter to Ruge a few years earlier. But in the *Introduction* Marx is still prepared to write that:[126]

> The German nation must therefore link its dream history to its present conditions and subject not only these conditions but also their abstract continuation to criticism.

The differences, then, between the *Introduction* and the *Communist Manifesto* cannot be reduced to just a change in the empirical content of the conception of the proletariat, nor are they merely 'minor changes in theories and ways of presenting them' as Bertell Ollman,[127] in another context, suggests that they might be. Rather, the differences are substantial theoretical differences. The morally defined proletariat and the dominating revolutionary role of philosophy in the *Introduction* hark back to the 'very idealistic' theory of the letters to Ruge rather than forge ahead to the 'materialistic' theory of the *Communist Manifesto*.

IV

It has been shown in this chapter that Marx's early social and political ideas are not static or simply elaborated, for he does not merely add to or fill out a position previously stated in each new piece of writing. In the *Critique* Marx argues that the history of the state must be understood in terms of the history of man. The writings which follow are the result of a restless attempt to develop this idea into a full theory of man's oppression and liberation. The first step in this advancement occurs when Marx drops the assumption of the *Critique* that emancipation from alienation can be achieved politically, through a democratic development of the political state. He simultaneously drops the assumption that the cause of alienation can be located in the division between the state and civil society, although the bifurcation of man's individual being — which results from this division — continues to be regarded as a feature of alienation. In *On the Jewish Question* Marx begins to analyse civil society in an attempt to discover the cause of alienation, and concludes that money is responsible for man's estrangement. This notion too is abandoned in the *Economic and Philosophic Manuscripts*, where money is described as the phenomenal form of alienation, and where it is argued that the root of estrangement is in the process of labour under conditions of private property. Each new position formulated by Marx is not merely a development of the previous one, but an alternative to it.

On the more directly political plane, Marx has argued in *On the Jewish Question* that the universality of the democratic state is illusory and that democracy can liberate man only politically, leaving his alienation in civil society unaffected and itself constituting a political alienation. In the *Introduction to the Critique of Hegel's Philosophy of Right* the proletariat, rather than the citizenry of the *Critique*, is designated the universal class. Marx thus discovers the relevance of class for the transcendence of estrangement as early as 1843 in the *Critique*. But in that work the class which overthrows alienation is not the proletariat, it is the entirely differently conceived 'class of citizens'. In the *Introduction* the proletariat is the revolutionary class, but the particular conception of the class of historical transformation is here quite unlike that of Marx's later thought.

It can be seen that Marx's theoretical development does not simply occur through an 'epistemological break', in which he embarks on a new departure by apprehending a single new problematic. His development is incremental and step by step. Marx develops a series of new positions in sequence rather than all at once. But neither is Marx's development in the form of a continuing elaboration of a unit of theories which persists throughout his work, nor even throughout the works of the early period. It has been shown that during the relatively short period of 1843 to 1845 Marx's understanding of alienation, and up to 1847 the possible agency of human emancipation are represented by a number of different theories which are held only as long as it took him to construct a quite different theory, which he regarded to be more adequate than the one preceding it.

Chapter Six

Politics

Many of the themes dealt with in earlier chapters continue to occupy our attention in this final chapter. There is a continuation here of the discussion initiated above of alienation theory, the development of the class concept in Marx, the relation between Marx's early theory and liberal democratic theory, and the influence of Adam Smith's thought on Marx's early writing. Some new questions also are broached in the discussion of Marx's political theory and its development.

It was shown in Chapter 4 that there is a marked distinction between Marx's early and mature theories of alienation. In Chapter 5 it was argued that the early theory of alienation itself underwent several stages of development from the *Critique of Hegel's Philosophy of Right* to the *Economic and Philosophic Manuscripts*. During this period the conception of the precipitating cause of alienation and the process of human emancipation were modified by Marx, although the theory of the state as alienated social power is common to all of his early writings irrespective of variations on these other matters. A dimension of alienation not discussed in earlier chapters is outlined and evaluated in the present chapter. It is shown that Marx's early conception of man's alienation in the state resembles the early liberal democratic theory of state sovereignty. The argument that there is a connection between Marx's early theory of alienation and classical liberalism is enhanced by the claim that the theory of the state as alienated social power is sustained by Marx's adaptation of a notion of social class drawn from Adam Smith. When he rejected Smith's class model, Marx rejected also the early theory of the state and developed an alternative to it.

As it was shown in Chapter 4 that the economic dimension of the early theory of alienation is not absorbed by the later theory, but is transcended by it, so it is shown in the present chapter that Marx's theory of the state as alienated social power has no place in his mature theory of the state as a class instrument. The chapter goes on to argue that as Marx's analysis of class relations became more sophisticated so too did his mature theory of the state. Whereas in its first expression in *The German Ideology* the mature state theory tends to assume that the capitalist state is the capitalist class in politics, he argues in later writings that social classes and the political state occupy different fields of operation. The later development of Marx's mature theory also demonstrates that the state, as part of the social formation, plays a role in the development of social classes, a factor which escapes his early formulation of the mature political theory.

This final chapter concludes on the influence of revolutionary theory on Marx's intellectual development. It is shown that his political and social thought derive from conceptions of political and social reality which are formed in the experience of, or through a study of revolutionary upheaval. The intellectual origins in Enlightenment and later revolutionary democratic thought of Marx's mature theory of the state are discussed briefly and his original contributions to the revolutionary tradition of political theory are noted.

I

While Marx constantly revised his explanation of the cause of alienation and its transcendence, the analysis of political democracy remained more or less the same during the period 1843 to 1845. Marx perceives that in civil society, where man leads an atomic existence as an egoistic being, isolated from his fellows in the pursuit of private interests and the satisfaction of particular needs, man loses his essential sociality, his natural faculties and powers. The theory of alienation which attempts to explain how man loses his essential nature, and how he might regain it, takes various forms in the different writings of the period. They all acknowledge, however, that the political state is an expression of man's alienation, that it is the political form of his alienation. Political alienation is a special form of alienation. Whereas the alienation of labour in its economic dimension robs man of his true community in creating objects which are wholly independent of him, in his political alienation man creates the state in which his alienated social power resides and where he exists in some form of community. In being a political community the state is only a partial community, an alienated community, but none the less man's existence in the state is quite distinct from his existence in civil society where he is devoid of community. The state as alienated social power can be characterised by three fundamental features, then. As a consequence of alienation it derives from or is based upon civil society. The distinct nature of political alienation means that the state is strictly separated from civil society. And as man's social power, which is alienated in civil society, comes to form the political state, man's political life takes the form of a communal life. In what follows the conception of the state as alienated social power will be elaborated and examined.

Marx took from Feuerbach the notion that man's alienation is a consequence of those things produced by men which become independent of them. This is very clearly expressed in the *Economic and Philosophic Manuscripts* when Marx says that:[1]

> The alienation of the worker in his product means not only that his labour becomes object, an external existence, but that it exists outside him, independently, as something alien to him, and that it becomes a power of its own confronting him.

It is Marx's intention that the products of alienation be understood as not only material objects, but also the institutional consequences of the alienated relation. On the page before the one on which the above sentence appears Marx describes religion as one such product, and he might have added there, as he did later in the *Manuscripts*, that the state is another consequence of man's alienated situation. This view is also expressed in the *Critique* when Marx says that the state is a function of the individual's social capacity and that this capacity is alienated in the state.[2] Like all products of man's alienation the state is a consequence of his situation in civil society and comes to be a factor in his oppression.

As an alienated phenomenon the political state is conceived by Marx as the negation of man, that is, the negation of man's human social being. The argument that the state is both the result of alienation and an instrument of alienation is analogous to the discussion of private property in the *Manuscripts* where it is held that although private property appears to be the cause of alienation it is really its effect, but that once actualised it comes to be a supporting cause of man's alienation.[3] However, unlike private property the alienating magnitude of the state is two-fold and it is in this that its special nature lies. The state functions to preserve the egoism of civil society, and therefore reinforces the economic and social alienation of man. In its form, on the other hand, as the political community of man, the state itself constitutes a second, different type of alienation, political alienation *per se*.

In the *Economic and Philosophic Manuscripts* Marx describes the state as one of a number of 'particular modes of production' which fall under the general law of man's self-alienation.[4] 'Mode of production' is not understood here, as in Marx's later works, as the general form of social production, but rather as the facility productive of a particular function. The specific characteristic of the state is that it produces the means of preserving man's alienation in civil society. This is stated more directly and broadly when the function of the state is outlined in *On the Jewish Question*. Marx says that the political community is a 'means for the conservation of [the] so-called rights of man'.[5] The rights of man are distinguished from the rights of the citizen in so far as the former are the rights of the member of civil society only, thus strongly differentiating them from political rights.[6] The rights extended to civil man by the state are predominantly the rights of property, of self-interest, the right to be without community.[7] The state therefore functions to preserve the primary basis of man's egoism and alienation, according to Marx's argument. In summary, the state is an alienating institution in the sense that it provides juridical support to the economic and social alienation which characterises man's existence in civil society. The state functions to maintain primary alienation, and thus contributes to it.

In its function the political state is not the cause of primary alienation, its contribution to man's estrangement in this respect is the degree to which it supports alienation by legally sustaining private interest. But in conjunction with its function, the form of the state directly produces a secondary alienation, political alienation. Before examining fully the nature of man's political alienation in the state it will be necessary to consider the alienating dualism of the division between the state and civil society.

Marx argues that alienated man suffers a fundamental division in his life and being because as a member of civil society on the one hand, and of the state on the other, he is forced into two distinct and conflicting identities which must be held simultaneously. Man's political life, in which he exercises political rights, is conducted 'in community with others'.[8] Indeed, Marx adds that 'participation in the community, in the political community or state' is the very content of political rights. The political community exists in conjunction with civil society, so that while man is and regards himself to be 'a communal being' in the state, he is at the same time, as a member of the civil society, 'active as a private individual'.[9] These are not merely different spheres of man's being, but in vital respects contradictory spheres. Civil society is the sphere of 'egoistic man, separated from his fellow men and from the community',[10] whereas the state is itself community, the political community, in which man 'is considered to be a species-being'.[11] Thus Marx regards alienated man as a being rendered into two contradictory parts which exist side by side in the one person. But the political community and civil society are not simply parallel in Marx's account, for the state functions to serve civil society: 'political life ... [is] a mere means whose goal is the life of civil society.'[12] Man's communal life in the state is not only in contradiction with his life in civil society, but subordinate to it.

The alienation of man is evidenced in and partly constituted by the dualism of the state and civil society, the division between the citizen and the bourgeois in the single person. Not only does the state directly function to preserve civil society in safeguarding the rights of property and private interest, but the form of the state itself perpetuates the dualism. Marx explains that in the modern state man achieves political emancipation, for the modern state is sufficiently powerful to free itself from religion, private property and so forth. Man is not impeded, therefore, by his station or individual endowments from participating in the business of the state. The modern political state, unlike the feudal state, is the business of all the people, for the political state is 'constituted ... as a concern of the whole people'.[13] But this is precisely the point that Marx wishes to emphasise. The state 'only experiences itself as a political state and asserts its universality in opposition to these elements'.[14] Rather than liberate man from the forces which oppress him the political state merely declares them to be non-political. In this way it is able to provide a form of universality for all its citizens which must exist outside, indeed, in opposition to the tethers on man's freedom which confront him in civil society. It is the political form of the state, which establishes itself after stepping aside, as it were, from civil society, in which man's communal life takes an alienated form. For the political state is incapable of fulfilling its promise of universality. It gives man a universal existence, but only on the basis of an atomic, isolated and non-communal existence in civil society, which contradicts and dominates the political community. It is the merely political form of man's community in the state that constitutes his political alienation.

It has been shown that the state and civil society are not merely separate and distinct phenomena to Marx, but opposites: the 'political state is by its nature the species-life of man in opposition to his material life.'[15] Because the state cannot carry into effect its promise of universality the opposition between the state and civil society is not simply institutional but ontological. Man's real life, says Marx, is conducted in civil society, in the state his political life is airy and unactual. This view is expressed in all of his early discussions of the state. In amplifying Marx's conception of the state as alienated social power, it specifies what he regards to be the content of the political state. In the *Critique of Hegel's Philosophy of Right* Marx says that the political state exists 'alongside the real life of the people', that in civil society man 'stands in material opposition to the state', and that 'political life is the airy life, the aetherial region of civil society.'[16] In *On the Jewish Question* it is similarly claimed that in civil society man is 'in his immediate reality',[17] and that:[18]

> man as he is a member of civil society is taken to be the real man, man as distinct from citizen, since he is man in his sensuous, individual and immediate existence, whereas politically man is simply abstract, artificial man, man as an allegorical, moral person.

The proof of man's reality in civil society is precisely in the fact that civil society is the foundation of the political state, its material presupposition.[19] And the unreality of man in the political state is a consequence of the incomplete universality of the political community.[20] The content of the political state, therefore, is man as 'the imaginary member of a fictitious sovereignty, [man] divested of his real individual life and filled with an unreal universality.'[21]

While man's individual existence in civil society has a material reality, in matters of public or general concern, as opposed to individual concern, each individual serves 'the political function [which is] his universal function'.[22] Because the political state cannot affect the material reality of man's alienation, which leads to his individual existence, his universality in the state must be illusory. So that in community with others, in performing the general or political function, in the state, man is an 'imaginary member of a fictitious sovereignty'. The substance of political alienation derives from the nature of this sovereignty.

Marx describes the quality of sovereignty in the state when he says in *On the Jewish Question* that:[23]

> Political democracy ... regards man − not just one man but all men − as a sovereign and supreme being; but man in his uncultivated,

unsocial aspect, man in his contingent existence, man just as he is, man as he has been corrupted, lost to himself, sold, and exposed to the rule of inhuman conditions and elements by the entire organisation of our society — in a word, man who is not yet his true species-being.

This statement serves to differentiate political democracy from the feudal polity, in which the individual is excluded from the state, and also from monarchy, in which sovereignty is invested in a single person. In contrast to both of these the whole people are given sovereign authority by the democratic constitution. But Marx's major consideration is that the full sovereignty of man, the supreme power of man as man, which occurs only as a manifestation of man's species-nature, is denied in political democracy. Indeed, he says that its absence is the foundation of political democracy, for the state imbues the whole people as a sovereign force on the supposition that as individuals they will be without sovereignty in their social alienation. It is in this sense that Marx says that the sovereignty of man in political democracy is a merely fictitious sovereignty. It is only in their relations in the political community that men are sovereign. Man's true power of community is alienated from him and invested in the political state. The sovereignty of man in the political state is the sovereignty of citizenship, and it is the relationship between citizens which constitutes the political community of the democratic state.

II

As the theory of the state as alienated social power has been fully outlined, it can now be evaluated. It will be recalled from our discussion of the *Critique*'s political theory in the previous chapter that Marx identifies the state with citizenship. The difference between the political and the democratic states is a difference in the scope of citizenship; in the former man is a citizen in only half of his being, in the latter it embraces his entire being. In *On the Jewish Question* he similarly refers to 'citizenship, the political community',[24] although he now rejects the claim that there is a significant distinction between the political state and the democratic state. What is continuous, though, is that the state is conceived as the relation between men as citizens. We shall return to this point shortly. It has also been shown that the state, in being separated from civil society, divides man into two, each person is both a member of the political community and an individual non-communal member of civil society. As a citizen in the political community man fulfils a general need which is to be the 'means for the conservation of ... [the] rights of man' so that the citizen is 'the servant of egoistic man'.[25] The secondary alienation of man in the state — which is his social power invested in the political community — is to preserve the primary alienation of man in civil society. Basically, then, in his political alienation man provides the state with a sovereign community which functions to preserve his alienation in civil society, his egoistic being founded upon private property and private interest. This conception of the state bears a striking resemblance to the legal theory of democracy which was developed in the seventeenth and eighteenth centuries.

In general terms this theory argues that in democracy the people as a whole has vested its sovereign power in the legal structure of the state, which in turn protects the interests of the people. The political state represents itself as the embodiment of the general interest of the whole of society. The state's legitimacy and sovereignty derive from the participation of formally free and equal individual citizens, who form a single and unified political community through the suffrage. In surrendering their individual sovereignty to the political community the people as a whole receive in return the secular responsibility of the state towards the people. An early statement of this view can be found in John Locke's *Second Treatise on Government* where he says that:[26]

> Political Power is that Power which every Man, having in the state of Nature, has given up into the hands of Society, and therein to the Governours, whom the Society hath set over itself, with this express or tacit Trust, That it shall be imployed for their good, and the preservation of their Property.

The argument here is that man surrenders to the state a power he naturally possesses, with the purpose of preserving property.

Marx's theory of the state as alienated social power is not simply a restatement of early democracy theory, but all of the elements of the latter are in the former. First, man surrenders or alienates to the political community a power which he naturally possesses. Second, he participates in the community of the state as a free citizen, and it is from this that the state derives its sovereignty. Third, the political community stands apart from civil society and functions to preserve and safeguard its material foundation, private property. Marx's theory diverges from liberal theory, though, in having a critical dimension. Marx regards the state, as a product of man's essential powers which exists independently of his material existence in civil society, to be an object or institution which oppresses man. Thus Marx adds to the democratic theory of the state an element of Feuerbachian humanism. He also argues, where neither the democratic theorists nor Feuerbach do, that man's existence in the state as a citizen constitutes a secondary alienation. Man's community with others in the state, in being political, is merely partial, and in its partiality is an unreal community.

The philosophical aspect of the theory of the political state as alienated social power is a theory of sovereignty similar to classical democratic theory. Unlike democratic theory, though, there is implicit in Marx's theory a humanist critique of the state. The empirical component of Marx's theory of the democratic state is the proposition that the state is a system of relationships between men as citizens. This is consistent with his general theory of alienation, which argues that in his alienation man has imposed upon him particular roles. In the alienation of his labour, for instance, man is nothing but a worker. In his political alienation, *pari passu*, man is nothing but a citizen. These separate roles, when strung together, make up the single individual, but an individual devoid of integrity and divided into unrelated spheres of being. To the extent that there is a sociological dimension to Marx's early theory of the state it is the political sociology of roles. In his political alienation man has imposed upon him the role of citizen. The relationship of men in the citizenship role constitutes the state. In the *Critique* Marx says that 'the state cannot be regarded as a simple reality, it must be viewed as an activity, as a differentiated activity.'[27] This is because, according to Marx, in the political state man does not interact with others as men, but as role occupants.

Although it is not an exhaustive description, Marx's theory of alienation can be depicted as a version of role theory.[28] In arguing that man is fragmented in the alienation of his labour and in his political alienation, the conception of human estrangement entails that in occupying different roles man is oppressed. It thus shares with modern sociology the view that 'roles are a constraining force on the individual.'[29] The major difference between Marx's theory of estrangement and sociological role theory is that whereas Marx conceives of a situation in which man occupies no roles, role theory can conceive of no such situation. But in other respects the two are quite similar, especially in their focus of analysis and their analysis of institutions. It was shown in Chapter 3 above that Marx's early theory of alienation is without a sociology. In so far as role theory is concerned with the multifarious personae which man has imposed upon him by society, it focuses on the individual's 'meshing' of roles, which does not extend beyond the area of mediation between the individual and society.[30] In this sense role theory has no fully sociological conception of society, it occupies the catchment area between social psychology and sociology. Alienation theory and role theory are approximate in their omissions.

More importantly, there is a similarity between Marx's theory of alienation and modern role theory in the way they each depict institutions. According to both theories institutions are constructed from the roles occupied by men active in a particular capacity in social life. Peter Berger and Thomas Luckmann, for instance, have said that 'roles *represent* the institutional order';[31] and as C. Wright Mills has put it, 'an institution is a set of roles graded in authority.'[32] It would follow from this that the particularly political role of citizen would constitute the particularly political institution of the state. This is exactly Marx's position when he says that the state is the relation between men as citizens in the political community. The claim regarding the totalised citizen relationship which constitutes the state, and the argument concerning the democratic state's sovereignty as the community of alienated beings, are equivalent in substance. What one says in terms of empirical role categories, the other expresses in the language of traditional political theory.

III

The philosophical conception of the state's sovereignty is in principle neutral on the question of social class. Role analysis, on the other hand, need not ignore class; indeed, in *The German Ideology* Marx discusses class in something like role terms.[33] But the citizenship role, as it is related to the conception of democratic sovereignty, is an inherently non-class category. When Marx refers to the power of the state it is also as a non-class force. Man's alienated social power, the power of man's essential nature estranged from him, comprises state power. The early discussion of the instrumental aspect of the state is similarly couched in a non-class phraseology. The state preserves the egoism of civil society, or, more concretely, preserves private property. In all of this Marx's early formulations are quite unlike his later theory of the state. In his works after *The German Ideology* Marx describes the state in a specifically class context. On the question of citizenship, for instance, he says in *The Civil War in France* that the democratic suffrage allows the people to decide 'once in three or six years which member of the ruling class was to misrepresent [it] in Parliament'.[34] The state's power is a class power, in the celebrated words of the *Communist Manifesto*, '[the] executive of the modern state is but a committee for managing the common affairs of the whole bourgeoisie.'[35] Marx argues that the state in capitalist society is a capitalist state irrespective of which class is drawn upon in forming the government.[36] And the state's function, Marx says in *The German Ideology*, is to 'guarantee ... [the] property and interests' of the bourgeoisie.[37] For each non-class statement in Marx's early theory of the state, the later account stresses the class dimension.

It is necessary to remark here that the notion of the state as subordinate to the interests of particular social groups is not exactly absent from the writings in which Marx describes the political state as the community of alienated social power. According to the *Critique* the bureaucracy, as the state instrumentality, subverts the general interest of the state in representing a particular interest which conflicts with other interests.[38] What distinguishes this account from apparently similar claims in *The German Ideology* and later works is that here the particular interest represented by the bureaucracy is exclusively its own interest rather than that of the bourgeoisie, and the property it protects as its own is the state itself.[39] Elsewhere in the *Critique* Marx discusses in similar terms the relations between private property, particular interest and the state with reference to primogeniture and the entitled estate of land owners.

In an account which strikingly resembles his later discussion Marx says that:[40]

Whereas according to Hegel primogeniture represents the power of the political state over private property, it is in fact the power of abstract private property over the political state. He makes the cause into the effect and the effect into the cause, the determining factor into the determined and vice-versa.

This statement concludes a paragraph which opens with a comment on the observation that for Hegel 'primogeniture is merely an exigency of politics' in so far as the political need for social representation in the legislature is met by the entitled estate and that the mechanism by which the estate is maintained and perpetuated is primogeniture. This runs parallel to Hegel's more directly central view that the state embodies a General Interest from which derives the various Particular Interests of civil society. Marx's response to Hegel's claim that primogeniture is a consequence of a political cause is the counter claim that:[41]

> In reality primogeniture is a consequence of private property in the strict sense, private property petrified, private property (*quand même*) at the point of its greatest autonomy and sharpest definition.

When Marx says that 'primogeniture represents . . . the power of abstract private property over the political state,' he is merely extending the point he had earlier made concerning the bureaucracy. We have seen that he argues that the bureaucracy, conceptualised as the universal class by Hegel, uses the state as its private property in the satisfaction of its own particular interests. 'Primogeniture,' Marx says, 'is merely the particular form of the general relationship obtaining between private property and the political state.'[42] This general relationship is one in which the various functions of the state serve particular interests as the property of those interests and these interests, in their turn, direct the 'will' of the functionaries themselves.[43] 'Primogeniture is the political meaning of private property,' Marx continues, 'private property in its political significance, i.e. in its universal significance. Here then, the constitution is the constitution of private property.'[44] The landed estate, which is maintained through primogeniture, is best suited to the legislative function not because of its incorruptibility, as Hegel argues; rather it performs the legislative function because that function is its private property and it is its private property because private landed property bestows a political significance and role. The constitution is the private property of the entitled estate. The power of private property over the state exists in the absence of a General Interest in the state. Political processes are not understood here in terms of the material processes of production in society, but in terms of the multifarious interest groups which hold functional positions in the state.

In formulating his critique of Hegel Marx develops a critique of the political state. His comments on primogeniture and the state can be interpreted as meaning both that the constitution is the property of the landed estate and that the landed estate defends its landed property in and through the constitution. This latter interpretation is not foremost in the *Critique*, but is certainly implied in it and is similar to the position Marx articulated during 1842 in *Anekdota* and *Rheinische Zeitung* articles which condemned the advantage provided by certain laws to sectional interests.[45] These comments on the legal sanctions of material interests do not appear as a fully theoretical recognition of economic determination in political life, but are part of a critique of the political state based on very different premises. Unlike his mature writings, in which the state was condemned as a force of class oppression, the overthrow of which was the necessary condition of human liberation, Marx argues in the *Critique* (and the earlier essays) that laws such as these and the satisfaction of such interests are contrary to the true nature of the state which, as a rational organism, is capable of raising the true essence of man to its full station.[46]

It will be clear, then, that when in his early work Marx discusses the state as an instrument of particular interests he conceives this as an aberration, a perversion of the state's true role. Also, the notion of private property, from which the interests dominating the state derive, encompasses not merely property of a materially determinate nature, but also property in the purely functional sense of immanent possession, the right of access juridically prescribed, so that the state instrumentality is the property of the bureaucracy and the constitution the property of the entitled estate. As it is property in this sense which founds political interest expressed in the state, implying the state's subordination to particular social groups, the notion of the state as a class instrument in this context is quite unlike that first developed in *The German Ideology*. It might be added that while Marx's early insights on the place of private interest in the political state textually coexist with the theory of the state as alienated social power they are not integrated into it. Not only are they quite dissimilar in actual content and context from the analogous claims in Marx's later writings about the state as a class instrument, they do not feature as central propositions in a theory of the state, as do the similarly formulated claims in the mature work.

When the empirical insights of this early discussion of the relation between particular interest and the state are elaborated into a theoretical consideration of the class nature of the democratic state there occur certain modifications in Marx's analysis of the state as alienated social power. This latter conception is founded upon man's primary alienation in civil society. In his mature writings Marx continues to argue that the state has a material foundation, but not on the supposition of man's loss of essence in civil society. The state is founded, rather, on the class nature of society and, in particular, on the economic exploitation of labour which is at the basis of class relations.[47]

This may not appear to be fundamentally different from the early treatment of the state, for as we saw in Chapter 4 above, the early conception of the alienation of labour is analogous to the conception of a quantitative economic exploitation of labour. But its significance can be appreciated when it is recognised that whereas all men as citizens are alienated in the political community, according to the early theory, in the mature theory the state is an instrument of oppression wielded by one class against another. In *The German Ideology* Marx remarks that members of the ruling class enjoy 'personal freedom' in the state.[48] The relationship between the proletariat and the state is seen to be of a very different order. In a draft of *The Civil War in France* Marx says that 'the state machinery and parliamentarism are not the real life of the ruling classes, but only the organised general organs of their domination.'[49] In serving one class the state is an instrument of oppression to another. The claim that there is a differential class experience of the state is dissimilar to the assumption of the early theory that all are equally alienated in it.

A separate issue, which can be dealt with here, is that when Marx argues that the state is not the real life of the ruling class, he indicates that the state cannot be regarded as a class 'community'. In the mature writings the state is not primarily a relationship between citizens, but a structure of governance which serves the interests of the ruling class in the long term. We say in the long term because Marx argues — especially in his discussion of the Factory Acts in *Capital* — that the capitalist state guarantees certain economic interests of the working class and contravenes the short-term economic interests of the factory owners.[50] He also recognises that the state and the capitalist class sometimes meet in antagonism.[51] Thus the capitalist state is not the bourgeoisie in politics, but an instrument guaranteeing the dominance of bourgeois production and property. Some scholars have argued that there is a second theory of the state in Marx's mature writings which proposes that the state, rather than being an instrument of the superordinate class, exists independently of classes and constitutes itself as the dominant force in society.[52] This is relevant to our discussion because Shlomo Avineri has suggested that this second theory is a restatement of Marx's earlier view of the state.[53]

The argument that there are two distinct theories of the state in Marx's mature writing is based upon a misunderstanding. It is certainly the case that in one context Marx refers to the state as an appendage or instrument of the dominant economic class, and in another he refers to the state as a force which is independent of all classes and stands above them. But these different accounts do not assume different theories of the state. A formal statement of the first description of the state will show that it implies the second. To say that something, call it S, is an instrument of something else, call that C, entails both that S be distinct from C and that S provide some functional value to C. In the discussion of Bonapartism, for instance, where Marx allegedly develops the second theory of the state, the state still serves a class function, but in a contradictory manner:[54]

> As the executive authority which has made itself an independent power, Bonaparte feels it to be his mission to safeguard 'bourgeois order'. But the strength of this bourgeois order lies in the middle class. He looks on himself, therefore, as the representative of the middle class and issues decrees in this sense. Nevertheless, he is somebody solely due to the fact that he has broken the political power of this middle class and daily breaks it anew. Consequently, he looks on himself as the adversary of the political and literary power of the middle class. But by protecting its material power, he generates its political power anew. The cause must accordingly be kept alive; but the effect, where it manifests itself, must be done away with.

What is important here is that in maintaining social order the state serves the material interest of the capitalist class. And this because the social order is itself based on economic exploitation and class domination. What have been claimed to be two theories of the state are really two theorems of a single theory. The theory that the state in capitalist society is a capitalist state means that the state serves the interests of the capitalist class even though it is independent of it. When he emphasises the independence of the state from social classes Marx does not cease to consider it in class terms, as he did in his theory of the state as alienated social power.

Marx's early considerations of the state as a citizenship relation, while not central to his later discussion, do not disappear from it. They do, though, figure in a different context than that of the early writings in so far as the concept of class is taken into the core of political analysis in the later works. The class concept is not absent from Marx's early theory of politics, however, as was shown above in the discussion of the *Introduction to the Critique*, in which proletarian revolution is a central category. It remains, then, to explain this apparent anomaly of an absence of class considerations in the early theory of the state as alienated social power.

The most advanced appreciation of class in Marx's early writings can be found in the *Economic and Philosophic Manuscripts*. The concepts of class struggle, the two-class model and the proletariat, which are generally understood to be the characteristically Marxist class categories, appear in the *Manuscripts* when any one of them may be absent or less than clearly formulated in the other works of the period. The *Manuscripts* open with the claim that it is 'the antagonistic struggle between capitalist and worker' which determines wages.[55] In the section on 'Estranged Labour' Marx says that in the modern development of the economy 'the whole of society must fall apart into two classes – the property-owners and the propertyless workers.'[56] And the proletarian is defined as 'the man who, being without capital and rent, lives purely by labour.'[57] While the class categories employed in Marx's mature thought are already assembled in the *Economic and Philosophic Manuscripts*, the conception of class in the latter is quite different in one fundamental respect from that developed in *The German Ideology* and elaborated in Marx's works thereafter. In the 1844 *Manuscripts* class is conceived aggregatively, as a collection of individuals who merely share particular individual attributes. The explanation of the absence of class in the early theory of the state must begin with this point.

When discussing the relations of exploitation in the *Manuscripts* Marx focuses on the individual worker and rhetorically asks to whom does the worker's alienated activity belong. The answer is that 'it belongs to some *other man than the worker*.'[58] He goes on to explain that:[59]

> Through estranged, alienated labour, then, the worker produces the relationship to this labour of a man alien to labour and standing outside it. The relationship of the worker to labour engenders the relation to it of the capitalist, or whatever one chooses to call the master of labour.

The relation of worker to capitalist is thus described as an individual relation between one man and the other. We know that what the worker loses to the capitalist is a part of his essential human being and, of necessity, this constitutes an individual loss. All individuals suffering the same individual loss comprise the working class, the individuals who command the benefit of that loss similarly amass into the capitalist class. The class concept of the *Manuscripts* assumes that empirically class is simply reducible to its individual members. This view is not confined to the *Manuscripts*. Although in other respects Marx's thought evolved considerably from the *Critique of Hegel's Philosophy of Right* to the *Economic and Philosophic Manuscripts*, the aggregative conception of class, which is also to be found in the *Critique*,[60] remains unchanged during the period.

In terms of Marx's later thought the reduction of class to its individual members is methodologically limiting, for it disembodies the social dimensions of the class relation. Classes are made up of individuals, but class as a social phenomenon cannot be reduced to its individual members. Classes have an historical existence which cannot be explained in terms of the biographies of the people who comprise them, they also have a social existence which cannot be accounted for through a knowledge of the behaviour and destiny of single persons. Rather it is one's position in the class structure which determines individual attributes, expectations and affiliations. It is 'crude and naive', as Henri Lefebvre has put it, to argue that the capitalist exploits the worker, for it is the class of capitalists which exploits the class of workers.[61] In Marx's mature writings economic class is conceived as a function of the mode of production. The relation between the two is located in the labour process. Marx says in the Preface to *A Contribution to the Critique of Political Economy*, that '[in] the social production of their existence, men inevitably enter into definite relations, which are independent of their will, namely relations of production appropriate to a given stage in the development of their material forces of production.'[62] The productive forces, the means of production and the social organisation of labour are irreducible to the individuals who occupy a place in them. Marx makes the same point himself in *Capital* when he says that 'individuals are dealt with only in so far as they are the personification of economic categories, embodiments of particular class-relations and class interests.'[63]

Marx's early conception of class is similar to that developed by Adam Smith, whose account of class is drawn upon in the *Economic and Philosophic Manuscripts*. At the end of the eighteenth century Smith was one of the first thinkers to recognise the importance of the class nature of modern society, but as we saw in Chapter 3 above, Smith's model of the social structure is one which builds upon individual persons each pursuing an individual interest motivated by an individual propensity. Throughout the first of the 1844 *Manuscripts* Marx treats class in a thoroughly Smithian fashion. He concludes from Smith that 'the governing power over labour and its products' is capital,[64] but conceives such a power to be purely economic. Indeed, Marx approvingly quotes Smith to the effect that such an economic dominance is irrelevant to a political understanding of class relations:[65]

> The person who either acquires, or succeeds to a great fortune, does
> not necessarily acquire or succeed to any political power. . . . The
> power which that possession immediately and directly conveys to
> him, is the power of purchasing; a certain command over all the
> labour, or over all the produce of labour, which is then in the
> market.

An analogous point is made in the third volume of *Capital* when
Marx contrasts the authority relations of pre-capitalist and capitalist
production.[66] Under capitalism the authority over labour of the
capitalist *qua* capital does not have political or theocratic dimensions,
he says. This is because in capitalist production individuals meet as
'autonomous' beings. It is certainly true that the fact that an individual
possesses capital wealth does not imply that he enjoys a proportionate
political power, nor that he has aspirations to acquire such. When the
conception of class assumes that class can be reduced to its individual
members any assumption regarding the political consequences of economic class relations must be without foundation or sense. But, as Marx
came to argue after the Paris *Manuscripts*, the relationship between
individual capitalist and labourer does not exhaust the depiction of
class relations. In the fully social sense the power of the capitalist class
is not to be reduced to the economic power of the individual capitalist.
In discussing the relation between capital and labour as a class relation
it is necessary to transcend the form of analysis predicated upon an
atomised model of class as aggregated individuals.[67]

In *The German Ideology*, where Marx conceives of class as a
function of the mode of production,[68] the political dimension of class
relations becomes apparent. Marx carefully outlines the relation
between the individual and social class. First, he recognises a tendency
in competition toward the individualisation of class, and a counter-
vailing tendency toward class cohesion through class struggle. Marx
says that '[c]ompetition separates individuals one from another . . . in
spite of the fact that it brings them together,'[69] for while 'they are on
hostile terms with each other as competitors' the 'separate individuals
form a class only insofar as they have to carry on a common battle
against another class.'[70] Second, the social consequence of class
relations, Marx argues, is that 'class . . . achieves an independent existence over against the individuals, so that the latter find their conditions
of existence predestined, and hence have their position in life and their
personal development assigned to them by their class, become subsumed

under it.'[71] Thus, while individuals comprise social classes, class cannot
be reduced to its individual members.

This new notion of class allows Marx to draw conclusions pertinent
to the political dimension of class which are denied by the conception
of class employed in the *Economic and Philosophic Manuscripts*. If
class is merely an aggregate of individuals, then an individual's ownership of property entails no more than that he has a command over
labour. The question of the relation between class and the political
state does not arise, and to have it raised against this background is
extraneous to the issues at hand. However, if class is conceived as a
phenomenon comprising more than the sum of its individual members,
that is, a social entity as opposed to a conglomeration of individuals,
the question of political power becomes a class question. This is Marx's
position in *The German Ideology*:[72]

> The conditions under which definite productive forces can be
> applied, are the conditions of the rule of a definite class of society,
> whose social power, deriving from its property, has its practical-
> idealistic expression in the form of the state.

As the conception of class develops in Marx's writings, there is an
associated development in the theory of the state. Marx's early theory
of the state as alienated social power corresponds to an individualised
conception of class; when he conceives of class as a function of the
mode of production and irreducible to its individual members the
state is described as an instrument of class rule.

The theory of the state in *The German Ideology* constitutes a new
departure of Marx's political theory, for it indicates that the theory
of the state as alienated social power has been abandoned. This new
development basically corresponds to the development of the class
concept in Marx's thought. When he argued that man's alienation is
not the result of the estrangement of an essential human nature, but
of an economic exploitation which is a function of class relations,
Marx advanced the view that the state is a social institution with the
specific task of preserving the relations of exploitation between the
classes. The view that the state is a repository of the social power
alienated from man in civil society proposes that all are equally alienated as citizens and that the political life of the people as a whole
constitutes the political community. The absence of class from this
political theory stands in sharp contrast to Marx's later theory of the
state. The critical element of both theories implies that the state must
be abolished if man is to achieve emancipation from alienation; but the

analytical content of the later theory, in explicitly specifying the political dimension of class relations, encourages Marx to develop a revolutionary programme dissimilar to the one advanced in his earlier thought. Integral to Marx's theory of the state as a class instrument is the programme of a revolutionary class struggle between the principal classes of labour and capital.[73] This is a precipitant of human emancipation which is absent from his early political and social theory, as discussion of the *Introduction* and the *Economic and Philosophic Manuscripts* in previous chapters has shown.

IV

In *The German Ideology* Marx says that the state:[74]

> is nothing more than the form of organisation which the bourgeois necessarily adopt both for internal and external purposes, for the mutual guarantee of their property and interests.

An entirely new theory of the state is reflected in this new conception of the state as 'the form in which the individuals of a ruling class assert their common interests',[75] a formulation quite different from the one which Marx had previously employed. In his earlier writings Marx describes the state as both a manifestation of man's self-estrangement and a vehicle in its maintenance; a consequence of man's alienated social power and a means for preserving the egoism of man in civil society. With a refinement in his works of the notion of class, it became apparent to Marx that the state's role in the preservation of property rights is a class function, and the state, therefore, is a class instrument, an instrument of class domination.

Arthur McGovern has noted that this theoretical development coincides with a shift in Marx's attention from industrially backward Germany to the more advanced countries.[76] It should not be forgotten, however, that Marx had already discussed the constitutions of America and France in his writings prior to *The German Ideology* without a suggestion that the state functions as an instrument of class rule. While empirical focus may be related to theoretical development, a more suggestive account of the genesis of Marx's conception of the state as a class instrument, an account which is acknowledged by McGovern, is that Marx reconstructed his theory of the state when the concept of 'mode of production' was first elaborated in *The German Ideology*. That is, with the advent of historical materialism Marx established a theory of society which, when applied to an analysis of the political domain, furnishes a theory of the state which relates it directly to the economic relations of society and the class relations which are there constituted.

In Marx's early writings the state appears as a relation between isolated monads, alienated men, and is a consequence of an alienated social power which exists outside of civil society itself. In *The German Ideology*, on the other hand, the state is an expression of the social power of a definite class in society, and that social power is not inherent in man as such but derives rather from the property of the dominant class.[77] Both theories of the state claim a basis for the state in man's condition. The 'presupposition' of the state according to *On the Jewish Question*, for instance, is 'egoistic man',[78] and in *The German Ideology* Marx says that the state 'continually evolv[es] out of the life-process of definite individuals'.[79] But man's condition is differently conceived in the two works. In *On the Jewish Question*, and other writings of the period, the human condition and the state are perceived in terms of a particular relation between individuals, such that individuals as citizens constitute the state in the alienation of their social power, and the individual condition of alienation is one in which the state divests man of 'his real individual life'.[80] In general terms this last point is not at issue in *The German Ideology*, but the analysis acquires a new content as Marx now argues that the common class interests of the bourgeoisie lead it to participate in the state 'not as individuals but as members of a class',[81] and as a member of the ruling class the individual bourgeois enjoys a personal freedom through the state which is denied to others,[82] even though others may 'have given themselves collective expression . . . [in] the state' as citizens.[83] The citizenship notion here is descriptively employed without the theoretical assumption that it derives from alienated social power. The class content ascribed to the state is contrary to the earlier formulation in which participation in the state is strictly in terms of a political community of alienated individuals who all exist in it as mere citizens.

While the theme of the denial of individual autonomy under capitalism, which was developed in the earlier writings, is maintained in *The German Ideology*, the state is seen in the latter work as an instrument of class aspiration rather than merely the denial of human fulfilment, as Marx had previously conceived it.[84] The state satisfies class needs and interests, as well as detracting from fully human needs. In a sense these are not contradictory formulations, for class needs are not themselves human needs, but on the contrary needs generated in a society which denies fully human capacities and interests. In this sense, it could be argued that the proposition that the state satisfies class needs merely clarifies the proposition that the state denies human needs. However, in moving from an analysis which focuses on the individual and his alienation to one in which class is not reducible to its individual members, Marx constructs a theory in which the state is based on the social power of a definite class rather than the alienated power of man in a citizenship relation. The difference between the two is not merely that the character of alienation is differently depicted in each, but also that alienation is no longer conceived as uniform and universal in the state, but differentiated in the different class conditions. The state power is no longer conceived as an abstract force of uniform oppression in alienation, but as an instrument in the service of one class enforcing the alienation of another.

Not only does the conception of the state change when the focus shifts from individual citizen to social class, but the historical genesis of the state is differently conceived in the two theories. In the early writings the modern state is seen primarily as a consequence of a political revolution, a revolution which in destroying the corporate distinctions of feudal society created the nation state. The argument of *On the Jewish Question*,[85] for instance, is that the distinction of estate and corporation, which defined the relation of the individual to civil society by the relations between his corporation and the state, was destroyed by the political revolution. The political revolution, then, destroyed the bonds of the feudal state and the political character of civil society. In so doing the political revolution both reduced civil society into its basic elements, egoistic men, and created a political community of the entire nation. The emergence of the modern state is thus explained strictly in terms of political emancipation, and the state is regarded as being based on the power of society which had been released by the political revolution and alienated from the medieval corporations. The alienation of the individual egoistic beings provides the content of the state form thus created.

In *The German Ideology* Marx accounts for the origins of the modern state in the development of private property and the emergence of the class power of the bourgeoisie.[86] In the *Economic and Philosophic Manuscripts* Marx describes the emergence of the capitalist class as a function of the development of private property,[87] but says nothing which relates to the formation of the modern state except that '[movable property, i.e. capital] claims to have obtained political freedom for the people.'[88] The discussion of *The German Ideology*, on the other hand, is quite explicit in claiming that private property, emancipated from communal determination, corresponds on the one hand to a class of individual owners who have in common their property interests, and on the other the national state which serves those interests. The description of the state as the form of organisation which the bourgeoisie adopts to guarantee its property follows naturally from the conception of class employed for the first time by Marx in *The German Ideology*.

A major characteristic difference between the theory of the state as alienated social power and the theory of the state as an instrument of class rule is that in the former the state is strictly separated from civil society and exists in antagonism with it, as was shown above, whereas in the latter the state serves a social class and is therefore conceived as a part of the social formation. The difference between the two positions is that the concept 'civil society', as it is defined in terms of individual egoistic needs, entails that the state must be radically distinct from civil society. The concept 'social formation', on the other hand, as it is defined in terms of social classes and institutions, entails that the state is a part of the social formation.

Some of Marx's formulations in *The German Ideology*, however, and indeed in works after *The German Ideology*, resemble those found in statements of the early theory of the state. This has led some writers to argue that in his later works Marx did not abandon the conception of the state as an alienated social power,[89] that it exists in tension with a conception of the state as a class instrument,[90] even though Marx may have concentrated more on this conception of the state in his later analysis.[91] Others, however, have argued – as it will be argued below – that after the mid-1840s the later conception of the state alone prevailed.[92] While there is a verbal similarity in various statements of Marx's two theories of the state, this cannot be interpreted to signify a theoretical continuity. Where scholars have perceived the two theories of the state coexisting in Marx's later writings they have failed to distinguish between the form of the state and its function, and assume that Marx's account of the state's form in his later writings is an account of the state as alienated social power.

V

In *The German Ideology* Marx describes the state as an 'illusory community' which has 'an independent existence in relation to' the individuals who comprise it.[93] Although not specifically referring to the state he goes on to say, in the manner of the earlier discussion of the division between the state and civil society, that 'there appears a division within the life of each individual.'[94] There is also in *The German Ideology* a description which claims that the state is part 'of the idealistic superstructure'.[95] These formulations are similar to ones in the early writings where the state is conceived as alienated social power. In the *Critique of Hegel's Philosophy of Right*, for instance, Marx says that man's 'political life is the airy life, the aetherial region of civil society,'[96] and in *On the Jewish Question* the citizen is described as 'the imaginary member of a fictitious sovereignty'.[97] The subject of Marx's discussion is made clear when he says in *The German Ideology* that the social power of the ruling class 'has its practical-idealistic expression . . . in the *form* of the state'.[98] There are basically two issues here. In both conceptions of the state the form of the state is distinct from civil society, but the nature of the distinction or separation between state and society is dissimilar. Secondly, the 'idealistic' nature of the state is differently conceived in the two theories.

It has already been argued above that the form of the state as alienated social power is the citizenship relation, in which man's essential sociality is posited in the sovereignty of the democratic state. In *The German Ideology*, on the other hand, the state is 'the form in which the individuals of a ruling class assert their common interests'.[99] The question of citizenship is not germane to this definition. In both conceptions of the state the state as a formal organisation is separated from the society on which it is based, but the nature of the separation is different in each case. In the early writings the state is separated from civil society in an almost ontological fashion. The content of man's being in civil society is fundamentally different from and antagonistic to the content of his being in the state, for in civil society man is without community and exists in egoistic isolation, in the state he is a communal being, existing in a condition of universality, even though it is partial.[100] The basis of the distinction between the state as a class instrument and society is identified in *The Civil War in France* when Marx says that the state power is 'wrought after the plan of a systematic and hierarchic division of labour'.[101] This indicates that it is the particular function of the state which separates it from the rest of society. The promulgation and administration of laws for the regulation of social life as a whole is the sole activity of the state apparatus; it is the performance of these activities which institutionally separate it from the rest of society. Although the state as a class instrument stands apart from society, Marx says that it only *'apparently* soar[s] high above society',[102] for it functions as a social institution in the service of a social class.

The claim in *The German Ideology* that the state is an idealistic expression of the social power of the ruling class is not a statement asserting that man is an 'imaginary member of a fictitious sovereignty' in the state, as Marx argues in *On the Jewish Question*. Rather it is a statement concerning the causal subservience of the state to the class which it serves. This is explained by Marx when he says that 'civil society is the true source and theatre of all history, . . . absurd is the conception of history . . . which neglects the real relationships and confines itself to high-sounding dramas of princes and states.'[103] The state is described as 'illusory' and 'idealistic' in *The German Ideology* in order to emphasise that it is a 'reflection' of social classes and the productive forces which produce them. Thus when Marx confines his remarks to the form of the state, there is a superficial similarity in his discussion of the state as alienated social power and as a class instrument. Beneath this apparent uniformity, however, are quite different conceptions of the state's form.

In his full account of the state Marx distinguishes between the form of the state and its function, as Michael Evans has suggested.[104] It has already been shown that the function of the state which corresponds to the different conceptions of the form of the state is also different in the case of the state as alienated social power on the one hand and the state as a class instrument on the other. In the former the state functions to preserve the egoism of civil society, in the latter it functions as an organ of class rule. Thus when Marx writes of the state in his mature works as an institutional form which is quite separate and distinct from economic and social relations, that is a purely political and national apparatus, he is not providing an account of the state which stands as an alternative to his description of the state as an institution which functions to safeguard the common and general interests of the economically dominant class in society. These are not contradictory formulations, but references to the state's form on the one hand and its function on the other.

Robert Tucker fails to make this distinction when he says that there is a:[105]

> definite tension in the thought of Marx and Engels between their conception of the state as alienated social power and their functional definition of it as an organ of class rule. Whereas the one

view propounds a dichotomy of state versus society, the other
treats the state as an instrumentality of class, which in turn is
part of society.

In *The German Ideology* and the writings thereafter, where Marx
describes the state as being in a dichotomous existence with society,
he merely acknowledges that the state is a political institution separate
and distinct from other formal aspects of the social structure. This is
not in tension with his description of the state's class function. Marx's
later discussion of the state as a form which exists 'outside' society,
is somehow 'alien' to society, may encourage the idea that he regards
the state as alienated social power, as he did in the early writings. But
to argue that this is actually the case, as Tucker does, is to fail to
distinguish between alternative representations of the form of the
state in Marx's early and later writings, as we have done above. Tucker's
argument, therefore, is based upon two misconceptions. He fails to
distinguish between alternative representations of the form of the
state in different periods of Marx's writing, and also fails to distinguish
between the form of the state and its function.

Shlomo Avineri has developed another interpretation of Marx's
theory of the state which argues that Marx:[106]

conceives the modern state as a perpetual tension between the idea
of universality, ideally a bulwark against the particularistic interests
of civil society, and these antagonistic interests themselves.

This claim can be supported by citations from the *Vorwärts!* article of
1844, *The German Ideology* and *Capital*. In *Critical Notes on 'The King
of Prussia and Social Reform'* Marx says that 'the state is based on . . .
the contradiction between *public* and *private life*, between *universal*
and *particular interests*.'[107] As the state is frustrated in attaining universality because it is a political state, Marx concludes that it 'must
confine itself to *formal*, *negative* activities'.[108] *The German Ideology*
similarly argues that in the division of labour there arises a contradiction between 'the interest of the separate individual . . . and the
communal interest', and also that the latter 'takes an independent form
as the *State*'.[109] In *Capital* Marx gives a concrete example which can be
seen as a confirmation of the argument of *The German Ideology*. The
nineteenth-century Factory Legislation, which limited the working
day, is described by Marx 'as an all-powerful social barrier'[110] which
capital accepted, he says, only 'under compulsion from society'.[111]
Thus Marx argues that the interest of the class of labour is satisfied by

the state's cognisance of a general interest, which was opposed by the particular interest of capital, against whom the legislation was passed. The first question which arises from this is whether the conception of the state's inclination towards universality, expressed as a general interest embodied in the political state, is the same in the early and later conceptions of the state. Secondly, it is necessary to know what relationship there is between the class function of the state and the fact that it serves a general interest.

Although dispersed over many sources Marx's mature discussion of the relation between particular and general interests is fairly detailed. In *The Eighteenth Brumaire of Louis Bonaparte* Marx differentiates between the 'private interests' of the bourgeoisie and its 'general class interests, that is, its political interests'.[112] Although he does not say so here, the private interests of the bourgeoisie − as opposed to its political and general interests − can be regarded in Marx's writings to be the economic interests of the different sections of the capitalist class. Both types of interest are class interests, one general and long-term, the other narrow and short-term. This contention is given support in the discussion of the Factory Acts in *Capital* where Marx argues that while in general terms the capitalists have good reason to ensure the protection of the working class provided by the legislation limiting the working day, their narrow economic interest compels them to oppose such legislation.[113] Thus while the general class interest of capital would lead the class as a whole to support the legislation, the particular interest of capital led the factory owners to oppose it. Marx goes on to show that the general interest of capital, in the instance of the Factory Legislation, was a consequence of the fact that 'the spokesmen and political leaders of the manufacturing class . . . had entered upon the contest for the repeal of the Corn Laws, and needed the workers to help them to victory.'[114] In order to repeal one set of laws, which served the landed proprietors, the parliamentary representatives of the manufacturers enacted the Ten Hours' Bill, even in the face of opposition from the manufacturers themselves. While the economic interest of the manufacturers, as they conceived it themselves, was contravened by the new legislation, the general interest of capital as a whole was advanced. The repeal of the Corn Laws, which required working-class support, was to cheapen the cost of bread and therefore reduce the wages bill.

With the example of the Factory Acts − 'made by a state which is ruled by capitalist and landlord'[115] − Marx in effect demonstrates that the liberal maxim is false, which claims that the aggregate satisfaction of individual interests leads to the satisfaction of a general interest. For he argues that in order that the general interest be served capital must be restrained and regulated in the pursuit of its particular economic interests. The implication of Marx's analysis is that there is a disjuncture between the particular economic interests and the general political interests of capital. The purpose of the Factory Acts was to 'curb the passion of capital for a limitless draining of labour-power'.[116] In the pursuit of its immediate economic interests capital was led to exploit labour to the point of extinction and it could not stop itself from doing so. The general interest, which is of a political rather than a narrow economic nature, and therefore not limited by narrow considerations of particular requirements, saw that 'the limiting of factory labour was dictated by the same necessity which spread guano over the English fields'.[117] 'Factory legislation,' says Marx, is 'just as much the necessary product of modern industry as cotton yarn, self-actors, and the electric telegraph.'[118] Thus while Marx holds that there is a disjuncture between particular and general interests, he regards them both to be capitalist interests. The general interest of the capitalist class requires that certain of its particular interests be denied. So that while there may be conflicts between the particular interests of society and the attempts of the state to serve a general interest, there is no tension between the conception of the state as an instrument of the capitalist class and the conception that there is a general interest embodied in the state.

Marx's argument seems to be that in the separation of the state from the economy, the former is encouraged to develop a perspective which both transcends the particular interests of capital and orchestrates its general interests. The state itself is not concerned to make a profit, but to ensure that the social order based upon profit continues to function satisfactorily. When Marx acknowledges that the state performs a public function as well as a class function, as when he says that:[119]

> supervision and all-round interference by the government involves both the performance of common activities arising from the nature of all communities, and the specific functions arising from the antithesis between the government and the mass of the people,

he is not asserting that the two are not related. He makes it clear that 'regulation and order are themselves indispensable elements of any mode of production',[120] and their good management, therefore, serves the general interest of the ruling class whose dominance is based upon the mode of production.

Marx therefore does conceive of the state as something like a 'bulwark against the particularistic interests of civil society',[121] as Avineri says, for the interests arising in the antagonistic relations between the classes of labour and capital, and within the classes themselves, are managed and resolved by the state in the satisfaction of a general interest. But the general interest of the state is the general interest of capital, which takes a political form in the state, serving the capitalist class as a whole by maintaining the capitalist social order. That the state in capitalist society satisfies certain working-class interests does not mean, for Marx, that the state ceases to serve the interests of capital. The satisfaction of such particular interests is regarded by him as a means of ensuring the continuance of capitalist production and therefore a necessary measure to ensure the social dominance of capital. The conception of the state as an instrument of class rule entails that the state encapsulate the general political interest of capital, which requires that it restrain certain narrow and particular economic interest manifest in the capitalist class. The general interest embodied in the state is not conceived in terms of the 'idea of universality'[122] according to Marx's mature writings, for it is the general interest of capital which, in the state, sanctions and satisfies the interests of capitalism as such by preserving a social order conducive to capitalist production.

Avineri's interpretation of Marx's conception of the state as a perpetual tension between the idea of universality and antagonistic social interests is justified for Marx's early account of the state only. According to the theory of the state as alienated social power the universality of man's essential sociality is given partial expression in the political community. The political function of man as citizen is 'his universal function'.[123] But because the state's 'universality [is] in opposition to' the particular differences — and competitive interests — of men in civil society, the political limitations of the state and its function in safeguarding the egoism of civil society,[124] places it in a condition of tension between these two poles. Indeed, Marx says that the political state is 'unthinkable in the absence of an organised antithesis between the universal idea and the individual existence of man'.[125] The conception of universality in this context is based upon the assumption of an essentialist human nature. The state is a merely partial community precisely because man is estranged from his essential universality in his individual existence in civil society.

The state's inclination towards universality, which is restrained by and in tension with its presupposition and protection of the egoism of civil society, is fundamentally different from the conception of a general interest embodied in the state as a class instrument. In the early theory of the state there is a contradiction within the state between its communal universality and its political particularity. In the later theory the general interest embodied in the state is not in conflict with its class function, although in serving the general interest of capital the state may find itself in conflict with particular capitalist interests and working-class interests. Whereas the state as alienated social power is in principle in a condition of internal tension, there is no necessary internal tension within the state as a class instrument. Secondly, the universality of the state as alienated social power is based upon a philosophical anthropology of man's essential nature; the generality of the state as a class instrument is based upon the material reality of a mode of production in which the general interest of the dominant class is expressed politically in the form of the state. Finally, the particularity of civil society on which the state as alienated social power is based is the result of the alienation of man from his essential nature. The particular interests of capitalist society which the state as a class instrument subordinates to its general interest, are the class interests of a society in which the alienation of some serves the direct economic needs of others.

While there is a superficial similarity between the theory of the state as alienated social power and the theory of the state as a class instrument in so far as they both indicate that there is a tension between universality or generality on the one hand, and antagonistic particular interests on the other, the content of the tension is not the same in either case. There is no basis, therefore, on this supposition, to argue that Marx's later theory of the state merely subsumes the earlier theory, for they are quite different in their comprehension of the basis and condition of the state and offer significantly dissimilar analyses of the state.

The discussion so far has attempted to demonstrate that in *The German Ideology* Marx abandons the theory of the state as alienated social power, which was developed in the *Critique of Hegel's Philosophy of Right* and *On the Jewish Question*, and reflected in other works of the period. In proposing that the state is a class instrument Marx formulates a theory of the state which continues to be fundamental to all of his later political thought. The first statement of the new theory is not its final form, however, and in two specific areas of the account of the state in *The German Ideology* Marx develops an analysis which he later went on to seriously modify. In his first discussion of the state as a class instrument Marx tends to reduce the

capitalist state to the capitalist class. He also argues that the bourgeoisie 'purchases' the state without realising, as it is argued in *Capital*,
that the state plays an important role in the historical development of
the capitalist class. It is to these issues that we will now turn.

VI

The German Ideology was begun in September 1845 after Engels had
completed his survey of the conditions of English labour[126] and both
he and Marx had spent six weeks in England researching economic
literature.[127] The work was begun, therefore, only after both authors
had had first-hand experience of the most advanced capitalist nation in
the world at the time; it also brings together a wealth of historical
material.[128] But it was not until 1847, with *The Poverty of Philosophy*,
Wage-Labour and Capital and the *Communist Manifesto*[129] that Marx
began in earnest a general analysis of the capitalist mode of production.
The full theoretical account of capitalist production was not completed until a decade later when Marx outlined the theory of surplus
value in the *Grundrisse*. *The German Ideology* is largely Marx's last
full-scale grapple with German philosophy, and while it presents numerous arguments concerning the empirical relations of class and power,
it uses them to illustrate methodological and philosophical points
rather than to develop a theory of capitalism and the capitalist state.
Many of the ideas expressed in *The German Ideology* are certainly
early statements of Marx's broad analysis of capitalist society and
politics which occupies his later writing, but we should be aware that
the relations of property, class and state outlined in the work are
subject to subsequent clarification. The limitations of *The German
Ideology* in this regard are clearly evident in the way in which Marx
draws the relationship between the bourgeois class and the organisation
of its political power.

According to Marx's argument in *The German Ideology*, the state is
the ruling class in politics, for he says that 'the bourgeois . . . are forced
to constitute themselves as "we", as a moral person, as the State, in
order to safeguard their common interests.'[130] This is seen by Marx as
an historical consequence of the fact that as 'a *class* and no longer an
estate, the bourgeoisie is forced to organise itself no longer locally, but
nationally, and to give a general form to its mean average interest' in
the state.[131] He does say, however, that the political power of the class
is not exercised directly by the class as a whole, for the 'collective

power thus created' by the formation of the propertied class into the state 'is delegated[d] . . . to a few persons', 'if only because of the division of labour'.[132] Thus Marx argues that the state is formed by the bourgeoisie and exists as an apparatus delegated with its class power. The direct nexus between the state and the bourgeoisie is indicated further in Marx's association of the will of the state as law with the will of the bourgeoisie.

The real basis of the state, Marx says, is 'quite independent of the *will* of individuals', for it rests on the 'material life of individuals . . . their mode of production and forms of intercourse'.[133] He goes on to say that:[134]

> The individuals who rule in these conditions, besides having to
> constitute their power in the form of the state, have to give their
> will, which is determined by these definite conditions, a universal
> expression as the will of the state, as law — an expression whose
> content is always determined by the relations of this class.

Marx makes it clear that the enforcement of bourgeois will as law is not an arbitrary expression of individual wills, but the collective or average will of the bourgeoisie as a class, 'determined by their common interests, [which] is law'.[135] Thus law is not based on will, but on material relations of production; however, the general interest of the capitalist class rising from these relations is given expression in its common will as the will of the state in law. Marx's analysis is highly significant in terms of the history of legal theory, for to the classical jurist conception of law as the 'will of the state', he adds a factor which demonstrates the fictitious character of the state's sovereignty; he shows that the content of law has a class determination based upon the property relations of society, and thus that the state's will is not original but derivative. While this account of law which holds that law changes to suit the commercial and economic necessities of capitalist production remains central to Marx's later discussion of the subject, the direct relation drawn in *The German Ideology* between the bourgeoisie and its will in the state and law is shown, in later writings, to be inadequate for a general theory of the capitalist state.

In works subsequent to *The German Ideology* Marx argues that the relation between the capitalist class and the state personnel is historically variable. In an article published in the *New York Daily Tribune* of 1852 Marx describes the Whigs as 'the aristocratic representatives of the bourgeoisie . . . [who] abandon to them . . . the monopoly of government and the exclusive possession of office'.[136] An aristocratic government in this situation, Marx says, means that the state serves the bourgeois interests, for in their monopoly of government the Whigs administer a 'course of social and political development [which] have shown themselves to ... [be] unavoidable and undeniable'[137] as a consequence of the dominance of bourgeois property. In the opening paragraphs of *The Class Struggles in France* it is argued, on the other hand, that there is a deleterious consequence for the government of society in one faction of the bourgeoisie holding state power.[138] Because of the difference between the particular and the general interests of the bourgeoisie, the administration of the state in favour of the interest of one faction of the ruling class disrupted the equilibrium of national production as a whole. Thus Marx argues that the capitalist state may function adequately as an instrument of class rule even though the bourgeoisie is not directly represented in the state, and also that a narrow representation of a particular bourgeois interest in the state apparatus may be disruptive of its proper functioning.

In *The Eighteenth Brumaire of Louis Bonaparte* Marx describes a situation in which it is in the interests of the bourgeoisie to relinquish 'its own rule'. He says:[139]

> that in order to preserve its social power intact, its political power must be broken; that the individual bourgeois can continue to exploit the other classes ... only on condition that their class be condemned along with other classes to like political nullity; that in order to save its purse, it must forfeit the crown, and the sword that is to safeguard it must at the same time be hung over its own head as a sword of Damocles.

The political power to which Marx refers is the bourgeoisie's power in the state, not its power of the state. It is 'in order to preserve its social power intact', that 'the sword that is to safeguard it' must be out of the hands of the class itself. Such different factors as the weight of aristocratic traditions, the involvement of the working class in politics through the universal suffrage and disruptive political divisions within the bourgeoisie, have, at different times, made untenable the prospect of a state manned by members of the bourgeois class.[140] Marx's general point is that the government of a bourgeois state need not be drawn from the bourgeois class.

It is sufficient that the state safeguards the capitalist relations of property and production for the social power of the capitalist class to remain intact. It is upon this power, according to Marx's argument, that the state rests, for 'each mode of production produces its specific legal relations, political forms, etc.'[141] The administration and creation of law, on this account, is not reliant upon the direct expression of a class 'will', as it is in *The German Ideology*. Marx says that 'in general, the relationship between the political . . . representatives of a class and the class they represent' is that 'in their minds [the former] do not get beyond the limits which the latter do not get beyond in life, that they are consequently driven, theoretically, to the same problems and solutions to which the material interests and social position drive the latter practically.'[142] In conducting the business of state, which is the business of maintaining social order, the state personnel are led to resolve as problems of policy and law what are, on the economic plane, problems of production and the relations of property. Who directly manages the state is, in this sense, irrelevant to Marx's theory of the state. The imperatives of the economic relations of society, which determine the real course of social and political development, thereby determine the activities of the state and in broad terms set the limits of its charter and conduct. The state power is based upon the economic relations of society, which constitute the power of the bourgeoisie. The state power, therefore, is the power of the bourgeoisie, even though it may not hold office.

The relationship between the capitalist class and the capitalist state in Marx's mature theory is even less direct when the question of the social composition of the bureaucracy is considered. While the capitalist nature of the state is indifferent to the class origins of the government, the professional administrators of state power are not conceived in class terms at all. Officialdom, in Marx's theory of the state, is merely a social stratum. The bureaucracy produces nothing but regulations, it administers state power rather than the power of productive forces, it neither produces nor appropriates value directly but lives on taxes, it exists alongside the real classes of society, serving one and oppressing the other, but remaining distinct from both.[143] Although individuals in the higher echelons of the state administration may have been born into the capitalist class, as members of the bureaucracy they are without class. But in their bureaucratic production they serve the interests of the bourgeoisie by serving the state power. Thus the relation between the capitalist class and the organisation of its political power is socially most distant in the bureaucracy, although politically quite direct, for the bureaucracy has a specific vocational interest in the administration of state power and therefore the power of the capitalist class.

The basic assumptions of *The German Ideology*, that the power of the state is the power of the capitalist class and that law is the generalised will of the bourgeoisie, are developed in Marx's later writings on the capitalist state. The relation between the capitalist class and the state, and between the capitalist class and law, however, are later shown to be less direct and much more complex than Marx describes them in the first statement of the theory. The basic proposition of the theory of the state as a class instrument, that the power of the state rests upon the power of property relations which give the bourgeoisie its social dominance, is not subsequently changed by Marx; but the relationship between the capitalist class and the organisation of its political power is later described in terms of different mechanisms than it is given in *The German Ideology*.

In both *The German Ideology* and *Capital* Marx dates the beginnings of the capitalist state from the advent of the national debt.[144] In *The German Ideology* the situation is described as one in which the bourgeoisie simply purchases the state and enhances its own wealth in doing so. In *Capital* and other writings of the period the relations are more dialectically drawn. Instead of an undifferentiated and already existing class merely purchasing the state, Marx outlines a process in which the national debt acts as a means of primitive accumulation for the emerging bourgeoisie, bringing forth a finance faction of the class, altering the composition of the class as a whole, and, with the introduction of a banking system, altering also the institutional nature of the economy. The relations of property, class and state are seen to be more subtle in Marx's later treatment of the subject than the description in *The German Ideology* allows.

The historical origins of capitalism, according to Marx, are to be located in the mercantile period of economic development. As a system of commerce the major feature of mercantilism was that it gave the economy a national rather than a local character, and established the state on a foundation of private property. Marx says in *Capital* that the national character of the mercantile system was a matter of real substance, for in their concern for the wealth of the nation and the resources of the state the mercantilists 'pronounce the interests of the capitalist class and the amassing of riches in general to be the ultimate aim of the state'.[145] He goes on to say that the 'foundation of national power' rests upon 'the development of the interests of capital and of the capitalist class'.[146] So that although Marx comments in the *Communist Manifesto* that the bourgeoisie has ruled for 'scarce one hundred years',[147] he can also say, in *Capital*, that the 'English

Parliament . . . for five hundred years, [and] , with shameless egoism . . . [has served] the capitalists.'[148] For while the political dominance of the capitalist class in the state has endured for a century, the satisfaction of the capitalist interest by the state has a history five times as long.

Marx explains[149] that the international trade and commerce of mercantilism, and the colonial system which it developed, involved the emerging nations of Europe in trade wars. The contradictory consequence of this early phase of capitalism was that while the incipient national capitalist class, and through it, the nation, accumulated great wealth, the state, in prosecuting commercial war in defence of the national interest, became impoverished. The state could finance its navy and the advancement of the interests of the nation only by levying taxes and inaugurating a system of public credit or national debt. This need for state finance set in motion a complicated set of reactions which not only consolidated the capitalist mode of production, but undermined the absolute monarchy which had overseen the mercantile system, replacing it with a more directly capitalist state form. In *The Poverty of Philosophy* Marx quotes James Steuart to the effect that monarchy, unlike limited government, 'imposes taxes upon people who are growing richer. . . . Thus the monarch imposes a tax upon industry', and adds that:[150]

> the English bourgeoisie, on attaining its political constitution under
> William of Orange, created all at once a new system of taxes, public
> credit and the system of protective duties, as soon as it was in a
> position freely to develop its conditions of existence.

Marx argues that the problems of state finance, consequential upon the growing national wealth of the mercantile period, were resolved in a manner which not only produced the modern systems of taxation, fiscal policy and banking, but which further advanced the development of the capitalist class and enhanced its political power.

In *The German Ideology* Marx says that:[151]

> the modern State [was] purchased gradually by the owners of
> property by means of taxation, [and] has fallen entirely into
> their hands through the national debt, and its existence has become
> wholly dependent on the commercial credit which the owners of
> property, the bourgeois, extend to it, as reflected in the rise and
> fall of State funds on the stock exchange.

This assessment of the situation is consistent with Marx's later accounts, but his subsequent arguments add that the capitalist class not only acquires the state, but is itself significantly restructured through the development of the state. The system of the public debt, Marx says in *Capital*, functioned as 'one of the most powerful levers of primitive accumulation', for it endowed 'barren money with the power of breeding and thus turns it into capital'.[152] The money lent to the state was converted into national bonds issued to the lender. These continued to circulate as negotiable notes and served the same function as cash in the economy. Thus a state loan did not deprive the capitalist of spending power, it enriched his money wealth through the interest it earned and gave rise to associations of capitalist financiers who formed themselves into joint-stock companies and forerunners of the modern banks. Thus the national debt created a section of the capitalist class which Marx says was essential to the full development of capitalism itself.

Marx argues that during the period of the mercantile system the production process could hardly be distinguished from that of the pre-capitalist era; it lacked the intense technical division of labour typical of capitalist production proper. At the time of royal absolutism the only difference between manufacture and the handicraft trades of the medieval guild was that of scale, in early manufacture the 'workshop of the medieval master handicraftsman is simply enlarged.'[153] The fully capitalist organisation of production requires a financial infrastructure, the appearance of which marks the consolidation of the capitalist mode of production, for the 'social character of capital is first promoted and wholly realised through the full development of the credit and banking system.'[154] But this development, as we have just seen, was not a spontaneous consequence of the development of property and the propertied class, for it was facilitated by an innovation in state finance. Marx's argument, then, is that the enhancement of the capitalist interest and the capitalist economy was historically affected through the direct and indirect efforts of the state. The absolutist state directly defended national mercantile wealth and indirectly, in floating public loans, enriched the extant wealth of the bourgeoisie and gave rise to finance capital which further promoted the development of the capitalist mode of production. These changes led the capitalist class to acquire political ambitions of its own against the monarchy, and provided it with the means of direct political power, through the banking and credit systems, with which it could realise those ambitions.

'The subordination of the kingship to Parliament,' Marx says in a review article on English history, 'was its subordination to the rule of a class.'[155] The factor which gave the bourgeoisie its 'control over the state'[156] was the growth of finance capital which culminated in the institution of the Bank of England in 1694, a fact deplored by its Tory detractors who protested that 'Banks are republican institutions'.[157] Thus as Marx had argued in *The German Ideology*, it was through the national debt that the state had fallen out of the hands of the royal house into the pocket of the bourgeoisie. 'Each step in the development of the bourgeoisie,' claims the *Communist Manifesto*, 'was accompanied by a corresponding political advance of that class.'[158] The subject of this comment is the political evolution of the French bourgeoisie, but the point is a general one. The consolidation of the capitalist class as a political force is possible only after the consolidation of the capitalist mode of production. The financial sustenance of the absolute monarchy created the modern credit and banking system which provided the capitalist class with a lever which gave it the political impetus to rule on its own behalf. But the basis of the economic development of the bourgeoisie which undermined the absolute monarchy was the creation, through the state, of finance capitalists who endowed the capitalist class as a whole with the economic means to acquire full political power.

The complex interrelation between the development of money property, the changing requirements of the state and the structural development of the capitalist class, demonstrated in Marx's later discussion of the relation between the class and political power, indicate the limitations of his earlier tendency to reduce the state to the capitalist class. In Marx's later discussion it is implicit that the state had served the interests of capital prior to the full development of the capitalist class, and that the maturity of the class followed upon the development of the national debt in the state. It was only after this state sponsored development of the class in the creation of finance capital, according to Marx's later discussion, that the bourgeoisie could begin to fully acquire the state as its own. Marx has not fundamentally revised the early formulation of the theory of the state as a class instrument, but he has modified it in order to show that the state, in its promotion of national wealth, provided an instrumental value to the capitalist class before it was wielded by the bourgeoisie as its own. Secondly, Marx's later account of the state shows that the consolidation of the capitalist mode of production and the crucial development of the capitalist class were as much a consequence of the evolution of the state as the changing political nature of the state was a consequence of the evolution of capitalist property.

VII

Marx's general proposition that the state is an expression of class domination, while breaking radically with the philosophy of German Idealism and Hegel in particular, has its precursors in the Western tradition of political theory.[159] This assessment is acknowledged by Marx when he says in *The German Ideology* that:[160]

> The modern French, English and American writers all express the opinion that the State exists only for the sake of private property, so that this fact has penetrated into the consciousness of the normal man.

Writers who had studied the political and economic changes of seventeenth- and eighteenth-century Europe were aware of the fact that changes in the form of property gave rise to corresponding changes in the political structure, and that newly acquired political power functioned to defend and advance the emergent property relations. Marx breaks with the earlier materialist political thought by analysing the political organisation of class rule in terms of the relations of social production, and also in the implications he draws from this. Before discussing Marx's contribution to political theory, we will consider the tradition to which Marx is heir.

Although the seventeenth-century historian of the English Civil War seems not to have influenced Marx, nor is he referred to in Marx's writings, James Harrington deserves to be mentioned as an intellectual forebear of the theory of the state as a class instrument. Harrington is widely regarded to have discovered the law that political power follows property, that economic phenomena have a decisive influence on political structure and function.[161] He argues that the English Civil War was a mere readjustment of the political 'superstructure'[162] to the economic reality of the movement of landed property from the crown and the nobility to the bourgeoisie and the lower gentry. Harrington also recognised that in the commercial cities of the Netherlands the distribution of capital was responsible for the configuration of political power. Harrington's conception of property, however, is legalistic. He saw property as a legal institution, believing that the distribution of property could be changed by law, and that by such means government could bring about a distribution of property favourable to its rule. Notes jotted in Marx's excerpt-books for the years 1879 to 1881 explicitly repudiate the juristic notion of property,[163] but the general thrust of Harrington's political sociology is impressive in its similarity to Marx's discussion of the material basis of the political state and the changes affected in the form of the state through changes in property relations.

The resemblance between the analysis of political power in terms of property developed by the participant-historian of the French Revolution, Joseph Barnave, and Marx's materialist interpretation of history has also been noted by various writers.[164] Barnave argues that:[165]

> a new distribution of wealth produces a new distribution of power. Just as the possession of land raised the aristocracy, so does industrial property raise the power of the people,

and:[166]

> just as landed property is, in all large states, the basis of aristocracy and federalism, so is capital the principle of democracy and of unity.

This can be read as almost a summary of Marx's discussion in the *Communist Manifesto*.[167] Henri Saint-Simon similarly explains political relations in terms of economic conditions and argues that property is primary over politics in so far as government and political institutions in general are subject to the property relations of society:[168]

> La form du gouvernement n'est qu'une forme et la constitution de la propriété est le fond; donc c'est cette constitution qui sert véritablement de base à l'edifice social.
> [The form of government is merely a form and the constitution of property is the basis; therefore it is this constitution which is really at the base of the social edifice.]

As with Harrington, neither Barnave nor Saint-Simon went as far as Marx's model of economic causation in their theorising. Both French thinkers maintain that economic development is a consequence of intellectual advancement, whereas Marx argues that in the development of their material production men develop their knowledge. In political theory, however, the ancestry of Marx's analysis of the material foundation of politics can be clearly discerned in these historians of the French Revolution. In the case of Saint-Simon Marx owes a direct intellectual debt.[169] The cultural milieu in which he developed in the Germany of the 1830s was as strongly Saint-Simonian as it was Hegelian. Marx's elders, peers and teachers were in varying degrees followers of Saint-Simonian ideas.[170] And, as the critique of Karl Grun in *The German Ideology* indicates, Marx had a good working knowledge of the Saint-Simonian texts.[171] Saint-Simon's plea for a unified science and his positivism are echoed in the *Economic and Philosophic Manuscripts* and *The German Ideology*.[172] It is, indeed, difficult to discuss the development of Marx's social theory and the theory of the state without at least a passing reference to Saint-Simon.

The materialist tradition of political analysis continued to be expressed in the work of writers contemporary to Marx. The French historian and statesman, François Guizot, for instance, argued in his various books on European and French history that in order to understand political institutions, one must examine the various strata existing in society and their mutual relationships, and that in order to understand these various strata, one must first know the form and the relations of landed property.[173] And John Stuart Mill, commenting on European ideas which had influenced him, mentions the proposition 'that government is always either in the hands, or passing into the hands, of whatever is the strongest power in society, and what this power is does not depend on institutions, but institutions on it.'[174] The general approach outlined by these writers to the consideration of political institutions is strikingly similar to Marx's, and all the more interesting for the fact that Marx polemicised against them.

The precursors of Marx's theory of the state have in common an historiography based on the study of revolution. Revolution not only creates new social order and establishes new political power, but in laying bare the social roots of political organisation it also introduces new political discourse. Reasoning which argues from society to state rather than from state to society is the intellectual product of revolution. The vocabulary of such a methodology was alien to German thought until the revolution of 1848, although it had been established in England by the seventeenth century and in France by the eighteenth. German intellectuals at the time of Marx's early development accepted the power of the state as the effective factor in social events and looked to the absolute monarchy of Frederick William IV for social reform. The wave of academic repression and press censorship of 1842-3 merely confirmed their belief in the potency of the state over society. Marx's theoretical strength lies in the fact that he based his research on the intellectual tradition of revolutionary historiography rather than the tradition which dominated Germany at the time. While in Paris during the end of 1843 Marx made an avid study of the French Revolution and planned to write a history of the Convention. The book was abandoned before it was begun, but the work he put into its preparation undoubtedly led Marx to develop the theory of the state as an instrument of class rule based upon the power of the dominant class in society.[175]

Marx went beyond the materialist tradition of political analysis upon which he built his mature theory of the state by analysing the political organisation of class rule in terms of the relations of social production, and drew implications from his model which opened a new phase in political theory. Earlier theorists had understood property either legally, as with Harrington, or functionally, relating it to particular occupations and different sources of income. Marx argues that the relations of property are ultimately the relations of social production, the former being merely a legal term for the latter.[176] This introduces a consideration absent in earlier writers. Property is conceived by Marx in terms of the social appropriation of the product of labour, rather than merely in terms of the appropriation of the product of nature. The relationship between ruler and ruled is ultimately taken back, therefore, to the social relations of production on which the relations of property rest. Thus Marx specifies that the different relations of property, on which different state forms are founded, can be understood only in terms of the social mode of production. The importance of this factor to the analysis of politics is that it explicitly relates the class nature of political rule to the instrumental value of the state as an organ of class domination. Whereas previous materialist appreciations of political organisation went no further than to argue that the power of the state derives from the power of property, Marx explicitly specifies that the state relates back to the economic relations of social production as a force of oppression against the class of direct producers. The state serves as an instrument of class rule, according to Marx, in maintaining the relations of production and enforcing the subordination of the working class to them. Earlier political theories had emphasised the oppressive nature of the state, but none of them, including Marx's early theory of the state as alienated social power, had argued that the state's oppression is a class oppression and that the state is an oppressive instrument of class rule.

The basic proposition of Marx's political analysis, that the state is the political expression of class domination, leads him to make two further points which are essential to his political theory. In its rise to social power the proletariat, Marx argues, must seize the state and turn it against the bourgeoisie. Secondly, in the post-capitalist society of communism, in which class and class oppression have been abolished, the state is without a purpose and will therefore disappear with the last vestiges of class antagonism.

Marx argues that although the material basis of communism is inherent in the dynamic of capitalist development,[177] in pursuance of its general interest in class struggle it is imperative that the proletariat capture the state and neutralise the political power of the bourgeoisie. In the *Inaugural Address of the International Working Men's Association* Marx describes the conquest of political power as 'the great duty of the working classes',[178] and he explains in the *Critique of the Gotha Programme* that:[179]

Between capitalist and communist society lies the period of the revolutionary transformation of the one into the other. Corresponding to this is also a political transformation period in which the state can be nothing but the revolutionary dictatorship of the proletariat.

In its ascendancy to social power and economic dominance the proletariat is compelled, as the bourgeoisie was before it, to turn the state into the political instrument of its class rule. Marx's concept of the 'dictatorship of the proletariat' is an expression for the historical form of the state under the conditions of proletarian superiority during the period of revolutionary transformation from capitalism to classless communism.[180] The dictatorship of the proletariat, in Marx's political theory, is the post-bourgeois form of the state which expresses the political power of the working class.

Unlike previous forms of the state, however, the class rule of the proletariat is not to sanction the class relations over which it is dominant, nor is it to advance the particular interests of the proletariat as a ruling class *vis-à-vis* the defeated bourgeoisie, it is to undermine the basis of class rule itself. Marx's discussion in *The Civil War in France* of the difference between the proletarian state and the capitalist state indicates that as the former is 'the political form ... [of] the emancipation of labour' it is 'to serve as a lever for uprooting the economical foundations upon which rests the existence of classes, and therefore of class-rule'.[181] This is because, as Marx stated in the preamble to the *General Rules of the International Working Men's Association*, 'the emancipation of the working classes means ... the abolition of all class-rule.'[182] The dictatorship of the proletariat, therefore, is regarded by Marx as a form of political transition from the capitalist state to stateless communism. This is a logical consequence of Marx's theory of political power as 'the official expression of [class] antagonism', for with the demise of class the social basis of the state, the instrument of class domination, is removed.[183] The claim that the state will disappear in communism is not an expression of anarchist thought in Marx's political theory. Unlike the anarchists, Marx does not argue that the abolition of the state will break the power of the ruling class, but rather that as a consequence of social development and revolution, through which classes are abolished, there is no place for the political organisation of class domination.[184] The theory of the state as an instrument of class rule entails that in the classless society there will be no state.

Although Marx's mature theory of the state continues a tradition of Western political thought, the particular interpretation which he gives to the view that political power is based on the social power of property leads Marx to develop a political theory which is profoundly original. By arguing that property relations derive from the relations of social production, Marx is able to show that political rule is the rule of the dominant class in society, and that the state is the instrument of class oppression which, in maintaining the relations of social production, is an oppressive force against the class of direct producers. Secondly, as the form of the state is appropriate to the class relations of the society in which it functions, the rising working class is led to capture the capitalist state, change its form, and exercise it as an instrument for the abolition of class in the quest for its emancipation from wage-labour. And finally, as the state is the organisation of political power for class domination, the state will disappear in the classless society of communism. These three fundamental tenets of Marx's political theory are unique to his mature theory of the state as the instrument of class rule.

Chapter Seven

Conclusion

Discussion throughout this book has been concerned with the development of Marx's methodology and the theoretical underpinnings of his social and political thought. There has been no attempt in the above chapters to measure Marx's theorising against the reality he seeks to explain. The failure to consider the success or otherwise of Marx's account of social processes and their economic foundations should not be read as indifference to such questions. It is simply that an examination of Marx's correctness of explanation would have required another type of book. Since Bernstein's *Evolutionary Socialism*[1] there has been a constant flow of words on Marx's understanding of and capacity to explain reality. The resulting literature is enormously varied in every respect.[2] Perhaps the point made in this book, that there are a number of significant turning points in the development of Marx's apprehension of his subject, can go some way toward accounting for the fact that quite different conclusions have been drawn by those who have written on this theme.

Rather than catalogue where Marx was right or wrong we have attempted a general presentation of his intellectual development, indicating its sources and presuppositions. Lenin's famous statement that the sources of Marxism are 'German philosophy, English political economy and French Socialism' is widely regarded as a fair summary. It does require documentation and substantiation, though. The literature concerned with these matters is less than complete. The debate about Marx's sources has largely focused on German philosophy, and within that substantially on Hegel. It has been shown in Chapter 2, without directly taking issue with the Hegelisation of Marx, that another side of German philosophy, in the form of Ludwig Feuerbach, exercised considerable influence on Marx's thought and its development. Where most commentators, following Plekhanov,[3] have seen Feuerbach's influence in terms of Marx taking an idea or set of ideas from Feuerbach as his own, a quite different situation is presented here. Marx made Feuerbachian theory consistent by developing Feuerbach's incomplete conceptualisations. In enhancing the competence of Feuerbachian theory contradictions within it became manifest. Marx's transcendence of these contradictions in *The German Ideology* is at the same time a new theoretical beginning.

Our treatment of English political economy, Lenin's second source of Marxism, is somewhat broader than generally found in discussions of Marx's development. Chapter 3 documents the similarity between Marx's early theory of civil society and that found in classical liberal theory (of which political economy is a part), especially the theoretical proximity between the underpinnings of Marx's early model of communist society and liberal conceptions of a harmonised commercial society. More specifically, the theoretical similarity between aspects of Marx's Paris Writings and the work of Adam Smith, which has been relatively neglected by many interpreters of Marx's early thought, is discussed not only in relation to the concept of 'social harmony', but also, in Chapter 4, with regard to the concept of social class and that part of Marx's early theory of alienation which deals with the labour process in general and labour productivity in particular. Lenin's third source of Marxism, French Socialism, is not treated here. It is shown in Chapter 6, though, that the materialist theory of history and politics developed by Marx is part of a democratic revolutionary tradition which is not confined to French Socialism.

In discussing the presuppositions of Marx's theoretical development a number of general issues are touched upon without being adequately dealt with. For instance, the social action/social system dichotomy is mentioned in Chapter 3, the irreducibility of social phenomena is suggested in Chapters 3 and 6, and so on. These and other issues are central to the philosophy of social science and to sociological theory, and it is clear that Marx's formulations address them. These themes, however, have not been explored. It was felt that the discussion of Marx's development would only be interrupted with questions of general interest. Any frustration arising from this omission will be doubled as it is not possible to treat these matters in a separate chapter.[4] Two issues of general significance arising out of our treatment of Marx will be briefly dealt with here, though. They are the interaction of political orientation and social explanation, and the connection between theory and critique.

It is clear from our description of Marx's development that throughout his career there is a strong interaction between political interest and methodology. This is not to suggest that Marx's social theory can be adequately described in political terms. Rather, the understanding of social reality provided by Marx's theorising was guided by and has considerable importance for political objectives. It is not being claimed that Marx conceived of theory as an instrumental science in the Baconian sense that underlying the scientific enterprise is vested the possibility of technical control. But in so far as a social theory analyses and interprets structures and relations, and explains their historical development, it is able to inform a political movement on the limitations of its means of action and the nature and weaknesses of the forces to which it is opposed. Indeed, one measure of a social theory's strength is the extent to which it can fulfil these requirements. It is in this sense that Marx's social theory is politically instrumental. This cognitive-political aspect of Marx's formulations returns our attention to its significance for an understanding of theoretical development in his thought.

It was the continuing programmatic aspect of social revolution and, from the 1843 *Introduction*, proletarian revolution, which led Marx to discard the idealist interpretation of history and historical change advocated in the works up to and including the *Theses on Feuerbach*. Not only were his early writings to become polemically and tactically inept, they were also inadequate for Marx's revolutionary purposes because of their failure to develop a comprehensive analysis of the oppressive social order which Marx sought to see overthrown. Marx's early revolutionary politics were based upon an idealist expectation that revolutionary change could be achieved through the realisation of philosophy, and upon a social analysis premised upon the ethical supposition that abject poverty and degradation were necessary conditions for the insurrectionary mobilisation of the proletariat. Marx came to abandon these and related notions in his attempt to elaborate a theory of capitalist society which identified the operative variables of social dynamics, and the social processes which provided levers of action to the agents of social revolution.

In the course of his endeavour to construct an operative science of capitalist society Marx developed a number of different specific theories, theories which provide analyses of social and political structures and relations, of the oppressive conditions to which man is subject, and of the means by which exploitation and its associated conditions can be overcome, or, rather, overthrown. Marx's primary concern was to elaborate a social and political theory integral to a political programme of fundamental social change. This led him to constantly revise his interpretation of social reality and to outline what were (in terms of an earlier statement) often significantly new theories. Various aspects of this process in Marx have been traced in some detail above. In particular, it was shown, for instance, that in his critique of political economy and the categories of phenomenal forms Marx constructs concepts of the essential or real relations of capitalism. These theoretical formulations are aspects of Marx's critique of capitalism and of the socialist movement against capitalism.

In his mature essentialism Marx develops an intentionally critical science. With the discovery of the real relations of capitalist production Marx discovers the material conditions which engender the ideology of the age, that is, the phenomenal categories which in everyday parlance account for the direct experience of life and labour and render innocuous what Marx shows to be unequal relations of exploitation. In Marx's science of society is his critique of capitalism. Marx's science was developed in the service of his revolutionary aspirations; in order to change the world he had to interpret it operatively, understand it scientifically. Marx's critical science, then, is an integral part of a wider revolutionary framework.

The argument set out in the chapters above, and briefly summarised here, is implicitly rejected in a recent statement of the argument that Marx was both a scientist and a practical moralist.[5] In Alvin Gouldner's lively account of Marx's theoretical formation 'primary Marxism has a "nuclear contradiction" [which] generates ... two boundaried subsystems of elaborated theory that I will call Scientific Marxism and Critical Marxism.'[6] Thus Gouldner argues that the really serious split in Marx's theory is not between the early and later writings, but between two quite different theories of praxis or social action which coexist antagonistically throughout the entirety of Marx's work. According to Gouldner, Marx conceives of 'praxis' as both 'the constrained labour that reproduces the status quo' and 'the free labour contributing toward emancipation from it'.[7] In terms of the first form of praxis, Gouldner goes on to say, 'persons submit to necessity', whereas in the second 'they undertake a deliberate and Promethean struggle against it.' Thus Marxism is both a science of political economy and also a philosophy of praxis, according to Gouldner, or, as he goes on to say, 'a tensionful conjunction of science and politics, theory and practice'. Associated with Scientific Marxism is determinism and necessity, associated with Critical Marxism is voluntarism and freedom.

Gouldner's argument, interesting and illuminating as it is, is based on a fundamental misunderstanding of Marx's science and critique.

The two Marxisms which Gouldner identifies are not at all contradictory in Marx's statement of them. It has already been indicated that the essential relations which are the subject of Marx's critical science are precisely those which lead to fundamental social change when affected by revolutionary intervention. Certainly Marx's science of capitalism presupposes an existing structure of relations which constrain the actions of individuals and groups. It also assumes, though, not just that the structures are transmutable, because they are dynamic, but that they are not necessarily indifferent in their course of development to human intervention. Human action *can* produce an outcome that would otherwise not occur. Quite simply put, it would be unnecessary for Marx to elaborate a science of capitalism if socialism were inevitable (as Gouldner claims Scientific Marxism holds). Science is necessary precisely for those who want to intervene in the order its laws describe, to bring about (or prevent) change. If a desired situation is to arise through an independent dynamic, there is no need to understand the processes through which it occurs, no requirement that its course be understood and analysed.

Marx's scientific theory of capitalist society is an account of its contradictions which both develop out of a given situation and tend to undermine it. Thus the contradictions which Marx's science focuses upon are opportunities and resources for groups that Marx assumed would know how and when to act through an understanding of social processes. In developing an operational understanding of capitalist dynamics Marx not only wishes to make the point that each 'law' of capitalist development, which expresses its *essential* relations, 'is modified in its working by many circumstances'.[8] Just as important is the safeguard against optimistic opportunism which seeks advantage in immediate situations without being aware of their limits and without understanding the nature and character of its means of action. Thus Marx reminds us that men and women cannot make history 'just as they please', although they may mistake the imperatives of law-bound social relations for their own private motives.[9] And certain endeavours are condemned to failure because the economic form of society allows no possibility of success.[10] Actions which change economic 'laws', in Marx's view, are those which make use of the opportunities made available to them by the working of those laws.

In Marx, science is critique, necessity the basis of freedom, and theory the precondition of action.

Notes and references

The abbreviation *MESW*, used in footnotes throughout, refers to Marx and Engels, *Selected Works in Three Volumes* (Moscow: Progress Publishers, 1969-70). For all other references full bibliographic detail is given in the first citation for each chapter.

Introduction

1 The surviving manuscript is incomplete and begins with a discussion of Hegel's sec. 261.

Chapter 1 Epistemology

1 *Early Writings* (Harmondsworth: Penguin, 1975), pp. 185-6; emphasis added.
2 *Ibid.*, pp. 87-89.
3 Marx also uses the terms 'material state' and 'unpolitical state' to designate what he calls the 'real state'. The term 'constitutional state' is sometimes used for 'political state', cf. *ibid.*, pp. 90, 119, 120, 129.
4 *Ibid.*, p. 88; cf. also pp. 143-4.
5 *Ibid.*, p. 87.
6 *Ibid.*, p. 148.
7 'the real subject, man, remains the same and does not forfeit his identity in the various determinations of his being', *ibid.*, p. 149.
8 *Ibid.*, p. 131; emphasis in original.
9 *Ibid.*, p. 183.
10 *Ibid.*, p. 77-8; emphasis in original.
11 *Ibid.*, p. 176; emphasis in original. 'Concrete state' means here 'real state'.

12 *Ibid.*, p. 89.

13 *Ibid.*, pp. 128-9; emphasis added.

14 Easton and Guddat (eds), *Writings of the Young Marx on Philosophy and Society* (New York: Anchor Books, 1967), p. 141.

15 Cf. Richard Hunt, *Political Ideas of Marx and Engels*, Vol. 1 (London: Macmillan, 1975), p. 40.

16 Cf., for example, *Early Writings*, pp. 63, 73, 98. Hegel does not deny the fact of social and economic forces. He assumes, though, that they are merely the mechanisms through which the World Spirit operates.

17 *Ibid.*, p. 80. Feuerbach's 'transformative method' basically consists of reversing the primacy Hegel attributes to the Idea or Spirit over Man and Nature, so that for Feuerbach Mind is a function of Natural Man. Feuerbach's critique of Hegel amounts to his pointing out that Man, the proper subject of both history and philosophy, has been turned by Hegel into a mere predicate. The transformative method revises and corrects what it conceives to be a conceptual inversion. Cf. especially Ludwig Feuerbach, 'Preliminary Theses on the Reform of Philosophy', *The Fiery Brook* (New York: Anchor Books, 1972), p. 152. The question of Marx's relation to Feuerbach will be more fully dealt with in the next chapter.

18 *Early Writings*, p. 87. This is immediately followed by a statement of the Feuerbachian critique of religion.

19 *Ibid.*, p. 99; second emphasis added.

20 Marx's internal critique of Hegel includes more than his application of the Feuerbachian subject-predicate inversion. An important but almost totally ignored aspect of the *Critique* is an elaboration of a revolutionary interpretation of Rousseau's political theory, in opposition to the interpretation of Rousseau implicit in Hegel's *Philosophy of Right*. It is inappropriate to discuss this here, but the following points, which would be central to such a discussion, may be mentioned. A significant aspect of Hegel's philosophy of the state is an elaboration of Rousseau's notion that man's essence is in the ideal of freedom, which is expressed in the state. Marx's critique of Hegel can be read as an interpretation of Rousseau's *Social Contract* which stresses the revolutionary implications of primary or direct democracy, namely, that any state which is not a congress or union of people in an expression of the General Will is not an expression of a free rational will. Marx's discussion of whether 'all, as individuals' should share in deliberating and deciding on political matters of general concern (*Early Writings*, pp. 185-95) shows that he is much more sensible to Rousseau's distinction

between the General Will and the Will of All than is Hegel. Lucio Colletti, *From Rousseau to Lenin* (London: New Left Books, 1972), pp. 185-7, gives support to this interpretation.

21 Louis Dupre, *The Philosophical Foundations of Marxism* (New York: Harcourt, Brace and World, 1966), pp. 92-3.

22 *Early Writings*, p. 62.

23 Marx, of course, is critical of Hegel's generous ascription of rationality to empirical existence, for the political state is rational to Hegel. Cf. *Early Writings*, p. 63. It should be noted, though, that some of Hegel's views in the *Philosophy of Right* ran counter to the practices of the Prussian state, especially those relating to censorship and the treatment of minority groups, both in 1821 — when Hegel's work was first published — and in 1843.

24 *Early Writings*, pp. 91, 98, 113. Hunt, *Political Ideas of Marx and Engels*, Vol. I, pp. 82-4, makes this point strongly. A more sustained discussion which argues for the same proposition is Horst Mewes, 'On the Concept of Politics in the Early Work of Karl Marx', *Social Research*, 43(2), 1976.

25 *Early Writings*, p. 89.

26 Plato outlines his theory of ideas in *The Republic* (London: Oxford University Press, 1972), Chapter 35, and in 'Phaedo', *Portrait of Socrates* (London: Oxford University Press, 1953), pp. 165ff.

27 *Early Writings*, p. 88; emphasis added.

28 Herbert Marcuse, *Reason and Revolution* (London: Routledge & Kegan Paul, 1973), p. 271, on the other hand, regards Marx's epistemology as Hegelian. It is true, of course, that there is much Platonic expression in Hegel — especially the *Encylopaedia* — and that Marx's view of Plato is mediated through Hegelian eyes. But these points should not detract from the case argued here.

29 *Early Writings*, pp. 154, 156; emphasis added. A very different critique of Hegel's concept formation is developed by Marx in *The Holy Family* (Moscow: Progress Publishers, 1975), pp. 68-9.

30 Marx says that democracy 'is the first true unity of the particular and the universal', *Early Writings*, p. 88.

31 Easton and Guddat, *op. cit.*, pp. 61-2.

32 *Early Writings*, p. 208.

33 The *Introduction* to *A Contribution to the Critique of Political Economy* was written in 1857. According to the 'Preface' to *A Contribution...*, the *Introduction* was not published because it 'anticipate[d] results which still have to be substantiated', *A Contribution...* (Moscow: Progress Publishers, 1970), p. 19. The significance of the *Introduction* to our argument is that it falls in the period during which Marx is widely regarded as having

'returned to Hegel'.

34 *A Contribution* . . . , pp. 205, 206.
35 *Ibid.*, p. 207. Cf. also the comments in Engels, *Anti-Dühring* (Moscow: Progress Publishers, 1969), p. 116.
36 *A Contribution* . . . , p. 206.
37 *Ibid.*, emphasis added.
38 *The German Ideology* (Moscow: Progress Publishers, 1968), p. 57. Marx criticises Feuerbach for leaving the historical dimension out of his materialism; cf. *ibid.*, pp. 59-60.
39 *A Contribution* . . . , p. 207; emphasis added.
40 *Ibid.*, p. 210; *The Poverty of Philosophy* (Moscow: Progress Publishers, 1966), pp. 91-2, 95.
41 *Early Writings*, pp. 148, 88, 150, 208.
42 Cf., e.g., *Capital*, I (Moscow: Progress Publishers, n.d.), p. 300; *Capital*, III (Moscow: Progress Publishers, 1971), p. 817.
43 *Capital*, I, p. 85, note 1.
44 *Capital*, I, p. 291; *Capital*, III, p. 830. A metaphor of the difference between scientific and vulgar economy can be found in the 'Critique', *Early Writings*, pp. 158-9.
45 *Capital*, I, pp. 503, 530.
46 The important distinction between 'phenomena' and 'phenomenal categories' escapes Jean Hyppolite, *Studies in Marx and Hegel* (New York: Basic Books, 1969), p. 139, although Henri Lefebvre, *The Sociology of Marx* (New York: Vintage, 1969), p. 62, understands it better. Marx's formulations sometimes fudge the distinction, such as when he says, for instance, that vulgar economy 'on principle worships appearances only', *Capital*, I, p. 504. None the less, the distinction is amply clear in *Capital*.
47 *Capital*, I, p. 78; emphasis added.
48 *Ibid.*, p. 77.
49 *Ibid.*
50 Compare Marx's comments on the invisibility in everyday categories of capitalist exploitation, with his comments on the stark visibility of exploitation under serfdom, *Capital*, I, pp. 82, 314-15, 505, 533.
51 *Capital*, I, p. 76.
52 *Capital*, I, p. 503. Marx's critique is conducted in *Capital*, I, Chapter 19.
53 *Ibid.*, p. 501; emphasis added.
54 *Ibid.*, pp. 501-2.
55 *Ibid.*, pp. 503, 504.
56 *Ibid.*, p. 503.
57 *Ibid.*, p. 504.
58 This is not merely biological subsistence, but subsistence under-

stood historically and morally and includes the cost of training and education as well as the maintenance of the labourer's family; cf. *Capital*, I, pp. 167-9.

59   *Ibid.*, p. 504.
60   *Ibid.*, I, p. 505.
61   *Ibid.*
62   *Ibid.*, p. 506.
63   *Ibid.*, p. 505.
64   *Ibid.*, p. 507.
65   *Ibid.*
66   *Ibid.*, pp. 505-6.
67   *Ibid.*, p. 79.
68   Cf. *Capital*, I, pp. 85-6, note; *Capital*, III, pp. 791-2.
69   *A Contribution . . .* , p. 202.
70   Marx raises this point as an objection to classical political economy on numerous occasions, although he did say that 'the analysis carried out by the classical economists themselves nevertheless paves the way for the refutation of this conception,' *Theories of Surplus Value*, III (Moscow: Progress Publishers, 1971), p. 501.
71   'Critique of the Gotha Programme', *MESW*, III, 19. Cf. also *A Contribution. . .* , pp. 200-2.

Chapter 2   Feuerbach

1   M. Gagern, *Ludwig Feuerbach: Philosophie und Religionskritik* (Munich and Salzburg: Anton Pustet, 1970); M.W. Wartofsky, *Feuerbach* (London: Cambridge University Press, 1977).
2   Cf., e.g., A. James Gregor, 'Marx, Feuerbach and the Reform of the Hegelian Dialectic', *Science and Society*, 29(1), 1965, pp. 72-4, and David McLellan, *The Young Hegelians and Karl Marx* (London: Macmillan, 1969), pp. 107-10.
3   *The German Ideology* (Moscow: Progress Publishers, 1968), p. 57.
4   Istvan Meszaros, *Marx's Theory of Alienation* (London: Merlin Press, 1970), p. 234; Karl Korsch, *Karl Marx* (New York: Russell & Russell, 1963), pp. 173-4.
5   Louis Althusser, *For Marx* (London: Allen Lane, 1969).
6   McLellan, *op. cit.*, p. 112. Engels was the first to coin the term 'historical materialism', which he did, with some embarrassment, in the 'Special Introduction' to the 1892 English edition of *Socialism: Utopian and Scientific, MESW*, III, p. 103. While the

term is not Marx's there is no good reason to abandon the established practice of calling the methodology he did develop 'historical materialism'. The term is no more than a summary of his own description of the method outlined in *The German Ideology*; cf. *MESW*, I, pp. 29-30.

7   Eugene Kamenka, *The Philosophy of Ludwig Feuerbach* (London: Routledge & Kegan Paul, 1970), p. 119. Cf. also Sidney Hook, *From Hegel to Marx* (Michigan: Ann Arbor, 1962), p. 272.

8   These take the form of sarcastic allusions to the Young Hegelian usage. In the *Communist Manifesto*, written in the following year, the repudiation is more explicit, cf. *MESW*, I, p. 131. But see also the novel interpretation of this by Shlomo Avineri, *The Social and Political Thought of Karl Marx* (London: Cambridge University Press, 1970), p. 123. It will be argued in Chapter 4 below that while there is a theory of alienation in Marx's mature work it is fundamentally unlike the theory of alienation presented in the *Manuscripts*.

9   Korsch, *op. cit.*, p. 172.

10   Frederick Engels, 'Ludwig Feuerbach and the End of Classical German Philosophy', *MESW*, III, p. 344.

11   A.J. Gregor, *op. cit.*, p. 68; Robert Tucker, *Philosophy and Myth in Karl Marx* (London: Cambridge University Press, 2nd edn, 1972), pp. 80, 95.

12   Franz Mehring, *Karl Marx* (Michigan: Ann Arbor, 1962), p. 52. Cf. also Z.A. Jordan, *The Evolution of Historical Materialism* (London: Macmillan, 1967), pp. 18-19.

13   McLellan, *op. cit.*, p. 72.

14   For a detailed treatment of this period see David McLellan, *Karl Marx: His Life and Thought* (London: Macmillan, 1973), pp. 40-61.

15   'Luther as Arbiter between Strauss and Feuerbach', in Loyd Easton and Kurt Guddat (eds), *Writings of the Young Marx on Philosophy and Society* (New York: Anchor Books, 1967), p. 95.

16   Cf. McLellan, *Karl Marx*, p. 67 note 3.

17   Feuerbach, 'Preliminary Theses on the Reform of Philosophy', in Zawar Hanfi (ed.), *The Fiery Brook: Selected Writings of Ludwig Feuerbach* (New York: Anchor Books, 1972), pp. 154, 168.

18   *Ibid.*, p. 164.

19   *Ibid.*, p. 172.

20   *Ibid.*, p. 165.

21   Marx, 'Critique of Hegel's Philosophy of Right: Introduction', *Early Writings* (Harmondsworth: Penguin, 1975), p. 250.

22   *Ibid.*, pp. 250, 251, 257.

23   *The Holy Family* (Moscow: Progress Publishers, 1975), pp. 109-10, 147.

24   It should be said that even here Feuerbach is defended against Bauer.

25   Meszaros, *op. cit.*, pp. 234-7, says that Marx had only a verbal debt to Feuerbach by 1844 and had no political use for him thereafter.

26   Marx to Arnold Ruge, 13 March 1843; quoted in Avineri, *op. cit.*, p. 10.

27   Cf. Meszaros, *op. cit.*, pp. 234ff; McLellan, *Karl Marx*, p. 78.

28   *Early Writings*, p. 243.

29   *The Holy Family*, pp. 109-10, 147.

30   Marx to Feuerbach, August 1844; quoted in Meszaros, *op. cit.*, p. 235, and a slightly different translation in McLellan, *Karl Marx*, p. 124.

31   Feuerbach regarded Marx and Ruge as too impatient for action and held that 'the time was not yet ripe for a transition from theory to practice, for the theory had still to be perfected', McLellan, *Karl Marx*, p. 78.

32   For statements of a contrary view, cf. Althusser, *op. cit.*, p. 34; Maurice Godelier, *Rationality and Irrationality in Economics* (London: New Left Books, 1972), pp. 115, 118 note 18; McLellan, *Karl Marx*, p. 140; and also Engels, 'Forward to *Ludwig Feuerbach* . . . ', *MESW*, III, p. 336.

33   Marx's letter to Ruge, quoted in Avineri, *op. cit.*, p. 10.

34   *Early Writings*, p. 251; *Economic and Philosophic Manuscripts* (Moscow: Progress Publishers, 1967), p. 71; *The Holy Family*, p. 140.

35   *Early Writings*, p. 244.

36   *Ibid.*, p. 249, 250, 251.

37   'Theses on Feuerbach, I', *MESW*, I, p. 13.

38   *Economic and Philosophic Manuscripts*, p. 102.

39   *Ibid*.

40   *Ibid*, p. 146.

41   *Early Writings*, p. 244.

42   Cf. *Economic and Philosophic Manuscripts*, pp. 99, 144-5.

43   *Economic and Philosophic Manuscripts*, p. 146.

44   'Preliminary Theses on the Reform of Philosophy', in Hanfi (ed.), *op. cit.*, p. 163.

45   *Economic and Philosophic Manuscripts*, pp. 102-4.

46   'Preliminary Theses . . .', *op. cit.*, p. 162.

47   *The Holy Family*, p. 111.

48   'Theses on Feuerbach, I', *MESW*, I, p. 13.

49   *Economic and Philosophic Manuscripts*, p. 144.

50 *Ibid.*, emphasis added.
51 'Theses on Feuerbach, III', *MESW*, I, pp. 13-14. Cf. also *The Holy Family*, p. 153.
52 Cf., e.g., Hook, *op. cit.*, p. 293; Joachim Israel, *Alienation: From Marx to Modern Sociology* (Boston: Allyn and Bacon, 1971), p. 56; George Lichtheim, *Marxism: An Historical and Critical Study* (London: Routledge & Kegan Paul, 2nd edn, 1971), p. 42.
53 'Theses on Feuerbach, VI', *MESW*, I, p. 14.
54 'Theses on Feuerbach, IV', *ibid.*
55 Cf., e.g., *The German Ideology*, p. 32.
56 'Theses on Feuerbach, V', *MESW*, I, p. 14.
57 *The German Ideology*, p. 38.
58 'Theses on Feuerbach, VII', *MESW*, I, p. 14.
59 *Early Writings*, p. 244.
60 Cf., e.g., Louis Dupre, *The Philosophical Foundations of Marxism* (New York: Harcourt, Brace and World, 1966), p. 113; Israel, *op. cit.*, p. 32.
61 *Early Writings*, p. 250.
62 Easton and Guddat (eds), *op. cit.*, p. 237.
63 *Economic and Philosophic Manuscripts*, p. 135.
64 *Early Writings*, p. 99. Marx no doubt got this notion from Feuerbach, compare *ibid.*, p. 78, with 'Preliminary Theses . . .', p. 172.
65 'Theses on Feuerbach, VII', *MESW*, I, p. 14.
66 *Early Writings*, p. 148.
67 'Theses on Feuerbach, VI', *MESW*, I, p. 14.
68 *Ibid.*
69 Hanfi (ed.), *op. cit.*, p. 244.
70 'Theses on Feuerbach, VI', *MESW*, I, p. 14.
71 E.g., Bertell Ollman, *Alienation: Marx's Conception of Man In Capitalist Society* (London: Cambridge University Press, 1971), p. 116.
72 'Theses on Feuerbach, VI', *MESW*, I, p. 14.
73 'Principles of the Philosophy of the Future', Hanfi (ed.), *op. cit.*, p. 215.
74 *Economic and Philosophic Manuscripts*, p. 134; *The Holy Family*, p. 147.
75 'Theses on Feuerbach, VIII and XI', *MESW*, I, p. 15.
76 'Theses on Feuerbach, VIII', *ibid.*
77 'Theses on Feuerbach, X', *ibid.*
78 'Theses on Feuerbach, IX and X', *ibid.*
79 'On the "Essence of Christianity" in Relation to "The Unique and His Property" ', quoted in *MESW*, I, p. 536, note 22.
80 Cf. Sec. 33 of 'Principles of the Philosophy of the Future', Hanfi (ed.), *op. cit.*, pp. 225-6.

81   *The Holy Family*, pp. 152-3.

82   *Ibid.*, p. 154.

83   *Economic and Philosophic Manuscripts*, p. 99. The role of love in sociality is more directly Feuerbachian in Marx's manuscript notes on James Mills's *Elements of Political Economy*; cf. *Early Writings*, p. 277.

84   *Economic and Philosophic Manuscripts*, p. 95; emphasis in original.

85   Cf. *ibid.*, p. 131.

86   *Ibid.*, p. 119.

87   Cf., e.g., *ibid.*, pp. 92, 114.

88   Marx talks vaguely and not a little obscurely of 'communist action' which will arise out of history in the form of a developing need. Cf. *ibid.*, pp. 106, 115. This is discussed more fully in Chapter 3 below.

89   *The Holy Family*, p. 43.

90   *The German Ideology*, pp. 69-70.

91   Cf. the discussion concerning the consequence of the rise of the political working-class movement on the liberal theory of human nature in C.B. Macpherson, *Democratic Theory: Essays in Retrieval* (London: Oxford University Press, 1973), p. 202.

92   Lucio Colletti, 'Introduction', to Marx, *Early Writings*, pp. 48, 56; Meszaros, *op. cit.*

93   It is for this reason that the *Manuscripts* are often seen as a 'bridge' between Marx's earlier philosophical writings and his later economic works, and also as the starting point of the later thought; cf., e.g., Daniel Bell, 'The Debate on Alienation' in *Revisionism*, Leopold Labedz (ed.), (New York: Praeger, 1962), p. 201, McLellan, *Karl Marx*, p. 128.

94   Published in the *Deutsch-Französische Jahrbücher* of 1844 and appears as an appendix to the Moscow edition of the *Manuscripts*. For a discussion of the importance of Engel's essay in Marx's writing of the *Economic and Philosophic Manuscripts*, cf. John Maguire, *Marx's Paris Writings* (Dublin: Gill & Macmillan, 1972), pp. 55-8.

95   *Economic and Philosophic Manuscripts*, p. 19; emphasis in original.

96   *Ibid.*, p. 19; emphasis added.

97   *Ibid.*, p. 20.

98   *Ibid.*, pp. 133, 134.

99   *Ibid.*, pp. 135, 149.

100   *Early Writings*, pp. 243, 244-245.

101   *Economic and Philosophic Manuscripts*, p. 77.

102   *Ibid.*, p. 96.

103 *Ibid.*, pp. 69, 75.
104 Dupre, *op. cit.*, p. 121; Maguire, *op. cit.*, p. 7.
105 Ernest Mandel, *The Formation of the Economic Thought of Karl Marx* (London: New Left Books, 1971), p. 158; but cf. also Maguire, *op. cit.*, p. 154.
106 Herbert Marcuse, *Reason and Revolution* (London: Routledge & Kegan Paul 1973), p. 258. Marx makes a similar claim in *The German Ideology*, p. 259. The philosophical nature of the *Manuscripts* is stressed, however, in Marcuse's earlier 'The Foundations of Historical Materialism', *Studies in Critical Philosophy* (Boston: Beacon Press, 1973), pp. 3-10.
107 *Economic and Philosophic Manuscripts*, p. 20.
108 *Ibid.*, p. 18.
109 *Ibid.*, pp. 64-5.
110 *Ibid.*, pp. 104, 103. Cf. also Feuerbach, 'Preliminary Theses . . .', *op. cit.*, p. 172.
111 Hanfi (ed.), *op. cit.*, p. 97.
112 *Ibid.*, pp. 97-8.
113 *Ibid.*, p. 98.
114 *Economic and Philosophic Manuscripts*, p. 146; emphasis in original.
115 *Ibid.*, p. 71.
116 *Ibid.*, pp. 71-2.
117 *Ibid.*, pp. 96, 101.
118 Cf., e.g., *Capital*, I, p. 477.
119 *Economic and Philosophic Manuscripts*, pp. 64-78.
120 *Ibid.*, p. 67.
121 *Ibid.*, p. 68.
122 *Ibid.*, pp. 69-70.
123 *Ibid.*, p. 72; emphasis in original.
124 *Ibid.*, p. 73.
125 *Ibid.*, p. 76.
126 *Ibid.*, p. 120.
127 *Ibid.*, p. 70.
128 *Ibid.*, p. 72.
129 *Ibid.*, p. 67.
130 *Ibid.*, p. 71.
131 *Ibid.*, p. 72.
132 *Economic and Philosophic Manuscripts*, p. 71.
133 *Ibid.*, p. 97; cf. also *ibid.*, p. 95.
134 *Ibid.*, p. 103; emphasis in original.
135 'Preliminary Theses . . .', *op. cit.*, p. 169. Cf. also Kamenka, *op. cit.*, p. 86.
136 'Preliminary Theses . . .', *op. cit.*, p. 172. Cf. also Sec. 54 of the

'Principles of the Philosophy of the Future', *op. cit.*, p. 243.

137   *Economic and Philosophic Manuscripts*, p. 137; 'Preliminary Theses . . .', *op. cit.*, p. 164.
138   *The German Ideology*, p. 58.
139   *Economic and Philosophic Manuscripts*, p. 103.
140   *Ibid.*, p. 102.
141   *Capital*, I, p. 173.
142   *Ibid.*, pp. 173, 180.
143   *Ibid.*, p. 173.
144   McLellan, *Karl Marx*, p. 122.
145   *The German Ideology*, p. 31.
146   *Ibid.*
147   *Ibid.*, pp. 36, 96-7.
148   *Ibid.*, p. 51.
149   *Ibid.*, pp. 43-4, 46, 49.
150   *Ibid.*, pp. 86-7.
151   This theme will be taken up in Chapter 5 below.
152   *Ibid.*, pp. 54, 102, 105.
153   *Ibid.*, p. 57.
154   McLellan, *The Young Hegelians and Karl Marx*, p. 112.

Chapter 3 Society

1   *Economic and Philosophic Manuscripts* (Moscow: Progress Publishers, 1967), p. 98; emphasis in original. This passage is read as a sociological critique of liberalism in Isaac Balbus, 'The Concept of Interest in Pluralist and Marxian Analysis', *Politics and Society*; 1(2), 1971, p. 167; Joseph O'Malley, 'Introduction' to Marx's *Critique of Hegel's Philosophy of Right* (London: Cambridge University Press, 1970), pp. xliii-xliv; Paul Walton and Andrew Gamble, *From Alienation to Surplus Value* (London: Sheed & Ward, 1972), pp. 2-3.
2   Irving Zeitlin, *Marxism* (Princeton: Van Nostrand, 1967), p. 34; T.B. Bottomore and M. Rubel, 'Introduction' to *Karl Marx: Selected Writings in Sociology and Social Philosophy* (Harmondsworth: Penguin, 1965), p. 33.
3   Shlomo Avineri, *The Social and Political Thought of Karl Marx* (London: Cambridge University Press, 1970), p. 88.
4   'Excerpts from James Mill's *Elements of Political Economy*', *Early Writings* (Harmondsworth: Penguin, 1965), p. 266.
5   *Ibid.*, p. 265.
6   *Ibid.*, p. 266.
7   *Ibid.*, pp. 267, 269; emphasis in original.

8   *Ibid.*, pp. 277-8.
9   *Early Writings*, p. 229.
10   *Ibid.*, p. 230.
11   *Ibid.* The notion that in civil society the individual is a 'self-sufficient monad' corresponds to Robert Paul Wolff's description of society in liberal theory as 'a system of independent centres of consciousness', *A Critique of Pure Tolerance* (London: Jonathan Cape, 1969), p. 37.
12   *Economic and Philosophic Manuscripts*, pp. 71, 73.
13   *Early Writings*, p. 230.
14   *Economic and Philosophic Manuscripts*, p. 120.
15   *Ibid.*, p. 124.
16   *Early Writings*, pp. 236-41, 259-65; *Economic and Philosophic Manuscripts*, pp. 126-31.
17   *Early Writings*, p. 240.
18   After Smith the concept of 'sympathy' became integrated into liberal thought generally; cf., e.g., John Stuart Mill, *Utilitarianism, Liberty, Representative Government* (London: Dent, 1960), pp. 29, 31.
19   Adam Smith, *The Theory of Moral Sentiments* (London: Bell & Daldy, 1869), p. 120. It is interesting to note that from the 1890s liberal theory has paradoxically held that such naturally social sanctions require state support.
20   *Economic and Philosophic Manuscripts*, p. 130.
21   *Early Writings*, p. 260.
22   *Economic and Philosophic Manuscripts*, p. 115.
23   *Early Writings*, p. 232.
24   *Ibid.*, p. 233.
25   'The Eighteenth Brumaire of Louis Bonaparte', *MESW*, I, p. 477.
26   *Early Writings*, p. 233.
27   *Economic and Philosophic Manuscripts*, p. 82; cf. also *ibid.*, p. 60.
28   *The Holy Family* (Moscow: Progress Publishers, 1975), p. 137; emphasis in original.
29   'Critical Notes on the Article "The King of Prussia and Social Reform" ', *Early Writings*, p. 412.
30   *Early Writings*, p. 232; emphasis in original.
31   *Ibid.*, p. 233.
32   *Economic and Philosophic Manuscripts*, p. 82.
33   *Early Writings*, p. 233.
34   *Economic and Philosophic Manuscripts*, p. 81; emphasis added.
35   *Grundrisse* (London: Allen Lane, 1973), p. 156.
36   Cf., e.g., David Thomson, *England in the Nineteenth Century* (Harmondsworth: Penguin, 1966), p. 57, and Eric Hobsbawm,

The Age of Revolution (London: Weidenfeld & Nicolson, 1962), p. 27.

37   Karl Polanyi, *The Great Transformation* (Boston: Beacon Press, 1968), pp. 73, 157.

38   *Early Writings*, p. 220; cf. also *Economic and Philosophic Manuscripts*, p. 73.

39   *Early Writings*, p. 234.

40   *Ibid.*, p. 90.

41   *Economic and Philosophic Manuscripts*, p. 96.

42   *Ibid.*, p. 95.

43   *Ibid.*, p. 96.

44   *Ibid.*

45   *Ibid.*

46   *Early Writings*, pp. 277-8.

47   *Economic and Philosophic Manuscripts*, p. 97; emphasis in original.

48   *Ibid.*, p. 96.

49   *Ibid.*, p. 106.

50   *Ibid.*, p. 85.

51   *Ibid.*, p. 97; emphasis in original.

52   *Ibid.*, p. 92; emphasis in original.

53   *Ibid.*, p. 103; emphasis in original.

54   *Ibid.*, pp. 102, 71.

55   *Economic and Philosophic Manuscripts*, p. 115.

56   *A Contribution to the Critique of Political Economy* (Moscow: Progress Publishers, 1970), p. 21. The absence of class categories here is explained politically by A.M. Prinz, 'Background and Ulterior Motive of Marx's "Preface" of 1859', *Journal of the History of Ideas*; 30(3), 1969, but historiographically by E. Hobsbawm, 'Introduction' to Marx's *Pre-Capitalist Economic Formations* (New York: International Publishers, 1969), pp. 10-11.

57   *The German Ideology* (Moscow: Progress Publishers, 1968), pp. 86-7.

58   Quoted in *Economic and Philosophic Manuscripts*, pp. 120-1.

59   John Stuart Mill, *A System of Logic* (London: Longmans, Green & Co., 1930), p. 573.

60   Cf. L.T. Hobhouse, *Liberalism* (London: Williams & Norgate, n.d.), pp. 125-7.

61   *Capital*, I (Moscow: Progress Publishers, n.d.), p. 172.

62   Hannah Arendt, *The Human Condition* (Chicago: University of Chicago Press, 1970), pp. 43-4; cf. also Ellen Wood, *Mind and Politics* (Berkeley: University of California Press, 1972), pp. 152-4.

63 Liberalism accepts that social and individual interests conflict, but it also assumes that they are habitually and at least temporarily reconcilable.

64 *Economic and Philosophic Manuscripts*, p. 77.

65 *Ibid.*, p. 152.

66 *Ibid.*, pp. 109-10, 119.

67 *Ibid.*, p. 98.

68 The phrase is from Maurice Godelier, *Rationality and Irrationality in Economics* (London: New Left Books, 1972), p. 123.

69 Alan Dawe, 'The Two Sociologies', *British Journal of Sociology*; 21(22), 1970.

70 Quoted in *Economic and Philosophic Manuscripts*, p. 120.

71 John Stuart Mill, *Auguste Comte and Positivism* (London: Trubner & Co., 1866), p. 84.

72 *Economic and Philosophic Manuscripts*, p. 97.

73 Ernest Mandel, *The Formation of the Economic Thought of Karl Marx* (London: New Left Books, 1971), p. 160; emphasis in original. Mandel refers specifically to *Economic and Philosophic Manuscripts*, pp. 65-6.

74 Mandel, *op. cit.*, p. 161.

75 *Ibid.*, p. 162.

76 John Maguire, *Marx's Paris Writings* (Dublin: Gill & Macmillan, 1972), p. 125. Maguire refers to *Economic and Philosophic Manuscripts*, pp. 70-4.

77 Cf., e.g., Anthony Giddens, *Capitalism and Modern Social Theory* (London: Cambridge University Press, 1975), pp. 19, 23, 229.

78 *Early Writings*, p. 226.

79 Z.A. Jordan, *The Evolution of Dialectical Materialism* (London: Macmillan, 1967), p. 43.

80 Maguire, *op. cit.*, p. 125.

81 *Economic and Philosophic Manuscripts*, pp. 106, 114.

82 *Economic and Philosophic Manuscripts*, pp. 75-6.

83 Mandel, *op. cit.*, p. 161, note 19.

84 *Economic and Philosophic Manuscripts*, p. 120.

85 Mao Tse-tung, *Four Essays on Philosophy* (Peking: Foreign Languages Press, 1966), pp. 26-8; Harry Eckstein, 'On the Etiology of Internal War', *Studies in the Philosophy of History*, George Nadel (ed.), (New York: Harper, 1965), p. 124. Cf. also Quinton Hoare and Geoffrey Nowell Smith (eds), *Selections from the Prison Notebooks of Antonio Gramsci* (London: Lawrence & Wishart, 1971), p. 178.

86 Jordan, *op. cit.*, p. 39; cf. also Avineri, *op. cit.*, p. 88.

87 *The Holy Family*, p. 142, quoted in Jordan, *op. cit.*

88 *The Holy Family*, p. 142.

89   Adam Smith, *The Wealth of Nations* (Harmondsworth: Penguin, 1973), p. 481.
90   *Early Writings*, p. 230.
91   *The German Ideology*, p. 49.
92   *Ibid.*, p. 41.
93   Cf. the discussion in Tom Bottomore, *Marxist Sociology* (London: Macmillan, 1975), Chapter 3.
94   V.I. Lenin, 'What the "Friends of the People" Are and How They Fight the Social-Democrats' *Selected Works*, I (Moscow: Foreign Languages Publishing House, 1946), p. 84.
95   *Capital*, III (Moscow: Progress Publishers, 1971), p. 791.
96   *Pre-Capitalist Economic Formations*, pp. 104, 105; *Grundrisse*, p. 502. The former is a translated section of the latter. References to both will be given, but the quotation will be from the former only.
97   *Capital*, pp. 82-3.
98   *Pre-Capitalist Economic Formations*, p. 108; *Grundrisse*, p. 505.
99   *Capital*, I, p. 668.
100 *Ibid.*; cf. also *Pre-Capitalist Economic Formations*, p. 111; *Grundrisse*, p. 507.
101 *Capital*, I, p. 698.
102 *Ibid.*, p. 477.
103 *Ibid.*, pp. 88-9, 550.
104 *Ibid.*, pp. 165, 166, 172.
105 *Pre-Capitalist Economic Formations*, p. 96; *Grundrisse*, p. 496.
106 *A Contribution to the Critique of Political Economy*, p. 189.
107 *Capital*, I, p. 43.
108 *Anti-Dühring* (Moscow: Progress Publishers, 1969), pp. 363-4.
109 *Capital*, I, p. 63.
110 *MESW*, II, p. 49; emphasis in original.
111 *Capital*, I, p. 96.
112 *Capital*, I, p. 114.
113 *Grundrisse*, p. 265. Cf. also *The Poverty of Philosophy* (Moscow: Progress Publishers, 1966), p. 67.
114 *Capital*, I, p. 79.
115 *Capital*, III, p. 831.
116 *Capital*, I, p. 78.

Chapter 4 Capitalism

1   Louis Althusser, *For Marx* (London: Allen Lane, 1969); Sidney Hook, *From Hegel to Marx* (Michigan: Ann Arbor, 1962), New Introduction.

2 Shlomo Avineri, *The Social and Political Thought of Karl Marx* (London: Cambridge University Press, 1970); Istvan Meszaros, *Marx's Theory of Alienation* (London: Merlin, 1970); Bertell Ollman, *Alienation* (London: Cambridge University Press, 1971).

3 David McLellan, 'Introduction to the *Grundrisse* (New York: Harper & Row, 1971); David McLellan 'The *Grundrisse* in the Context of Marx's Work as a Whole'; *Situating Marx*, Paul Walton and Stuart Hall (eds) (London: Human Context Books, n.d.); Martin Nicholaus, 'The Unknown Marx', *New Left Review*, No. 48, 1968; Iring Fetscher, 'The Young and the Old Marx', *Marx and the Western World*, Nicholas Lobkowicz (ed.), (Notre Dame: University of Notre Dame Press, 1967).

4 This position is cogently argued in Michael Evans, 'Two Translations of Marx', *Government and Opposition*; 7(2), 1972.

5 *The Poverty of Philosophy* (Moscow: Progress Publishers, 1966, p. 29; *A Contribution to the Critique of Political Economy* (Moscow: Progress Publishers, 1970), pp. 42-52; *Capital*, I (Moscow: Progress Publishers, n.d.), pp. 91-2, 110, 115, 170, 535-6, 547; *Theories of Surplus Value*, Part III (Moscow: Progress Publishers, 1971), pp. 259, 276, 466-7.

6 Daniel Bell, 'The Debate on Alienation', *Revisionism*, Leopold Labedz (ed.), (New York: Praeger, 1962), p. 204.

7 *Capital*, I, pp. 398, 407, 455.

8 Fredy Perlman, 'Introduction' to Isaak Rubin, *Essays on Marx's Theory of Value* (Detroit: Black and Red, 1972), p. xxv.

9 *Capital*, I, pp. 482-3.

10 *Ibid.*, pp. 340-1, 344, 604.

11 *The Poverty of Philosophy*, p. 29; *A Contribution to the Critique of Political Economy*, pp. 42-3, 56-7.

12 *Capital*, I, p. 536.

13 *Ibid.*, p. 535.

14 *Ibid.*

15 *Ibid.*

16 *Capital*, III (Moscow, Progress Publishers, 1971), pp. 814-15; 'Wage Labour and Capital', *MESW*, I, p. 161.

17 'Excerpts from James Mill's *Elements of Political Economy*', *Early Writings* (Harmondsworth: Penguin, 1975), pp. 259-60.

18 Perlman, *op. cit.*, p. xxiv; Paul Walton and Andrew Gamble, *From Alienation to Surplus Value* (London: Sheed & Ward, 1972), pp. 39-43.

19 'Wage Labour and Capital', *MESW*, I, pp. 163-7. A little later, though in the *Communist Manifesto*, the 'absolute impoverishment' thesis reappears; cf. *MESW*, I, pp. 114-15, 119.

20 *Capital*, I, Chapter 25, Sections 1 and 2.

21   *Economic and Philosophic Manuscripts* (Moscow: Progress Publishers, 1967), pp. 67, 66.

22   Although the notion is not entirely foreign to the *Manuscripts*, as on p. 29, Marx fails to integrate it into the theory of wages or alienation here.

23   *Economic and Philosophic Manuscripts*, p. 66.

24   *Ibid.*, p. 26.

25   *Ibid.*, pp. 26-7.

26   *Ibid.*, p. 66.

27   *Capital*, I, p. 313.

28   *Ibid.*, p. 400.

29   *Ibid.*, pp. 336, 341.

30   *Economic and Philosophic Manuscripts*, p. 69.

31   *Ibid.*, p. 110.

32   Bell, *op. cit.*, p. 203. Emphasis added. Cf. also George Lichtheim, *Marxism* (London: Routledge & Kegan Paul, 1971), p. 43.

33   This is denied by John O'Neill, 'The Concept of Estrangement in the Early and Later Writings of Karl Marx', *Philosophy and Phenomenological Research*; 25(1), 1964, p. 77.

34   *Economic and Philosophic Manuscripts*, p. 72.

35   *Ibid.*, p. 66.

36   Ernest Mandel, *The Formation of the Economic Thought of Karl Marx* (London: New Left Books, 1971), pp. 161-2.

37   *Economic and Philosophic Manuscripts*, p. 66.

38   *Ibid.*, pp. 66-7.

39   *MESW*, II, p. 55.

40   *Economic and Philosophic Manuscripts*, p. 24; cf. *ibid.*, p. 66.

41   *Capital*, I, pp. 164-5.

42   *Economic and Philosophic Manuscripts*, p. 95.

43   *Ibid.*, p. 71.

44   *Ibid.*, p. 152.

45   *Capital*, I, p. 26. Engels explains why in 'The Housing Question', cf. especially *MESW*, II, p. 373. Cf. also Marx's comment in a letter to F. Domela-Nieuwenhuis, 22 February, 1881; *Selected Correspondence* (Moscow: Progress Publishers, 1965), p. 338.

46   *MESW*, I, p. 121.

47   *Capital*, III, p. 820. Cf. also *The German Ideology* (Moscow: Progress Publishers, 1968), p. 93.

48   *Capital*, III, p. 820.

49   *Economic and Philosophic Manuscripts*, p. 71.

50   *Capital*, III, p. 819.

51   *Ibid.*, p. 820.

52   Lichtheim, *op. cit*, p. 197, is aware of this fact but not its significance.

53 *Economic and Philosophic Manuscripts*, pp. 75-6, 120.
54 *The German Ideology*, p. 49; *A Contribution to the Critique of Political Economy*, pp. 51-2; *Capital*, I, pp. 108, 340-1, 407.
55 *Capital*, I, p. 667.
56 *Ibid.*, p. 685.
57 *Ibid.*, p. 671.
58 *Ibid.*, p. 145.
59 *Ibid.*, p. 180.
60 *Economic and Philosophic Manuscripts*, p. 69.
61 *Capital*, I, p. 318.
62 *Ibid.*, p. 363.
63 *Ibid.*, p. 351.
64 *Ibid.*
65 The proposition that the essence of man is labour is an anthropological rather than an economic claim, but it implies that the labour process is dominated by the activities of the labourer rather than by the instruments of labour which he uses in production.
66 Heinz Lubasz, 'Marx's Initial Problematic: The Problem of Poverty', *Political Studies*; 24(1), 1976.
67 *Economic and Philosophic Manuscripts*, p. 64.
68 *Ibid.*, p. 24.
69 *Ibid.*, p. 30.
70 *Early Writings*, p. 256.
71 *Economic and Philosophic Manuscripts*, p. 88.
72 *Ibid.*, p. 81; emphasis in original.
73 *Ibid.*, p. 140; emphasis in original.
74 *Ibid.*, p. 96.
75 *Capital*, I, p. 174.
76 *Ibid.*, pp. 175-6.
77 *Economic and Philosophic Manuscripts*, p. 68; emphasis in original.
78 *Ibid.*
79 *Capital*, I, p. 320.
80 *Ibid.*, p. 398.
81 *Ibid.*, p. 329, note 4.
82 Marx had not developed the concepts 'constant' and 'variable' capital in the *Manuscripts*, but working from the vocabulary of classical political economy refers to 'fixed' and 'circulating' capital, *Economic and Philosophic Manuscripts*, p. 44. Cf. John Maguire, *Marx's Paris Writings* (Dublin: Gill & Macmillan, 1972), p. 55, for a discussion of the important difference between the two sets of categories.
83 *Capital*, I, pp. 329-30.

84   *Ibid.*, p. 355.
85   *Ibid.*, p. 369.
86   *Ibid.*, p. 399.
87   *Economic and Philosophic Manuscripts*, pp. 27-8. Compare with Marx's later discussion of the replacement of labour with machines as a consequence of the class struggle between capitalist and worker; cf., e.g., *The Poverty of Philosophy*, p. 122; *Capital*, I, Chapter 15, Section 5, especially pp. 407, 410-11. Cf. also Engels, *Anti-Dühring* (Moscow: Progress Publishers, 1969), pp. 324-5.
88   *Economic and Philosophic Manuscripts*, p. 109.
89   *Ibid.*, p. 33.
90   *Economic and Philosophic Manuscripts*, p. 27.
91   *Ibid.*, p. 124.
92   *Ibid.*, p. 120.
93   *Ibid.*, p. 30.
94   *Ibid.*, p. 123.
95   *Capital*, I, p. 329, note 4.
96   *Ibid.*, p. 325.
97   *Ibid.*, p. 340.
98   *Ibid.*, pp. 329-30.
99   *Ibid.*, p. 454.
100   *Ibid.*, p. 380.
101   *Ibid.*, p. 455.
102   *Ibid.*, p. 396.
103   *Ibid.*, pp. 331-2.
104   *Ibid.*, p. 332.
105   *Ibid.*, pp. 332, 336.
106   *Ibid.*, p. 334.
107   *Ibid.*, p. 336.
108   *Ibid.*, p. 335.
109   *Economic and Philosophic Manuscripts*, pp. 123-4.
110   *Ibid.*, pp. 68, 74; emphasis in original.
111   *Ibid.*, p. 66.
112   *Capital*, I, p. 335.
113   *Ibid.*, p. 336.
114   *Ibid.*, p. 335.

Chapter 5 Human emancipation

1   Shlomo Avineri, *The Social and Political Thought of Karl Marx* (London: Cambridge University Press, 1970); Jean Hyppolite, *Studies in Marx and Hegel* (New York: Basic Books, 1969);

Tom Kemp, 'Aspects of the Marxist Theory of the State', *Indian Journal of Social Research*, No. 2, 1964; Henri Lefebvre, *The Sociology of Marx* (New York: Vintage, 1969); Joseph O'Malley, 'Editor's Introduction' to Marx, *Critique of Hegel's Philosophy of Right* (London: Cambridge University Press, 1970).

2 Louis Dupre, *The Philosophical Foundations of Marxism* (New York: Harcourt, Brace & World, 1966), p. 93.

3 Theses on Feuerbach, XI, *MESW*, I, p. 15.

4 O'Malley, *op. cit.*, p. lii; cf. also Avineri, *op. cit.*, p. 34.

5 Marx, *A Contribution to the Critique of Political Economy* (Moscow: Progress Publishers, 1970), p. 20.

6 *Economic and Philosophic Manuscripts* (Moscow: Progress Publishers, 1967), p. 18.

7 *Ibid.*

8 David McLellan, *Karl Marx: His Life and Thought* (London: Macmillan, 1973), pp. 138-9.

9 *The German Ideology* (Moscow: Progress Publishers, 1968), p. 669.

10 Boris Nicolaievsky and Otto Maenchen-Helfen, *Karl Marx: Man and Fighter* (Harmondsworth: Penguin, 1976), p. 108.

11 Quoted in McLellan, *op. cit.*, p. 143.

12 *A Contribution to the Critique of Political Economy*, p. 22. Cf. also Engels's reminiscence in 'On the History of the Communist League', *MESW*, III, p. 179.

13 McLellan, *op. cit.*, p. 151; Nicolaievsky and Maenchen-Helfen, *op. cit.*, p. 112.

14 *Early Writings* (Harmondsworth: Penguin, 1975), pp. 143-4; emphasis in original.

15 *Ibid.*, p. 189; emphasis in original.

16 *Ibid.*

17 *Ibid.*, pp. 88-9.

18 *Ibid.*, p. 145.

19 *Ibid.*, p. 87.

20 *Ibid.*, pp. 89-90. Maurice Godelier, *Rationality and Irrationality in Economics* (London: New Left Books, 1972), p. 108, does confuse them.

21 *Early Writings*, p. 191; emphasis in original.

22 *Ibid.*, pp. 88-9.

23 O'Malley, *op. cit.*, p. lxiii.

24 *Early Writings*, p. 88.

25 *Ibid.*

26 *Ibid.*

27 For another interpretation cf. McLellan, *Marx Before Marxism* (Harmondsworth: Penguin, 1972), p. 151.

28 *Early Writings*, p. 253.
29 *Ibid.*, p. 411.
30 *Ibid.*, p. 417.
31 *Ibid.*, p. 418.
32 Cf. the remarks in 'The Class Struggles in France', *MESW*, I, pp. 222-3, 291.
33 *MESW*, I, pp. 135, 136.
34 *MESW*, II, p. 17.
35 Cf. Marx's letter to Wilhelm Liebknecht, 11 February, 1878, *Selected Correspondence* (Moscow: Progress Publishers, 1965), p. 314.
36 The contrary is asserted by Avineri, *op. cit.*, p. 34; cf. also McLellan, *op. cit.*, pp. 150-1.
37 *Early Writings*, pp. 219-22, 225-6.
38 *Ibid.*, p. 232.
39 *Ibid.*, p. 233.
40 *Ibid.*
41 *Ibid.*, emphasis in original.
42 Cf. *ibid.*, pp. 145-8, 158.
43 *Ibid.*, p. 219.
44 *Ibid.*
45 *Ibid.*, p. 222.
46 *Ibid.*
47 *Ibid.*, p. 219.
48 *Ibid.*, p. 223.
49 *Ibid.*, p. 222.
50 *Ibid.*, pp. 225-6.
51 *Ibid.*, p. 218.
52 *Ibid.*, p. 221.
53 *Ibid.*
54 *Ibid.*, p. 236.
55 *Ibid.*, p. 234.
56 *Economic and Philosophic Manuscripts*, p. 95.
57 *Ibid.*, p. 96.
58 *Early Writings*, p. 188.
59 Avineri, *op. cit.*, p. 18, maintains the contrary.
60 *Early Writings*, p. 239.
61 *Ibid.*, p. 236.
62 *Economic and Philosophic Manuscripts*, p. 65.
63 *Ibid.*, p. 130.
64 *Ibid.*, p. 128.
65 *Ibid.*, p. 129.
66 *Ibid.*, p. 127.
67 *Early Writings*, pp. 239-41.

68 *Economic and Philosophic Manuscripts*, p. 127.
69 *Ibid.*, p. 76; emphasis added.
70 Dupre, *op. cit.*, p. 129, says that this 'signals a new departure in [Marx's] thought'.
71 McLellan, *op. cit.*, p. 185.
72 Dupre, *op. cit.*, p. 112.
73 *Early Writings*, p. 144.
74 *Ibid.*, p. 146.
75 *Ibid.*
76 The bureaucracy provides an exception to this: 'The Medieval "Estate" survived only in the bureaucracy, in which civil and political positions are immediately identical,' *ibid.*
77 *Ibid.*
78 *Ibid.*, p. 147.
79 *Ibid.*, p. 146.
80 *Ibid.*, pp. 146-7.
81 Avineri, *The Social and Political Thought of Karl Marx*, p. 25.
82 Hegel, *Philosophy of Right* (London: Oxford University Press, 1967), pp. 149-50.
83 *Ibid.*, p. 150.
84 *Ibid.*, p. 131.
85 Avineri, *op. cit.*, pp. 57-9; Avineri, 'Hegelian Origins of Marx's Political Philosophy' in his *Marx's Socialism* (New York: Lieber Atherton, 1973). This position had been argued earlier by Bertrand de Jouvenel, *On Power* (Boston: Beacon Press, 1969), pp. 50-1.
86 *Early Writings*, p. 136.
87 *Ibid.*, pp. 107-9.
88 *Ibid.*, p. 144.
89 *Ibid.*, p. 112.
90 *The German Ideology*, p. 237.
91 *Early Writings*, p. 418.
92 *The German Ideology*, p. 669.
93 *Early Writings*, pp. 418-19.
94 Jean Hyppolite, *Studies in Marx and Hegel*, p. 122. A similar view is that of George Lichtheim, *Marxism* (London: Routledge & Kegan Paul, 1971), pp. 53-4.
95 *Early Writings*, p. 256.
96 *MESW*, I, p. 119.
97 Cf. for example, Ernest Mandel, *The Formation of the Economic Thought of Karl Marx* (London: New Left Books, 1971), p. 23.
98 *Early Writings*, p. 256.
99 *MESW*, I, p. 115.
100 In the *Communist Manifesto* the lumpenproletariat is described

as 'that passively rotting mass thrown off by the lowest layers of the old society', *MESW*, I, p. 118. For an economic analysis of the lumpenproletariat, cf. *Capital*, I, pp. 602-3.

101   *The German Ideology*, p. 220. Cf. also *MESW*, I, pp. 219-20. In the Paris *Manuscripts*, p. 27, Marx first identifies 'a section of the working class [which] falls into the ranks of beggary,' but does not enter into a discussion of it.

102   Marx's classic account of this process is in *The Eighteenth Brumaire of Louis Bonaparte*.

103   *MESW*, I, pp. 115-17. Hal Draper, 'The Principle of Self-Emancipation in Marx and Engels', *The Socialist Register* (London: Merlin Press, 1971), argues for a contrary position. He distinguishes between two types of proletarian revolution, one in which the proletariat carries out its own revolution, the other in which the proletariat is used to carry out a revolution, and notes that Marx was sensitive to the distinction (p. 81). Draper goes on to argue, however, specifically referring to the *Introduction*, that Marx never held the view that proletarian revolution involves that the proletariat be used to carry out a revolution (p. 94). Lichtheim, *Marxism*, p. 38, note 1, on the other hand, maintains that in the *Introduction* Marx was a 'German Jacobin for whom the proletariat existed primarily as the instrument of revolution'.

104   Lichtheim, *ibid.*, p. 54.

105   In the *Communist Manifesto*, on the other hand, Marx makes it quite clear that he regards the development of revolutionary theory as a consequence of the development of the proletariat, *MESW*, I, p. 134.

106   *Early Writings*, pp. 249, 251. It should be noted that the 'philosophy' to which Marx refers as having a revolutionary capacity is the critical philosophy of Feuerbach, discussed in Chapter 2 above. See also the discussion of Chapter 1, section II.

107   *Early Writings*, p. 244. Compare with *The Holy Family* (Moscow: Progress Publishers, 1975), pp. 100-1, 110, where the notion is given a more fully Feuerbachian treatment.

108   *Early Writings*, p. 252.

109   Cf. the discussion of practical and theoretical parties, *ibid.*, pp. 249-50.

110   *Ibid.*, p. 251.

111   *Ibid.*

112   *Ibid.*, p. 252.

113   *Ibid.*, p. 257.

114   Cf. Richard Hunt, *The Political Ideas of Marx and Engels* (London: Macmillan, 1975), Vol. I, p. 44.

115 *MESW*, I, pp. 115, 116. Cf. also *ibid.*, pp. 213-14.
116 *Early Writings*, p. 247.
117 *Ibid.* Cf. also the comments on Frederick William IV's rule, *ibid.*, p. 253.
118 *MESW*, I, p. 114.
119 *Early Writings*, p. 247.
120 'If one class is to be the class of liberation *par excellence*, then another class must be the class of overt oppression,' *ibid.*, p. 254.
121 'The proletariat is only beginning to appear in Germany as a result of the emergent industrial movement . . . the proletariat is . . . formed . . . from the mass of people issuing from society's acute disintegration,' *Early Writings*, p. 256. Cf. also *ibid.*, p. 248.
122 '. . . the system of industry and commerce . . . will lead much faster than the increase in the population to a rupture within existing society which the old system cannot heal . . .', *ibid.*, p. 205.
123 *Ibid.*, p. 209. In the same letter Marx rejects communism as a 'dogmatic abstraction', *ibid.*, p. 207. Writing in the *Economic and Philosophic Manuscripts* of the following year Marx declares his support for communism. This is actually less significant than it first appears as the *type* of communism he rejects in 1843 is also explicitly rejected in the *Manuscripts*.
124 David McLellan, *Karl Marx*, p. 77. Referring to this letter, George Lichtheim, *The Concept of Ideology and Other Essays* (New York: Vintage, 1967), p. 18, says that Marx 'was already a revolutionary, but not yet a materialist'.
125 *MESW*, I, pp. 18-19.
126 *Early Writings*, p. 249.
127 Bertell Ollman, *Alienation* (London: Cambridge University Press, 1971), p. xiii.

Chapter 6 Politics

1 *Economic and Philosophic Manuscripts* (Moscow: Progress Publishers, 1967), p. 67.
2 *Early Writings* (Harmondsworth: Penguin, 1975), pp. 78, 143.
3 *Economic and Philosophic Manuscripts*, p. 76.
4 *Ibid.*, p. 96.
5 *Early Writings*, p. 231.
6 *Ibid.*, p. 228.
7 *Ibid.*, pp. 229-30.
8 *Ibid.*, p. 227.
9 *Ibid.*, p. 220.

10 *Ibid.*, p. 230.
11 *Ibid.*, p. 220.
12 *Ibid.*, p. 231.
13 *Ibid.*, p. 232.
14 *Ibid.*, p. 219.
15 *Ibid.*, p. 220.
16 *Ibid.*, pp. 91, 143, 146.
17 *Ibid.*, p. 220.
18 *Ibid.*, p. 234.
19 *Ibid.*, p. 233.
20 *Ibid.*, p. 220. In the 'Critical Notes on "The King of Prussia and Social Reform" ' Marx comments that 'the state [is] an abstract totality which exists only through its separation from real life and which is unthinkable in the absence of an organised antithesis between the universal idea and the individual existence of man,' *ibid.*, p. 419.
21 *Ibid.*, p. 220.
22 *Ibid.*, p. 233.
23 *Ibid.*, pp. 225-226.
24 *Ibid.*, p. 231.
25 *Ibid.*
26 John Locke, *The Two Treatises of Government* (New York: New American Library, 1965 [1690]), p. 428.
27 *Early Writings*, p. 71.
28 Cf. Eduard Urbanek, 'Roles, Masks and Characters: A Contribution to Marx's Idea of the Social Role', *Marxism and Sociology*, Peter Berger (ed.), (New York: Appleton Century Crofts, 1969).
29 Ralf Dahrendorf, *Homo Sociologicus* (London: Routledge & Kegan Paul, 1973), p. 20.
30 *Ibid.*, pp. 6-7.
31 Peter Berger and Thomas Luckmann, *The Social Construction of Reality* (London: Allen Lane, 1969), p. 92; emphasis in original.
32 C. Wright Mills, *The Sociological Imagination* (Harmondsworth: Penguin, 1970), p. 38.
33 *The German Ideology* (Moscow: Progress Publishers, 1968), p. 95.
34 *MESW*, II, p. 221.
35 *MESW*, I, pp. 110-11.
36 'The Chartists', *Articles on Britain* (Moscow: Progress Publishers, 1971), p. 118; 'The Eighteenth Brumaire of Louis Bonaparte', *MESW*, I, p. 436. Cf. also Engels, 'Socialism: Utopian and Scientific', *MESW*, III, pp. 110-11.
37 *The German Ideology*, p. 79.
38 *Early Writings*, p. 106.

39 *Ibid.*, pp. 108, 109.
40 *Ibid.*, p. 167.
41 *Ibid.*
42 *Ibid.*, p. 177.
43 *Ibid.*, p. 169.
44 *Ibid.*, p. 177.
45 'Comments on the Latest Prussian Censorship Instruction', in Loyd Easton and Kurt Guddat (eds), *Writings of the Young Marx on Philosophy and Society* (New York: Anchor Books, 1967); 'Proceedings on the Sixth Rhenish Parliament: Third Article', in David McLellan (ed.), *Karl Marx: Early Texts* (Oxford: Blackwell, 1971).
46 Cf. *Early Writings*, pp. 128-9, 185-6. Cf. also Auguste Cornu, *The Origins of Marxian Thought* (Springfield: Charles Thomas, 1957), p. 78; Louis Dupre, *The Philosophical Foundations of Marxism* (New York: Harcourt Brace and World, 1966), pp. 106-7; Arthur McGovern, 'The Young Marx on the State', *Science and Society*; 34(4) 1970, p. 444.
47 *Capital*, III (Moscow: Progress Publishers, 1971), pp. 791-2; *A Contribution to the Critique of Political Economy* (Moscow: Progress Publishers, 1970), p. 193.
48 *The German Ideology*, p. 93.
49 *On the Paris Commune* (Moscow: Progress Publishers, 1971), p. 156.
50 *Capital* (Moscow: Progress Publishers, n.d.), I, pp. 257, 267, 279-80, 285-6, 451, 464.
51 Cf. e.g., *MESW*, I, pp. 433, 463.
52 John Sanderson, *An Interpretation of the Political Ideas of Marx and Engels* (London: Longmans, 1969), pp. 64-8; John Plamenatz, *German Marxism and Russian Communism* (London: Longmans, 1966), pp. 144-50; Ralph Miliband, 'Marx and the State' *The Socialist Register* (London: Merlin Press, 1965).
53 Shlomo Avineri, *The Social and Political Thought of Karl Marx* (London: Cambridge University Press, 1970), pp. 50-1.
54 *MESW*, I, pp. 484-5.
55 *Economic and Philosophic Manuscripts*, p. 23.
56 *Ibid.*, p. 64; cf. also *ibid.*, p. 58.
57 *Ibid.*, p. 31.
58 *Ibid.*, p. 74; emphasis in original.
59 *Ibid.*, pp. 75-6.
60 *Early Writings*, p. 147.
61 Henri Lefebvre, *The Sociology of Marx* (New York: Vintage, 1969), p. 121.
62 *A Contribution to the Critique of Political Economy*, p. 20.

63 *Capital*, I, pp. 20-1.
64 *Economic and Philosophic Manuscripts*, p. 37.
65 Adam Smith, *The Wealth of Nations*, quoted in *Economic and Philosophic Manuscripts*, p. 37.
66 *Capital*, III, p. 881.
67 This issue is debated by W.G. Runciman, 'Class, Status and Power?', *Sociology in its Place*, (Cambridge: Cambridge University Press, 1970), and G.K. Ingham, 'Social Stratification: Individual Attributes and Social Relationships', *Sociology*, 4(1), 1970.
68 The phrase 'mode of production' appears at least twice in the *Manuscripts*, pp. 96, 107, each time with a different meaning, neither of which coincides with the meaning given to the term in *The German Ideology*, pp. 31-2.
69 *MESW*, I, p. 63.
70 *The German Ideology*, p. 69.
71 *Ibid.*, pp. 69-70.
72 *Ibid.*, pp. 86-7.
73 *Ibid.*, p. 87.
74 *MESW*, I, p. 77.
75 *MESW*, I, p. 77.
76 Arthur McGovern, 'The Young Marx on the State', p. 431.
77 *MESW*, I, p. 40.
78 *Early Writings*, p. 233.
79 *MESW*, I, p. 24.
80 *Early Writings*, p. 220.
81 *MESW*, I, p. 68.
82 *Ibid.*, p. 66.
83 *Ibid.*, p. 67.
84 In the *Critique of Hegel's Philosophy of Right* Marx argues that the state bureaucracy uses the state to satisfy its own interests, but the argument is quite different from the one of *The German Ideology*, as shown above.
85 *Early Writings*, pp. 232-3.
86 *MESW*, I, pp. 76, 77.
87 *Economic and Philosophic Manuscripts*, pp. 82-5.
88 *Ibid.*, p. 84.
89 Robert Tucker, *The Marxian Revolutionary Idea* (New York: Norton and Co., 1969), p. 57; David McLellan, *The Thought of Karl Marx* (London: Macmillan, 1972), p. 181.
90 Tucker, *op. cit.*, p. 59.
91 McLellan, *op. cit.*, p. 181.
92 Daniel Tarschys, *Beyond the State* (Stockholm: Scandinavian University Books, 1972), pp. 82-3.

93   *MESW*, I, p. 66.
94   *Ibid.*
95   *Ibid.*, p. 76.
96   *Early Writings*, p. 146.
97   *Ibid.*, p. 220.
98   *MESW*, I, p. 40; emphasis added.
99   *Ibid.*, p. 77.
100 *Early Writings*, p. 220.
101 *MESW*, II, p. 217.
102 *Ibid.*, p. 219; emphasis added.
103 *MESW*, I, p. 38.
104 Michael Evans, *Karl Marx* (London: George Allen & Unwin, 1975), pp. 113-14.
105 Tucker, *op. cit.*, p. 59; emphasis in original.
106 Avineri, *The Social and Political Thought of Karl Marx*, p. 203.
107 *Early Writings*, p. 412; emphasis in original.
108 *Ibid.*, emphasis in original.
109 *MESW*, I, p. 34; emphasis in original.
110 *Capital*, I, p. 285.
111 *Ibid.*, p. 257.
112 *MESW*, I, p. 466. More precisely, Marx distinguishes between capitalist class interest in general — the interest in social relations of production which sustain the class — and particular or individual interests, formed through the competition for economic and social values available to the class as a whole. Marx also distinguishes between objective interests (general and individual) and the subjective interpretation of them.
113 *Capital*, I, pp. 256-7.
114 *Ibid.*, p. 267. A slightly different account is given in 'On the Question of Free Trade', *The Poverty of Philosophy* (Moscow: Progress Publishers, 1966), pp. 184-5.
115 *Capital*, I, p. 229.
116 *Ibid.*
117 *Ibid.*
118 *Ibid.*, p. 451.
119 *Capital*, III, p. 384.
120 *Ibid.*, p. 793.
121 Avineri, *op. cit.*, p. 203.
122 *Ibid.*
123 *Early Writings*, p. 233.
124 *Ibid.*, pp. 219, 231.
125 *Ibid.*, p. 419.
126 Frederick Engels, *The Condition of the Working Class in England*, first published 1845.

127 David McLellan, *Karl Marx* (London: Macmillan, 1973), pp. 141-2.
128 The bibliography of works referred to in *The German Ideology* covers fourteen pages, including two pages of periodical literature; cf. *The German Ideology*, pp. 708-22.
129 Published in February 1848, the *Communist Manifesto* was written between December 1847 and January 1848, by Marx; cf. David Riazanov, *Karl Marx and Friedrich Engels* (New York: Monthly Review Press, 1973), pp. 76-8.
130 *The German Ideology*, p. 399.
131 *MESW*, I, p. 77; emphasis in original.
132 *The German Ideology*, p. 399.
133 *Ibid.*, p. 366; emphasis in original.
134 *Ibid.*; cf. also *MESW*, I, pp. 78-9.
135 *The German Ideology*, p. 366.
136 'The Elections in England — Tories and Whigs', *Articles on Britain*, p. 112.
137 *Ibid.*
138 *MESW*, I, pp. 206-8.
139 *Ibid.*, p. 436.
140 Cf. Engels's discussion in *MESW*, III, pp. 110-11.
141 *A Contribution to the Critique of Political Economy*, p. 193.
142 *MESW*, I, p. 424.
143 *Ibid.*, pp. 477, 482-3.
144 *Ibid.*, p. 77; *The German Ideology*, p. 404; *Capital*, I, pp. 706-7.
145 *Capital*, III, p. 785.
146 *Ibid.*
147 *MESW*, I, p. 113.
148 *Capital*, I, p. 692.
149 *Ibid.*, Chapter 31.
150 *The Poverty of Philosophy*, p. 133.
151 *MESW*, I, p. 77.
152 *Capital*, I, p. 706.
153 *Ibid.*, p. 305.
154 *Capital*, III, p. 607.
155 'A Review of Guizot's Book *Why Has the English Revolution Been Successsful?*', *Articles on Britain*, p. 92.
156 *Capital*, III, p. 602.
157 Cited *ibid.*
158 *MESW*, I, p. 110; cf. also *MESW*, III, p. 218.
159 This is strongly denied by Arthur McGovern, 'The Young Marx on the State', p. 431, but affirmed by George Lichtheim, *Marxism* (London: Routledge & Kegan Paul, 1971), p. 373.
160 *MESW*, I, p. 77.

161 Lord Acton, *Lectures on Modern History* and *Historical Essays and Studies*, as quoted in G.E. Fasnacht, *Acton's Political Philosophy* (London: Hollis and Carter, 1952), p. 13; G.P. Gooch, *Political Thought in England from Bacon to Halifax* (London: Butterworth, 1939), p. 114; Harold Laski, *The Rise of European Liberalism* (London: George Allen & Unwin, 1947), p. 112. Harrington's major work, *Oceana*, was first published in 1656.

162 Harrington's expression, cited in Christopher Hill, 'The English Civil War Interpreted by Marx and Engels', *Science and Society*; 12(1), 1948, p. 130.

163 'Marginal Notes on Adolph Wagner's *Lehrbuch der politischen Ökonomie*', *Theoretical Practice*, No. 5, Spring 1972, pp. 57-8. Cf. also *A Contribution to the Critique of Political Economy*, pp. 192-3.

164 Laski, *op. cit.*, pp. 234-5; Ralph Miliband, 'Barnave: A Case of Bourgeois Class Consciousness', *Aspects of History and Class Consciousness*, 1; Meszaros (ed.), (London: Routledge & Kegan Paul, 1971), p. 28.

165 Joseph Barnave, *Introduction à la Revolution Française*, as quoted by Miliband, *op. cit.*, p. 33 and Laski, *op. cit.*, p. 232.

166 Barnave, *op. cit.*, as quoted by Miliband, *op. cit.*, p. 31.

167 *MESW*, I, p. 113.

168 Henri Saint-Simon, *L'Industrie*, as quoted by T.B. Bottomore and Maximilien Rubel, 'Introduction', *Karl Marx: Selected Writings in Sociology and Social Philosophy* (Harmondsworth: Penguin, 1965), p. 26; translation my own.

169 Cf. Lichtheim, *op. cit.*, pp. 61-2.

170 Z.A. Jordan, *The Evolution of Dialectical Materialism* (London: Macmillan, 1967), p. 119; Irving Zeitlin, *Marxism: A Reexamination* (Princeton: Van Nostrand), pp. 17-18.

171 *The German Ideology*, pp. 554-74.

172 *Economic and Philosophic Manuscripts*, pp. 102ff; *The German Ideology*, pp. 31, 36-7. Compare with the quotations from Saint-Simon in Herbert Marcuse, *Reason and Revolution* (London: Routledge & Kegan Paul, 1973), pp. 331-2.

173 Guizot's contemporary, Augustin Thierry, might also be mentioned in this context; cf. Marx's letter to Engels, 27 July, 1854, in *Selected Correspondence* (Moscow: Progress Publishers, 1965), p. 87.

174 J.S. Mill, *Autobiography* (New York: New American Library, 1964), p. 124.

175 The importance of Marx's study of the French Revolution is discussed by Bruce Brown, 'The French Revolution and the Rise of Social Theory', *Science and Society*; 30(4), 1966, pp. 423-4.

Cf. also Evans, *op. cit.*, p. 18.

176   *A Contribution to the Critique of Political Economy*, p. 21.
177   *Capital*, I, pp. 457-8, 472, 714-15.
178   *MESW*, II, p. 17.
179   *MESW*, III, p. 26.
180   Avineri, *op. cit.*, p. 204, denies the importance to Marx of the concept 'dictatorship of the proletariat' in this context. Cf. the critical discussion of Avineri's assertion in Chris Arthur, 'Two Kinds of Marxism', *Radical Philosophy*; No. 1, 1972, and Alan Gilbert, 'Salvaging Marx from Avineri', *Political Theory*; 4(1), 1976.
181   *MESW*, II, p. 223.
182   *Ibid.*, p. 19.
183   *The Poverty of Philosophy*, p. 151.
184   'Fictitious Splits in the International', *MESW*, II, pp. 285-6.

Chapter 7   Conclusion

1   Bernstein 'revised' Marx's theory to fit contemporary facts of economic development in 1899.
2   Compare, for example, Ralf Dahrendorf, *Class and Class Conflict in Industrial Society* (London: Routledge & Kegan Paul, 1959), C. Wright Mills, *The Marxists* (Harmondsworth: Penguin, 1963), Murray Wolfson, *A Reappraisal of Marxian Economics* (Baltimore: Penguin, 1968), Harry Braverman, *Labor and Monopoly Capital* (New York: Monthly Review Press, 1974).
3   George Plekhanov, *Fundamental Problems of Marxism* (New York: International Publishers, 1969), pp. 26-43.
4   The relevance of Marx to these questions is demonstrated in Anthony Giddens, *Central Problems in Social Theory* (London: Macmillan, 1979).
5   Earlier versions are in Dahrendorf, *op. cit.*, Joseph Schumpeter, *Capitalism, Socialism and Democracy* (London: George Allen & Unwin, 1966), Joan Robinson, *An Essay on Marxian Economics* (London: Macmillan, 1942).
6   Alvin Gouldner, *The Two Marxisms* (London: Macmillan, 1980), p. 14.
7   This and other quotations in the paragraph are from *ibid.*, pp. 33-5.
8   *Capital*, I (Moscow: Progress Publishers, n.d.), p. 603.
9   *MESW*, I, pp. 389, 421.
10   *Capital*, I, p. 96 note.

Index